T0114106

POSTMODERNISM AND THE POLITICS OF "CULTURE"

Cultural Studies Series

Paul Smith, Series Editor

POSTMODERNISM

AND

THE POLITICS OF "CULTURE"

ADAM KATZ

University of Hartford,
Southern Connecticut State University, and
Quinnipiac University

Routledge
Taylor & Francis Group

NEW YORK AND LONDON

Cultural Studies

First published 2000 by Westview Press

Published 2018 by Routledge
605 Third Avenue, New York, NY 10017
4 Park Square, Milton Park, Abingdon, Oxon OX14 4RN

Routledge is an imprint of the Taylor & Francis Group, an informa business

Library of Congress Cataloging-in-Publication Data
Katz, Adam.
   Postmodernism and the politics of "culture" / Adam Katz.
      p.   cm.—(Cultural studies)
   Includes bibliographical references and index.
   ISBN 0-8133-6807-3 (pbk. : alk. paper)
      1. Culture—Study and teaching.   2. Culture—Political aspects.   3. Politics and culture
4. Postmodernism.   I. Title.   II. Series.

HM623 .K38   2000
306—dc21
                                                                                    00-043793

ISBN 13: 978-0-8133-6807-8 (pbk)

CONTENTS

INTRODUCTION

I think it is time that we admitted that much of what we (progressive academics and intellectuals) are doing is not working.

—*Lawrence Grossberg (1998, 78–79)*

Imagine that your automobile is held up by armed bandits. You hand them over your money, passport, revolver and automobile. You are spared the pleasant company of the bandit. That is unquestionably a compromise. "Do ut des" ("I give" you money, firearms, automobile, "so that you give" me the opportunity to depart in peace). But it will be difficult to find a sane man who would declare such a compromise to be "inadmissible on principle," or who would proclaim the compromiser an accomplice of the bandits (even though the bandits might use the automobile and the firearms for further robberies). . . . One must learn to distinguish between a man who gave the bandits money and firearms in order to lessen the evil committed by them, and to facilitate the task of getting them captured and shot, and a man who gives bandits money and firearms in order to share in the loot. In politics this is not always as easy as in this childishly simple example.

—*V. I. Lenin (1940, 21–23)*

This book is a critique of what I call postmodern cultural studies and at the same time, by implication, of much of what passes for emancipatory theoretical politics today. The logic of postmodern cultural studies—part of a much broader liberal logic—is the production of the category of culture as a site of indeterminacy in order to dismantle the determinacy of the economic, of the category of radical democracy as the logic of history as opposed to the contradiction between the relations and forces of production, and of the privileging of struggles over representation as superseding class struggle. The broader theoretical-political logic underwriting these subversions, though, is the poststructuralist claim that the most radical act is resistance to closure. That is, the most radical act is to resist determinate understandings of causality—understandings tied to a simplify-

ing logic that seeks to both broaden and focus the scope of social struggles—and a rigorous mode of political responsibility in which knowledge,
theory, and action are mutually constitutive. The force of this theoretical
logic makes the establishment of reformist pragmatism appear to be the
limit of possible social transformation.

Such a critique is absolutely necessary today when a leading "journal of
committed writing" publishes friendly, chatty interviews with the publishers of academic presses and has sensationalistic special issues focused on
phenomena such as academic superstars, presumably passing this all off
as inquiries into the material conditions of intellectual work.[1] It is necessary when a prominent journal in the field of cultural studies has a special
issue on the institutionalization of cultural studies that is little more than
a virtual vocational seminar on how to publish/get a job/introduce cur-
ricular changes, etc.[2] And it is necessary when another of the founding
journals of cultural studies publishes a special issue supporting a graduate
student strike and the labor movement among exploited cultural workers
more generally without once bringing its activist commitments to bear
upon the postmodern theoretical discourses it promotes in every other issue (or vice versa).[3]

What has been systematically eliminated in postmodern cultural studies is polemic, in the sense of discourses organized around contending
concepts of the whole that attempt to bring to light the foundational principles of one's own and one's opponent's discourses and push such oppositions to their limits. This is largely a result of postmodern cultural studies' suppression of Marxism, which has functioned as a founding trauma
for contemporary cultural studies (and an excellent place to see this functioning is in the well-known volume *Cultural Studies*, many of the contributions to which I examine throughout the book). This point is crucial because the theoretical limits self-imposed on emancipatory thought, the
establishment of the Left as a self-regulating space based on local alliances and affiliations, the deployment of postmodern theory as the "general equivalent" protecting this space from consequential polemics, and
the suppression of Marxism (as the systemic articulation of mode of production, class, and revolution) are integrally connected.

In this introduction, I will accomplish three things. First, I will study a
current example of thinking about cultural studies through the writings of
one of its leading figures. Second, I will examine and engage a few recent
polemical texts to bring to light the (extremely narrow) limits of postmodern cultural studies and to begin to pressure those limits. And third, I will
explain the structure and aims of the book as a whole, in particular in relation to the problem of opening up some closed spaces within postmodern cultural studies and Left discourses within the academy and elsewhere.

Lawrence Grossberg's recent discussions of cultural studies have had a dual function. On one side, he has aimed at securing cultural studies' place within academic institutions by defending it against conservative attacks, the threat of co-optation, and critiques from what he calls "political economy." On the other side, he has advanced a critique internal to cultural studies, arguing against the prevalence of questions of subjectivity and identity in the field, which he furthermore links to a broader hermeneutical framework in which cultural studies is implicated. Grossberg's goal here is clearly to reconstruct the "inside" of cultural studies so as to enable it to adapt to these challenges coming from the "outside."

What is the current condition of cultural studies, according to Grossberg? It "is going through changes [but] not a 'crisis,'" he tells us, "for cultural studies has always been changing" (1997a, 343). Nevertheless, he acknowledges, cultural studies' position "has never been . . . more precarious"; it faces "serious dangers" and "threats" (272); its state is "troubled" (275) and its "viability" (272) is in question. But whether this constitutes a crisis depends upon how we answer two fundamental questions: Is there some coherence or identity to cultural studies? And is it a project and hence something that can be in crisis in the first place?

On one level, Grossberg is ready with answers here, providing a six-point definition of cultural studies. Still, if his definition is meant to combat what he apparently sees as the most insidious threat facing cultural studies—"as more people jump onto the cultural studies bandwagon, it needs to protect some sense of its own specificity as a way into the field of culture and power" (1997b, 7)—it doesn't seem very effective: In the end, he says, "cultural studies is perhaps best seen as a contextual theory of contexts as the lived milieux of power" (7–8). It is very hard to see what ground such a definition provides for rejecting the tendency, which Grossberg has deplored for years, to treat cultural studies as a label that can be slapped onto any discourse that in some way exceeds the limitations of a given discipline and pays some attention to its implication in institutional norms and structures. The problem of how to prevent cultural studies from becoming a "global intellectual commodity" remains (1997a, 344).

The trouble is that Grossberg wants the bandwagon without having too many people jumping on it. He is never very clear about whether the danger lies inside cultural studies or befalls it from without. Nor, for that matter, does he clarify why it is a danger at all, given that cultural studies has long abandoned the "romance of marginality" (1997b, 17). I will discuss this issue in more depth in Chapter 1, in terms of the constitution of cultural studies as an identity. Here, I want to focus on how one of cultural studies' leading voices constructs its identity in relation to its outside. Grossberg's definition of cultural studies works as what he calls an "umbrella," which he is all for unless "so many people [get] under the umbrella that it offers no protection" (1997a, 273): "When it rains, one seeks a good wide umbrella and, to continue the metaphor, progressive academics certainly need to come together not only to get in out of the rain but to ally their projects under a common banner" (272). The importance of cultural studies as a Left, progressive intellectual project is central to Grossberg's defenses and reformulations of cultural studies; it is the "we" he always has in mind. What he never really asks, though, is what makes "radical contextualism" Left and progressive? Why do progressive intellectuals need it? And why couldn't reactionary intellectuals also be radical contextualists? In what way is progressiveness any more than (to use a privileged term in cultural studies) a catachresis that retroactively posits progressive intellectuals as its referent, which, in turn, grounds the progressive credentials of cultural studies? That at least would explain why Grossberg's overriding concern in his defense of cultural studies is with a series of defensive maneuvers, the establishment of a series of inclusions and exclusions that systematically avoids questions of political principle.

Grossberg discusses "three criticisms [of cultural studies] that are worth considering in some detail" (1997a, 5). I will quickly pass by the first, which he identifies as the call for a "return to empirical researches" and which he claims presupposes "a larger celebration, even fetishization of the local" (6). I will only mention that although this seems to be a critique that comes from more traditional, disciplinary perspectives and hence can be easily dismissed, the only grounds on which a radical contextualism can reject this critique is that the disciplines fail to turn their empiricism on themselves and the conditions of academic work. The second and third criticisms strike closer to home.

> The second criticism of cultural studies is that it is little more than a populist celebration of media culture, reception/consumption, and consumer capitalism, and has given up any oppositional role. The third is that cultural studies ignores economics, including the institutions of cultural production, and thus that it is incapable of understanding the real structures of power, domination, and oppression in the contemporary world. Obviously, these two criticisms are often linked (6).

Although Grossberg acknowledges that these charges have some "local" value ("particular positions in cultural studies . . . have become too celebratory"; "there has been a tendency in some cultural studies to avoid detailed attention to the economic" [6]), still, he notes, with a richer contextualization of cultural studies, "the value of such criticisms all but disappears" (6).

Grossberg defends against the charge of populism first by resorting to what is, in essence, a presumably outmoded ("disciplinary") fact/value distinction. We need to distinguish, he claims, between "work on consumption (and reception) which looks at the complex and contradictory nature of consumption [and] work that . . . argues that any act of consumption is, by definition, pleasurable and therefore an act of resistance" (1997a, 7). In other words, he is asking what could possibly be wrong with analyzing consumption "in the wider context of social structures of power," in which case one would "of course" find that consumption has its "pleasures" and can be "empowering," while also being "manipulative" and "exploitative." Here, the academic credentials of cultural studies protect it against a political critique. Who could deny that good work can come out of studies on consumption? The problem for a knowledge formation, especially the Foucauldian/Deleuzean one Grossberg goes on to argue for, is accounting for the politics of this constitution of the object of cultural studies. In other words, the issue is not how manipulation and empowerment are balanced but how two central questions can be answered: What understanding of politics leads one to look for transformative potential in consumption in the first place? And how does this constitute a defense against the charge that cultural studies "has given up on any oppositional role"?

Grossberg's answers to these questions brings into focus the "front" he is defending here (ultimately far more important than right-wing anti-intellectual backlashes, which can't be all that effective if the biggest problem is keeping people off the bandwagon). The main enemies, he asserts, are the primacy of production relations in the explanation of the social and cultural realms, the "desire to return to a simpler model of domination in which people are seen as passively manipulated 'cultural dopes'" (1997a, 7), and "a still puritanical Left." The common thread here is a thorough rejection of any theoretico-political position outside of the contexts, complexity, nuances, and so on of the "lived milieux of power." The radical contextualism of cultural studies is predicated on the belief "that if one is to challenge the existing structures of power, one has to understand how [people's] complicity, [their] participation in power, is constructed and lived, and that means looking not at what people gain from such practices, but also at the possibilities for rearticulating such practices to escape, resist, or even oppose particular structures of power" (8). Effective opposition always comes from the inside, from experience, with the role of progressive intellectuals being to further contextualize this experience, which is to say articulate one context with another and so on. Again, where exactly is the "progressiveness" here? Reactionaries also challenge particular structures of power. In fact, the entire binary progressive/reactionary is irrelevant to the cultural studies described by Grossberg; it is extrinsic to its discourse and can only be seen as a legitimating effect of the field of knowledge/power articulated by policing texts such as Grossberg's own.

Grossberg's defense against the charges coming from political economy covers much of the same ground. He argues, for instance, that production and class are important but not the only things and that, anyway, cultural studies talks about class but about many other subjects as well; he contends that although "they" say we overestimate culture, "they," in fact, underestimate it; and he says that "reductionism" is bad and that "specificity" and "complexity" are good. But Grossberg uses an additional move worth pointing out. Returning to his call for an umbrella for progressive intellectuals, he pleads for "new ways of carrying on such internal debates and criticisms," ways in which "we" could avoid "accusing each other of evacuating politics altogether, of being traitors to the Left," which would entail "forget[ting] who the enemies are and where our allies (who may or may not be our friends) are to be found" (1997a, 13–14). Part of the problem here is that Grossberg has still not explained what makes the progressive intellectuals progressive, and not only that, he has just gone to great lengths to define cultural studies in such a way that it necessarily excludes political economy (i.e., Marxism, the puritans). Even more important, his argument seeks to dissolve the basic disagreements and the polemics, which are the only things that could possibly make cultural studies something more than an "intellectual commodity," into a narrowly institutional question. Grossberg displaces the "question of how economics should operate within cultural studies" onto a "failure of interdisciplinarity." The question, that is, is not one of fundamental political principles and theoretical concepts but of specific projects that are "unpredictable in advance"(14).

So much for Grossberg's defense of the inside against the outside—his proposal for a reconstruction of cultural studies would seem to render much of this advocacy of cultural studies irrelevant. In fact, it aggravates the problems. Grossberg argues for breaking with the entire structuralist/culturalist debate once articulated by Stuart Hall and the problems of identity and subjectivity associated with it, despite the fact that Hall's articulation (which I discuss in Chapter 1) was long ago firmly resolved in favor of a modified culturalism within the mainstream of cultural studies. Grossberg also advances what appears to be a thoroughgoing critique of cultural studies. Claiming that cultural studies is implicated in the modern separation of cultural from other practices and hence understood as a mode of mediation enabling the "decoding" or "interpretation" of subjectivity as progress, he concludes that "if cultural studies rests upon a philosophical discourse that is closely articulated into the very relations of power that it wants to dismantle, then it has to critically examine its own categories and the ways they are constrained by and articulated on this philosophical ground" (1997b, 20).

Contesting this philosophical framework, Grossberg proposes a "spatial materialism" relying on "the work of Foucault and Deleuze and Guattari (and their return to Spinoza)" (1997b, 20). The main philosophical assumption here is that "reality is nothing but the effects of its own rearticulation" (22) and that reality "produce[s] itself; it is both produced (contingent) and productive (real)" (21–22). In this case, "cultural practices are complex technologies and organizations that produce the real as maps of power" (22). This, of course, works very well with Grossberg's definition of cultural studies as radical contextualism: Cultural studies would then be the product of the cultural contexts that it, in turn, produces.

Grossberg's reconstruction of cultural studies—his production of cultural studies as a map of power—is aimed in particular at what he considers three retrograde binaries. First, there is the appearance/essence binary, which, for him, relies upon a practice of interpretation and decoding (that is, upon mediation), whereas, on his account, knowledge can be nothing more than a particular production of reality, interlocking with other cultural productions of reality. Second, there is the inside/outside binary—identity and difference—which is to be abandoned in favor of aggregations of mobilities and intensities. The central target here is the "position of the outsider" as providing a "standard of political and even intellectual judgment." Third, there is what we could call the top/bottom binary—"colonizer/colonized, oppressor/oppressed, domination/resistance, repression/transgression"—which seems "inapplicable to a spatial economy of power that cannot be reduced to simply geographical dichotomies—first world/third world, metropolitan/periphery, local/global" (1997b, 17). I will examine the consequences of this "spatial materialism" in the course of this introduction. For now, though, I want to return to the question I have been raising insistently all along: What, exactly, makes all this progressive? Put even more strongly, how does spatial materialism (which, after all, wants to eliminate a logic of temporality) not render the entire question of progressivism and opposition obsolete, part of the specifically modern technologies of power that need to be overcome?

Grossberg clearly does want to hold on to cultural studies ("I do not want to give up the ground or space of cultural studies" [1997b, 20]) as the umbrella project for Left and progressive intellectuals ("the creation of a better world"), but what makes one "mobility" or "intensity" better than another? If cultural practices "impose a particular conduct and organization not only on specific individualities, but also on particular planes of effects" (20), who, precisely, is imposing what on whom, why, and why (not how, which slips in a presupposition of the very progressiveness that needs explaining) should it be contested? The production of the power/knowledge space of cultural studies is predicated on the complete elimination of such questions along with the claim to have already answered them (by virtue of their having already been "produced" by the tradition of cultural studies—the point of Grossberg's biographical conclusion to his introduction to *Bringing It All Back Home*). But the most important question here is similar to one Grossberg raises ("Why has this [modern/Kantian] philosophical discourse had such powerful control for so long?" [20]): Why does the abolition of the Left, in the name of the Left, have such powerful control right now?

For Geoff Waite, the answer is "left-Nietzscheanism." In his *Nietzsche's Corps/e: Aesthetics, Politics, Prophecy, or, the Spectacular Technoculture of Everyday Life*, Waite begins with Georges Bataille's claim that "Nietzsche's position is the only one outside of communism" (1996, 1). He uses the concept of "Nietzsche's Corps/e" to map the current global order as the worldwide struggle between (now "victorious") capitalism and (now "dead") communism. He takes Bataille's claim most seriously: The Nietzschean text is "immunopathological," he says, a type of "viroid writing" which has penetrated throughout the capitalist social and cultural body," both "high" and (particularly) "mass" culture, and become more and more pervasive as its effects become less and less visible. "Nietzscheanism" must be relentlessly and unequivocally opposed if communism is to remain a future possibility.

The importance of Waite's argument is that the vast proliferation of the culture of surfaces in late capitalism (in Fredric Jameson's view of postmodernism), which supposedly leaves no conceivable alternative to the existing order, now has a name. To put it another way, the globalized paranoia that Jameson also suggests is essential to any possible critical stance under postmodern conditions (see Chapter 3) now has a real target, an intention—which, if it cannot quite be "hit" or captured, can at least be mapped, allegorized, and traced through its manifold appearances. The visible adversaries are Friedrich Nietzsche's "corpse," which is our own body as Nietzsche's life after death, and Nietzsche's "corps," the body of his (usually unwitting) disciples who, in the absence of explicit and knowing resistance, are, again, all of us.

Waite is, of course, quite aware of all the progressive appropriations of Nietzsche, which deconstruct his claims to intentionality and focus on his liberatory embrace of masks, multiple styles and identities, affirmative expression of intensities, and so forth. This Left-Nietzscheanism is, in fact, the central concern of Waite's book, insofar as it represents the strangulation of transformative possibilities from within. In fact, "even the greatest communist philosopher [Althusser] must be extracted from Nietzsche's web" (1996, 2–3). According to Waite, Nietzsche "designed his writing subliminally to program his readers to act in ways and for a single ultimate purpose that in theory they (we) can never fully grasp, and that works against the best interests of most of them (us)" (15). The deconstructions, the playfulness and ironies, and other apparently liberatory elements in the Nietzschean text mask the existence of a single self, which is channeled through the multiplicity of appearances and aimed at the death of communism. And this self has become embodied in all the latest modes of consciousness production: "'He' has become android . . . *is* TV and its mass media equivalents. He *is* the latest hardware on which national and transnational economies and militaries depend . . . Nietzsche is an 'influencing machine'" (15).

"Left-Nietzscheanism," of course, includes the vast majority of contemporary postmodern theorists (and, it goes without saying, cultural studies). Waite initially, then, needs to show that Nietzsche was unalterably opposed to all of the goals that could possibly be assigned to the Left. This is not all that difficult: The single most consistent and insistent theme in Nietzsche's text is the absolute necessity of orders of rank, domination and exploitation, explicit and unchallenged social hierarchies, and so on (as Waite says, some kind of "slave economy" is Nietzsche's "rigid designator" [1996, 183]). The more difficult questions are: Why do people think that Nietzsche can be "read" and "appropriated" differently? Why do they want to? And, for that matter, why can't they—why can't Nietzsche be read selectively, for example accepting his critique of metaphysics while rejecting his solidarity with the masters in their incessant struggle against slaves and their morality?

First of all, such hermeneutic approaches fail to grasp the logic of the Nietzschean text, which is simultaneously its causal effectivity: "its power to replicate itself in virtually any contingency" (Waite 1996, 25–26). Nietzsche(anism) produces a space, which is to say that reading Nietzsche involves always already having been read by him and thereby reading him on the terms he has already established. For example, if, in answer to my previous question—"Why do people think that Nietzsche can be 'read' and 'appropriated' differently?"—one answers (in accord with the prevailing cultural common sense, completely supported by the dominant cultural theories) that "of course" all texts are open to contrary and diverse appropriations, then one is already thoroughly and thoughtlessly within a Nietzschean space. Hence, insofar as different audiences pick up on one or another strand of Nietzsche's seemingly infinitely heterogeneous text, this has already been accounted for, programmed by, and incorporated into the text itself. Thus, there is no contradiction between the single-minded purposefulness of Nietzsche and the indeterminacy, multiplicity, and so on of Nietzscheanism. This is also why it is sheer illusion to imagine one could use Nietzsche for one's own purposes or reject the "unacceptable" portions of his text while rescuing the "liberating" ones.

Waite accounts for this structure by placing Nietzsche in the broader philosophical tradition of esotericism. Here, his aims are at least in part pedagogical: The "Left . . . has no deep understanding of esotericism generally." (1996, 31) Waite clearly thinks it should—the Left is much too trusting and has trusted Nietzsche. And Waite certainly pushes this logic of reading very far, perhaps to its logical conclusion. However, he states that, although the Left needs to understand esotericism, it should not practice it, but the matter is somewhat more complicated for Waite: "For if a writer *mentions* esotericism, it is possible, even likely, that the writer is also *using* it. At least this *must* be true for the Right in *principle*; if true also for the Left, it *ought* to be due to *contingent* circumstances" (32). And this naturally helps to save the "exoteric" tradition of Marxism in particular from the charges leveled at Nietzsche, despite Lenin's, Gramsci's, and Althusser's (and perhaps, in a sense, Marx's, as in his writings for British and American papers) resort to esotericism ("that cursed Aesopian language," as Lenin [1939, 7] called it).

But this distinction becomes problematic if Waite is using esotericism (since he mentions it) and if the contingent circumstances under which he is doing so comprise the world-historical effects of Nietzscheanism, whose "fasciod-liberal" viroid writing, unlike a particular regime or a prison sentence, has no clear end in sight. As I hope will become clear, I am not interested in deconstructing Waite's binary; rather, I hope to bring out some of the implications of his focus on the eso/exotericism question as a marker delineating the border between Right and Left. To begin with, I want to question his attempt to distance his own method of "reading between the lines" from that of Leo Strauss (another right-wing esoteric writer with his own "corps/e"). Drawing upon Jean Genet's *Un Captif Amoureux*, Waite distinguishes between writing and reading "between the lines" and "between the words." The latter is deemed less "linear" and "essentialist," in the sense of recovering and restoring an intact narrative; by contrast, reading and writing between the words implies a "vertical" relationship to the text, an attempt not merely to grasp the concealed narrative but also to find the representation "between words that resist narrativity in their more or less desperate search not (only) to capture or understand the real but (also) to appropriate and change it" (1996, 34).

First of all, it is not at all clear that Strauss's esotericism was aimed merely at uncovering a narrative. Here, Waite seems to ignore Strauss's distinction between ancient and modern esotericism: Whereas ancient esotericism (say, from Socrates to Maimonedes) aimed at maintaining the space of philosophy and its commitment to a rational questioning of all practices and beliefs, by protecting society from the corrosive effects of such questioning and thereby protecting philosophy from the inevitable reaction to that threat, modern esotericism (from Machiavelli to Nietzsche) aims at transforming society, at introducing "new modes and orders" and, as the following passage suggests, in ways not all that different from those Waite attributes to Nietzsche:

> By concealing his blasphemy, Machiavelli compels the reader to think the blasphemy by himself and thus to become Machiavelli's accomplice. One

cannot compare the situation of the reader of Machiavelli with that of a judge or prosecutor who likewise rethinks criminal or forbidden thoughts in order to bring the accused to justice and thus establishes a kind of intimacy with the criminal without however incurring the slightest suspicion of thus becoming an accomplice and without for a moment having a sense of guilt. For the criminal does not desire and invite this kind of intimacy but rather dislikes it. Machiavelli on the other hand is anxious to establish this kind of intimacy if only with a certain kind of reader whom he calls the "young." Concealment as practiced by Machiavelli is an instrument of subtle corruption or seduction. He fascinates his reader by confronting him with riddles. Thereafter the fascination with problem-solving makes the reader oblivious to all higher duties if not all duties. By concealing his blasphemies, Machiavelli merely avoids punishment or revenge, but not guilt (Strauss 1958, 50).

Waite is, I think, struggling to discover a mode of unnaive exotericism, which can uproot the structural logic of the enemy without duplicating that logic. In Genet's case, according to Waite, writing between the words is a "struggle for the *representation of reality* on behalf of the right of people . . . to *represent itself*"—which is, in fact, why writing between the words places one "in fields of historical *and* theoretical struggle" (1996, 34). Exotericism, in the sense of writing between the words, would surface and contest the silences produced by the violence of the esoteric without seeking to recuperate those silences in a self-legitimating manner. This would be a mode of ideology critique that confronts the centralized and concentrated force of ideology in defense of the conditions of possibility of the polemic of the other—it is this other polemic that is "between the words" in the sense that it implicates the reader in the opening of that historical and theoretical space.

I think Waite's association of exoteric writing with genuinely emancipatory discourses and esoteric writing with ultimately oppressive discourses is important and correct. Therefore, I want to pursue this topic further, marking the distinction as one between "opening" (exoteric) and "producing" (esoteric) a space. What effect, precisely, does really, essentially esoteric writing have, particularly on the Left? It is not so much that esoteric writing holds something back or even that it conceals the main point, its real intentions (this kind of thing can easily be attributed to "contingent" circumstances). It is more that esoteric writing transforms the inside/outside distinction (between those in the know who see the irony, who get the joke, etc., and those who don't) into a kind of technology that keeps producing that distinction over and over again. And it does this for a specific purpose: Although I can't claim that Waite would accept this formulation, I don't think I am at odds with his argument if I say that esotericism deploys the inside/outside distinction in order to undermine the surface/depth distinction. Thus, real knowing is shifted from a position outside the object, which allows one to see past the surface and attain a certain distance, to a position of being an insider promised access to the secret that only a few can share (a promise that can never quite be kept, since there is always a more "inside" layer to get to). And all this is done in order to make it impossible to challenge the top/bottom distinction, exposing this distinction once and for all, and naming it and transforming it into accessible targets.

This understanding can be productively brought to bear on Althusserian studies of ideology. Louis Althusser's notion of "interpellation" is recognizable as a mode not only of being "captured" and fixed by the dominant gaze (as it is usually read) but also of being "let in on" something; furthermore, Althusser's mapping of "theoretical ideologies," "practical ideologies," and the "practices" in which ideology is ultimately inscribed can also productively be seen as a series of layers, the most inside of which produces and conceals itself behind the more external layers. Waite's understanding of Nietzscheanism might also enable us to address an issue that most theories of ideology have assumed an answer to, without being able to actually provide this answer in any explicit way (which is also central to Waite's concerns)—that is, the question of accountability. As Waite says, "Nietzsche has contributed mightily to our loss of accountability" (1996, 38). But though ideology critique often finds it possible (even easy) to claim that a particular concept or discourse renders its user "complicit" with capitalism, racism, patriarchy, colonialism, etc., it tends to be a lot more difficult to explain where to assign the blame and why. Writing in and in the name of an open(ed) space might make this possible because one feature of the openness of any space is that "doers" and "deeds" *can* be associated with each other, which is why esotericism (Nietzscheanism) first of all aims at destroying such spaces.

But, then, how does Nietzscheanism infect the Left or, more accurately, induce the Left to infect itself? There must be some vulnerability on the part of the Left, and Waite doesn't explain what this might be. Part of the reason for this is that perhaps Waite himself needs to be "extracted" from Nietzscheanism, given his rather uncritical support of theorists such as Antonio Negri. Negri reconfigures the working class as a kind of Nietzschean "superman," a "will to power," which means that there is nothing very strange about his direct and indirect links to leading Nietzscheans such as Gilles Deleuze and his appropriation by American Deleuzeans such as Michael Hardt and Brian Massumi.

More generally, what can't be ignored here is what I will call the "esoteric foundations of subjectivity," a notion that holds for Left "subjects" as well as Right ones. In other words, the Left's vulnerability to Nietzscheanism is ultimately a result of its implication in specifically liberal-democratic categories, its at least tacit reliance upon liberal understandings of equality, freedom, democracy, etc. This reliance is tied to what must be seen as an attempt to gain some distance from liberal-democratic assumptions. By this, I mean the tendency to see these categories as "transitional" (i.e., formal) but with a concrete social content and thus filled with one content today, to be contested, so as to fill them with another tomorrow—rather than as a determinate, qualitative form taken by social relations, where the relation between doer and deed can be constituted. Politics is thus reduced to strategy, as in the uncritical use of these categories for denunciatory purposes via the yardstick of the "double standard": Practitioners of liberal democracy don't live up to their own principles, implying both a suppressed reality and a purely deceptive fictionality. In both cases, a paralyzing (at least intellectually paralyzing) mixture of cynicism and naïveté, instrumentalism and essentialism is involved. The assumption underlying such efforts is that of the inherent reversibility of the categories, from which it is not too difficult to reach the conclusion that their constant destabilization will lead to new, "democratic" subjectivities. This, in fact, constitutes the strongest tendency on the Left toward an esotericism of its own ("we" need to "construct" democracy in this way, for this audience and this purpose, etc.).

Chetan Bhatt's *Liberation and Purity: Race, New Religious Movements and the Ethics of Postmodernity* takes on an adversary similar to Waite's. Although his book deals with contemporary "religious authoritarianism" rather than Nietzsche(anism), his interest is also in how to defend Enlightened, progressive social transformation in the face of an antagonist who has penetrated, undermined, and appropriated the discourses of the Enlightenment from "within." On one level, Bhatt's book is set up in very traditional terms—with "faith" on one side and "reason" on the other; with faith associated with irrationality, dogmatism, and authoritarianism and reason providing the firm ground of democratic and egalitarian struggles. In his introduction, he recognizes that there is "short epistemological distance between some interpretations of modern science and the rationalities of religious faith"; that contemporary religious formations "appeal to some form of reason" and are "coherent discursive regimes"; and that reason has a "troubling" tendency to abdicate in the face of unanticipated consequences of "scientific-technical rationality" (1997, xi). But he says that ultimately, "religious ideologies do reach a point where their reason becomes exhausted," this limit being in their confrontation with "non-algorithmic, open-ended, anti-teleological natural and human science," which is faith's "only real intellectual enemy" (xii).

In many ways, then, Bhatt's book is set up as a classical Enlightenment critique of the "priests": What is most effective in combating religious authoritarians is showing them to be "irrational, unwarranted and wrong" (1997, 36). This mode of critique is displayed very clearly in Bhatt's forceful and uncompromising polemic against postmodern and postcolonial theory. What makes his critique of theorists such as Jacques Derrida, Michel Foucault, Homi Bhabha, and Gayatri Spivak so effective is that he consistently measures them against the standard of the resources they offer to fight effectively against religious authoritarianism; to put it differently, he tests these theories by putting them on the battleground between reason and faith.

So, one thread of critique involves postmodern and postcolonial theories' inadequacy in relation to and assault upon reason, realism, humanism, Enlightenment, and the like. One element of this critique concerns the dearth of analytical resources such theories provide. Their discussions of "alterity" and "difference" have little to do with either "the practices of the actual others" or their interests: As Bhatt writes, "It is not at all obvious that the others want to abandon rationality and reason, or history and humanism" (1997, 16). They fail to live up to "one task of historical methodology," which is to "distinguish the historical tendencies in modernity from the discursive claims about history within modernity," i.e., to examine "real institutions" (16). Finally, they are in many ways close to the basic assumptions of "religious authoritarianism" itself: "The prominence of binarism, complicated by a trinity, the work of the hidden hand, and absolute limit to the rationally knowable, some kind of transcendentalism, the privilege of some subject positions, sometimes combined with a unique and special incommensurability of some cultures or subjects, or the absolute decentreing of the subject in the presence of totality, infinity and ineffability all seem to be 'religious' themes" (34–35).

This implication of postmodern and postcolonial theories in antirational, religious themes, furthermore, means that they will be ineffective in combating religious authoritarianism, of even seeing it as something to be combated, even though "they would at the very least have a consistent *distaste* for the kind of chauvinism expressed through racism, sexism, homophobia—or religious authoritarianism" (Bhatt 1997, 5). Thus, their arguments are ineffective and irrelevant against the main enemies today and not only religious authoritarianism: "Racism, modernity, sexism, capitalism and imperialism are utterly unchanged by the act of deconstructing them" (15). Postmodern and postcolonial theories have no grounds for making political and ethical decisions. For example, they will be unable to distinguish between an authoritarian Muslim critique of Amnesty International using "universalist" (anti-imperialist) categories, even though "those critics of the West also do not *necessarily* want those Enlightenment products for themselves but want to use them strategically against the West and against dissenters," and "another directly opposed Muslim democratic tendency, which may itself criticize Western domination" but "will derive its authority primarily from humanism and rights"

(28). This "definitive and conclusive" political distinction is unintelligible to postmodern theories.

In addition, postmodern and postcolonial theorists fall short in their own attempts to critique the Enlightenment. They are themselves implicated in naive and outmoded Enlightenment assumptions and even in the most "obnoxious" (Bhatt 1997, 9) elements of the Enlightenment that need to be discarded. Bhatt describes them as "empiricist," "positivist," and "teleological" (16), as "Cartesian rationalists" (25), practicing "theoretical vanguardism" (25). They "explicitly attempt to provide grand totalizing theories of culture, domination, temporality, knowledge, reason, the Third World, modernity and the West" (25). The skepticism and cynicism of "much postmodern theory" (10) represents a regression to David Hume; its abstract concerns about identity and the transcendental subject are throwbacks to Jean-Jacques Rousseau, Immanuel Kant, and Georg Hegel (11). Finally, the postmodern theorists are ultimately hypocrites. They presuppose an "important but often clandestine political imaginary . . . affiliated with the value of social and cultural diversity (if not just difference) and profound ideas of liberty, radical democracy and, arguably, ultimate humanism" (5). But this political imaginary remains "clandestine," and moreover, these same theories systematically attack the very foundations of such goals. And in his analysis of Spivak's discussions of subalternity, Bhatt charges that, "despite her critique of the conditions in which alterity is claimed," Spivak "makes powerful associations between herself and the general figure of the 'Third World woman'" (22) and also thereby silences and exploits actual subalterns such as Shahbano who are not only "speaking" but are speaking out on the front lines in the battle against fundamentalism.

I am supportive of much of Bhatt's critique of the trajectory of contemporary theory, especially his claim that

> the harder work of the politically possible, the difficult issues of ethical accountability and moral necessity, the non-transient, often violent presence of institutional power, the endurance of the capital-labour relation and the manifest and real problems of judgement and evaluation seem to disappear under the debris of multiple antagonisms, indeterminate signification or even psychosis (1997, 4–5).

The first question I want to raise about Bhatt's critique is this: Which Enlightenment does he support and why? He asserts that "authoritarian forms of Hinduism or Islam" seem most "agitated when they are shown to be irrational, unwarranted and wrong" (1997, 36), yet he never actually substantiates this claim, even though the whole rationale behind his book presupposes it. In fact, as I will suggest, the most powerful elements in his book tend to call that claim into question. Second, as we saw earlier, the implication of postmodern and postcolonial theory in religious themes presumably discredits them in the struggle against religious authoritarianism. But Bhatt also makes more careful distinctions, for example, between the "young Muslims," an authoritarian group, and a "directly opposed Muslim democratic tendency" and in his insistence on noting that "the authoritarian religious movements described in the book are not to be considered equivalent to the religious traditions they claim hegemony over" (xiv). In other words, the problem is not with religious themes per se but with authoritarianism, with the *necessity* with which one can *only* use principles strategically and thereby protect one's own, fundamental principles from critical scrutiny.

Bhatt seems to employ a rather broad-based, even generic Enlightenment position, aimed largely at propping up struggles against religious authoritarianism, in the face of which not only postmodernism and deconstruction but also "Neo-Marxism" (1997, xv) and "black Marxism" have been ineffective. He gestures toward "the range and complexity of Enlightenment ideas" (10), and he does make some important distinctions and clarifications. For example, he distinguishes between a "transcendental subject of pure reason" (which implicates both postmodernism and religious authoritarianism) and a "practical rationality and a powerful appeal to the tribunal of humanism" (is this identical or fully compatible with what Bhatt goes on to identify as faith's "only real intellectual enemy," i.e., "open-ended science"?). He offers a useful critique of the political ineffectiveness of Jurgen Habermas's reconstruction of modern rationality (12–13). He also claims that "one can no longer easily resolve these issues by inserting a Marxian critique of the commodity form, the anthropology of labour, or a coming to self awareness of alienation" (8). (Along with this caricature of Marxism, Bhatt, like many humanists, conflates Althusser's critique of humanism with religion and poststructuralism.) In fact, he explicitly situates his book within the contemporary crisis of reason—"if nothing else, religious movements and regimes force us to rethink foundational issues in knowledge, ethics and the utopias we strive for" (xv). But he doesn't want to push this question very far: The necessity of "rethinking" reason and the other foundational concepts of modernity is perhaps too closely tied to their vulnerability.

Where Bhatt does seem to come down most unequivocally is in his contention that the claims religions make to be exempt from rational inspection must be rejected, i.e., they should be questioned and challenged on terms other than their own. This means that they should be explained, which finally leads to the conclusion that explaining them is a significant step toward defeating them: "Any critical assault on religious authoritarianism must start from the basis that there is nothing in those ideologies, or in the 'cultures' that gave rise to them, that is beyond the analytical reach of reason, rationalities or the forms of knowledge that we have" (1997, 35). And much of Bhatt's book is a sustained attempt to bring these ideologies within reach, involving extensive analyses of Hindu and Muslim doctrine, history, and institutions. But what is not clear is whether the "repetitive" and "iterative" form of this method—proving over and over again that "heavenly" claims have very "earthly" origins and causes, that they systematically misrepresent and misunderstand themselves—in fact addresses the main problem as Bhatt sees it, which is the fact that "virtually all of the tropes of Enlightenment political discourse appear foundationally in (Hindu and Muslim) authoritarian religious movements" (xvi).

The most important analytical issue raised by Bhatt's book lies in its grappling with the question of "space-time compression and its impact upon the meaning of politics in the contemporary period" (1997, xvii), of "how the global medium of electronic communications allows for the rehearsal of non-local 'cyber-spatial' identities and 'communities'" (xviii). His analysis of these new structures relies upon his focus on the necessity that authoritarian religious politics, insofar as it enters and seeks to conquer the public realm, must first protect its foundational, authoritative claims from critical scrutiny and then reproduce and extend this authority through incessant "repetition" and "iteration." Bhatt pursues this analysis via a discussion of the production of social space (as theorized, e.g., by Henri Lefebvre, Edward Soja, David Harvey, and others), in particular in relation to issues of postmodernity and globalization. He locates the force of authoritarian religious movements in the production of "trans-local" spaces, which extend beyond any sovereign national space without being "transnational" or "international" in the sense of corporations or political institutions.

The production of such spaces, according to Bhatt, is predicated upon a transcendental subject encapsulated within a narrative of liberation, which includes the projection of a never-ending series of antagonists and a "totalizing" theorization of obstacles faced by the movement and the necessity of its victory. The modernity of such movements—and their break from the religious traditions they claim to embody—is in their transformation of sacred texts into machines manufacturing bodies and relations between them, preempting and implicating possible hostile and critical responses and producing a circuit of responses and reactions immune to the "normal" workings of the media and other institutions. This accounts for their immediate relation to violence or at least the abstraction of the ever-present possibility of violence from any countervailing considerations and their viral relation to an "organic" but "sick" dominant social body unequivocally opposed to the subject of the movement.

Bhatt's analysis of the Salman Rushdie affair clearly demonstrates what this new mode of politics involves. Here, he examines the way in which a "tradition of a *global umma* that has never existed" (1997, 122) is invented and virtualized as a "hyper-real community" whose "motifs of solidarity, affinity and identity exist in their reproduction through electronic and print imagery" (132). Showing how the paralyzed progressive (multicultural, antiracist, feminist) formations in Britain could only comprehend the phenomenon through inadequate notions of race, fundamentalism, pluralism, etc., Bhatt contends that "it was the overwhelming presence of a symbolic transnational *umma* that silenced progressive opposition by virtue of its multiple and globally disparate presences and highly energetic representatives" (130). He is raising issues central to contemporary cultural studies and challenging its privileging of performativity and the subversion of modern rationalism as a political logic. But his discussion also returns us to an issue I raised before, which is whether contemporary forms of religious authoritarianism render the reason/faith binary Bhatt starts with obsolete: Is the reason proposed by Bhatt grasping religious authoritarianism or vice versa?

The Rushdie affair really does seem to present a strong challenge to existing modes of rationality. Bhatt writes, for instance, that "it transcend[ed] sociology and its object of study"; it was "not wholly describable in the political science of international relations"; it "problematized the ability of contemporary social and political theory to explain ideology, structure, action and collective agency"; it "refuted the idea of causally exclusive social and political explanation"; and it "could not be mapped as a reductive totality" (1997, 147). It is hardly surprising, then, that although "secular multiculturalism is extraordinarily necessary in opposing communalism . . . it increasingly looks defeated and vacant" (149). We are certainly well beyond simply showing religious authoritarianism that it is "irrational, unwarranted and wrong" or documenting the ways in which contemporary Muslim and Hindu politics "distort" the faiths they identify with.

Nevertheless, what is effectively shown in Bhatt's argument is that, like Waite's Nietzscheanism, despite the apparent fluctuations, multiplicity, incommensurability, and so on of these translocal, mass-mediated spaces, the *production* of the space itself relies upon very determinate "identity-claims" that "synthesize and make homogeneous for their subjects the various ontically different structures within the social formation" (1997, 124)—the "umma was constructed as a global presence that was unitary and universally, monologically hurt and offended by the book" (121). What Bhatt's book doesn't really answer is the following question: Is it the "content" of religious authoritarianism that needs most be contested, or is it this "form" (which is a kind of content on another level) of the production of space that is the adversary? Although his analyses seem to support the latter conclusion, this would significantly pressure the faith/reason contest he uses to construct his argument.

Bhatt's critique is torn between a real anguish regarding the weakness of progressives facing such forces (the "mythologies and transcendental fictions" of religious authoritarianism, claims Bhatt in concluding his book on the note of exposing the machinations of the "priests," "can be opposed by critical and realist engagements. But these seem incongruent and unsatisfactory outside of sustainable visions we can create for the future" [1997, 271]) and a very strong sense—never explicitly articulated—that progressives cannot simply appropriate the forms of this politics for "better" ends. In other words, the Left can't simply produce its own spaces, tied to a different, emancipatory, or utopian content. This conflict comes across in his very ambivalent analysis of the "new social movements," which often makes them sound quite similar to the religious authoritarians: As he describes them, they "tend to develop their own authoritarian discourses," they display a "profound neglect of democratic processes," and they are "marked by an obsession with cardinal differences, particularist distinctions, separateness and distance," even "creating the space for religious and absolutist revival and the repression of women's interests" (54). More generally, he says, "social movements manufacture an intelligible theory of the social formation that identifies the latter as a totality built of simple monologic structures that necessarily create systemic forms of oppression for their functional survival . . . a collective victim subjectivity is formed and a discourse of liberation is created that rests ultimately on the real or symbolic destruction of the totality" (55). Here, though, we really reach an impasse, since in this final quote, we can recognize much that would be central to any revolutionary theory—in particular, the reliance upon the *real* destruction of the (ultimately quite monologic) totality that necessarily creates systemic forms of oppression—the consideration of which doesn't seem to have a place in Bhatt's discussion.

In the end, then, Bhatt's argument for reason against faith (the founding polemic of modernity) not only cannot effectively ground and sustain its opposition to the most dangerous forms of modern irrationalism but also, in the name of a broad-based Enlightenment discourse, necessarily removes from the agenda the question of systemic, revolutionary transformation. Nevertheless, only this "foundational polemic" enables Bhatt to locate and surface the esoteric hiding places of religious authoritarianisms. If, as Bhatt says in a recent essay, one is to move "into the messy business of the evaluation of the democratic or authoritarian, egalitarian or totalitarian content of identities" (1999, 66) (for example, to contest the "universalistic" forms taken by racism and sexism[4]), it is necessary to take into account the constitutive esotericism of late-modern discourses on (post)identity. On another, more epistemological level, the absence of a foundational polemic makes it impossible to grasp the "production of space" as anything other than a series of cascading flows and implosions in Arjun Appadurai's Deleuzean formulations, in which case violence becomes a free-floating, multicausal stream of effects. In other words, a foundational polemic, radically severed from identity or subjectivities and yet capable of grasping the inner logic of viral ideological discourses, is necessary today for both objectivity and political judgment.

I will address another polemic that stakes out a position outside of the liberalism of postmodern cultural studies: the "strong" Left-Nietzscheanism of Tom Cohen. In doing so, I will take from Waite what I consider a highly productive "thought experiment," which enables us to read the contradictions of ideological texts by locating them somewhere on the series of inside/outside formations produced by specifically modern forms of esoteric writing (this, in turn, enables us to attribute political responsibility or to open a space wherein such responsibility becomes available). In addition, I will take from Bhatt the ongoing necessity of a foundational polemic freed from the "metaphysics of the subject and its easy philosophical identification with the metaphysics of the Volk" (1999, 68), which enables me to add that the "Enlightenment" is also constituted by and tends to conceal contending polemics.

Cohen's polemic against the "mimetic ideology" reproduced by contemporary cultural studies, in the antitheory identitarian mode that Grossberg also admits has become dominant, might be very helpful. For example, Cohen systemically undermines prevailing dialogisms that reduce culture to the endless reversals of self/other relations; more important, Cohen's polemic could help to expose and explain the mimeticism implicit in Grossberg's ("ghostly"?) invocation of leftism, progressivism, etc., even while installing theoretical machines that render such categories irrelevant. The problem is that, despite his antagonism toward linear narratives ("historicism"), Cohen wants to align himself with something like the Left: "The cultural left has made a central error in assuming that 'politics' must be defined in mimetic or representational terms alone . . . what has been suppressed . . . is the increasingly felt lack of a pre-mimetic or anti-mimetic politics" (1998, 32). He furthermore wants something like a notion of progress: "The return in the 80s to the *opposition* of history and language may turn out to have been, potentially, *a historical regression*" (39).

Unlike Grossberg's work, Cohen's text is clearer about why, for example, he wants to deploy rather mimetic narratives in order to stage his argument, despite his implication of mimetic logic in the depredations of a "globally destructive humanism" (1998, 22). The "icon of 'de Man,'" for example, was a "screen, a decoy, for other social and cultural energies to stage themselves against," in particular the "abjection of 'post-structural-ist' theory . . . and a *pragmatic* return to history and the social" (32–33). He has no problem with either linear or monocausal narratives: "Why, given the politicization of critical interests in the 80s, did we enter the mid-90s in so much more of a neoconservative and nationalist atmo-sphere? . . . Is it accidental that today, to be properly historical . . . the re-turn to the foundational subject on the left accorded with a right agenda that, at least institutionally, seems to have prevailed?" (33–34). Cohen is ready to return to the "properly historical," in other words, in order to es-tablish poststructuralist theory, especially its De Manian variant, as the real, albeit unrecognized and unappreciated, radical force of the 1980s and 1990s.

Still, there is something other than a contradiction here. Cohen's text it-self gives us the key to reading such claims when he explains his use of the "outmoded" or "eviscerated" concept of "ideology": The "mimetic history" of ideology is "penetrate[d]" by the "pre-phenomenal idiomatic (one might say idiocy)" of "inscription" (1998, 16). The "new" term pen-etrates the "old" in order to enable a Benjaminian "shock," "an abrupt break with programmed chains" (20)—and this involves, further, positing the "after" as, in fact, "before." The reversal of old and new, before and after is necessary because Cohen is, of course, not at all against "pro-grammed chains." A "proper" intervention will install "apparatuses that engulf and actively reconfigure the mimetic as such," that "all but [con-sume] its representational pretext" (4).

Cohen's discourse is set up in order to make the kind of questions I have been raising all along (what makes one "representational-temporal technology" [1998, 27] better than another, what makes a "multiplicity" of such technologies better than a "unifying code," etc.) appear hope-lessly naive and regressive. After all, the "'older' mimetic and binary log-ics [presumably including Left/Right, progressive/reactionary must, when encountered, be acknowledged as . . . cheerful points of translation and departure for the cultivation of chronographic networks and nervous sys-tems without models" (27). Cohen is quite honest about his "psychotic ethic . . . never mourn, incorporate" (31), and he is quite explicitly incor-porating, cannibalizing, infecting, etc., the Left, progressiveness, etc. He "had always wondered, maliciously, if de Man himself set a time bomb to disperse his own monumentalization" (32), which would allow a certain esotericism in de Man's discourse to work even more effectively (what, after all, is this talk of incorporation doing in a book so dedicated, at least exoterically, to undermining all interiority). Cohen's book, I would sug-gest, needs to be read as a time bomb of his own.

My point here is not that Cohen necessarily wants to destroy the Left or progressive critique but simply that he can't be trusted when he claims to want to "correct" that critique's errors. It is doubtful that Cohen expects to be taken seriously when he proposes Alfred Hitchcock, Walter Benjamin's fascination with drugs, and tourism as the avatars of a heretofore unthought radical discourse. And Cohen's actual political argument might become clearer if we read his effort to establish his radical credentials as a kind of preemptive premimeticism, aimed at disarming and implicating his opponents. His interest is in moving

> from an epistemo-aesthetic regime that had defined the "human" toward an altered and altering of the terrestrial itself. It forecasts a politics of "earth" in which that set of systems in which word-name we hear both *eat* and *ear* is not accorded status as ground *as such*. It is such an other "earth," not unconnected for man to traversing systems and competing laws of inscription, which Nietzsche commends as the *ethical* focus projected beyond the auto-referentialism of a globally destructive humanism (1998, 21–22).

Cohen's space-producing machines (and all that exists is such machines, so those who adhere to older, mimetic machines will be the products of the new series Cohen aims at producing), therefore, will get us closer to a politics of "earth." His distance even from de Man's "allegory," Cohen's main "switch" to move us from one trajectory to another, becomes clear here. His brief hint about "those intriguingly aware of a historical and perhaps survivalist bottleneck stalking the logics of reference in our culture" (1998, 27) indicates his sense of the stakes. What, then, is this earth that provides a "prefigural semiosis" (12) for a posthumanist politics? In his words, it is

> a proactive mimesis of infra-environmental camouflage, metamorphoses, chemical warfare, strategic imitation, counter-signatures between species, predatory and counter-predatory ritual that moves "forward" across diverse temporal planes and backloops by *re*marking technically anterior positions. . . . "Nature" in its chemical wars and camouflaging was already allomimetic, virtually linguistic or semaphoric, traversed by what is certainly an extra-terrestrial technicity—there is nothing specifically "earthly" about the trace—that interfaces life and death in a fashion which rewrites the hyperbolism of the former as a semiotic effect rather than a bio-logics (133).

This is the "State of Nature" meant to legitimate a full-fledged Nietzschean, "fasciod-liberal" politics: tactics without strategy, strategies without aims, appearances without essences, and signifiers without signified or, to put it another way, a hyperpragmatism extremely well suited to contemporary institutional transformations, capable of moving seamlessly from thoughtless brutality to subtle accommodations to systematic deception. This "sheer order of differential semaphores" is what Cohen calls a "radical publicness" (17), which I want to suggest is another example of reinscribing an "old" term out of existence. But I don't want to leave it there either, and so I will return to this point in a little while.

One thing I do agree with Cohen about, though, is that cultural studies, as presently constituted, is completely incapable of addressing his polemic (it is too explicit, it cannibalizes too much and too quickly)—or Waite's or Bhatt's. This is because cultural studies has become an inside/outside representational machine: Its leftist self-denomination is a means of exchange (internal negotiations), standard of measurement (production of obvious exclusions), and general equivalent (resistance to totalizing) all at once. The possibility of an outside as a space of theory implicated neither in local affiliations nor in the general cultural violence of representation has become unthinkable. Grossberg's arguments mark the highest stage in this process, but his attempt to bury the question of subjectivity simply makes the installation of a cultural studies identity all the more effective. This identity is predicated upon the very consistent, unequivocal attempt to produce resistance to closure as the preeminent political act.

Waite, in an important thrust, challenges the deconstructive (Nietzschean) move that unties description from prescription and hence truth from politics. He turns back this virulent inscription in a polemical move that, in effect, identifies the categories of causality and accountability: "For causation has to do, eventually, with political causes, and vice versa. It is also absolutely critical to remember—as Heidegger tends to 'forget' but this book will recall all along but most especially at its conclusion— that Greek 'cause' . . . once also meant 'culpability,' 'responsibility,' 'accountability'" (1996, 37). Waite then goes on to use Althusser's notion of structural causality to dissect the *intentions* virulently infiltrating, structuring, and commanding Nietzsche(anism). The point here is that the deconstructive operation showing that any claim to intentionality posits a naturalized ground from which that intention then claims to derive its legitimacy obscures the fact that both types of claim share a common presupposition, which is an "exoteric" or "open" space. By this, I mean, for now, simply a space where actions are free enough so that the beginnings and ends of acts can be associated by an outside position; the forms and materials of inquiry are similarly freed from obfuscations, making such an outside position possible. Principles such as equality, democracy, and freedom are variegated ways of bounding such a space, which is also to say they are not forms that can be filled with one content or another or means to achieve an extrinsic end or an immanent social process. These are the liberal-democratic assumptions that enable a deconstructive cannibalizing of these principles and that tie them to the ultimate esotericism: that of private property.

Poststructuralism (and Left-Nietzscheanism more generally) appears "radically democratic" because the operation of revealing the contingency of truth claims in their articulation with ethical and/or political claims seems to open up both sides of the equation and their articulation. However, this appearance subsides if we ask, Contestation over/for what? (I have discussed Cohen's text because he pushes these questions a bit further than most.) If the deconstructionist is honest, that is, if he or she does not relapse back into a banal recitation of the very liberal categories that have presumably been deconstructed, he or she will have to answer that resisting closure is itself the end of a properly deconstructive politics. But anticlosure, even on its own terms—i.e., presupposing its deconstructability—must itself rest upon closural assumptions, which is to say it must find its conditions of possibility in something external to itself. This something is the esotericism of private property, which—no matter how many regulators, no matter how free and aggressive a press, no matter how open the "books," no matter how many whistle-blowers, and, needless to say, no matter how thorough the deconstruction—will always be able to put forward one identity and hold back another, truly directive and hegemonic one.

What, then, would account for a space wherein deeds can be associated with doers, politics with truth? One way to begin delineating such a space is via Althusser's theorization of the institutional and social location of science, in his critique of "interdisciplinarity." In place of a relation between the disciplines (in particular science and philosophy) in which one discipline (philosophy) exploits the results of the other in order to ground and resolve contradictions in one of the "practical ideologies," Althusser argues for the "mutual constitution" between different fields. In this case, that would mean that materialist philosophy defends the sciences by opposing the exploitations of idealist philosophy and humanist practical ideologies while at the same time intervening in the spontaneous tendency of scientists themselves to draw conclusions from their scientific work that apply to the problems of "humanity" in general, thereby ultimately undermining the conditions of their own scientific work and of the power of scientificity more generally.[5]

Although Althusser doesn't say so, I would argue that something like this must also be the relation between science and politics: In this case, the very co-constitution of science and politics involves the common presupposition of openness and the simultaneous reliance of this openness upon the establishment of firm (i.e., not deconstructible) boundaries between science and politics. This is no longer a traditional binary relation in which we would have to determine a claim to priority (or subordination) or some natural relation between the two, since their relation is articulated by the aim of each to be open (exoteric) to the other as its outside. So, if the service science provides to politics is in explaining its conditions of possibility, eliminating as many false paths as possible, and demystifying obscurantist ideological generalities, this is, first of all, in the interest of a science that itself depends upon a politics that defends its conditions of possibility by opening spaces previously closed to scrutiny; furthermore, this displays before science the limits and terms of its own tasks, and it sets science in motion by opening itself for critique. Politics, likewise, is interested in a science that protects the foundational political categories upon which politics and science both depend—categories, in the case of Marxism in particular, whose demystification stands at the origins of the science itself and whose various appearances, semblances, and mystifications set the terms for science or revolutionary theory.

<o

It is amazing that cultural studies, with its focus on the constitution of subjectivities, has hardly, if at all, focused on the forms political accountability takes in everyday life. I don't just mean unmasking "universal" claims, such as those made at popular events ("We Are the World," etc.), or the way in which, for instance, the events surrounding the Rodney King beating are represented. Rather, I mean who, exactly, is accountable for what and why? For example, if we take international human rights law—increasingly proposed as a "cosmopolitan" model for progressive politics—seriously (in its strongest, Nuremberg Law terms), as well as the series of analogies it implicitly legitimates (crimes against humanity, crimes against women, eco-crimes), we could make a case that the vast majority of the citizens of at least the First World are complicit in a very literal sense. At the same time and by way of the very same process, the forms of public power that would be necessary for such levels of accountability have been increasingly eviscerated by transforming violations of human rights into calls for states of emergency. Why isn't this problematic and its manifestations in everyday life an interest of cultural studies, —not just in the sense of how "alternative" political spaces articulate themselves in relation to these categories or how the Left should relate to them but also in terms of what their political meaning is?

In fact, more popularly written books often address these issues, connecting analyses of culture with various forms of prepolitical and political action on the plane of the fundamental questions facing global society much more effectively than anything in cultural studies. For example, David Brin's *The Transparent Society: Will Technology Force Us to Choose Between Privacy and Freedom?* articulates a foundational polemic that traces a genealogy of "openness" from Periclean Athens through "a few other brief oases of relative liberty—the Icelandic Althing, some Italian city-states, the Iroquois confederacy, and perhaps a couple of bright moments during the Roman Republic, or the Baghdad Caliphate" (1998, 17) through to the modern "neo-West"; Brin ranges this genealogy against an-

other line originated and sponsored by Plato's reaction to Athenian democracy and traced through Hegel and up until twentieth-century totalitari-
anisms. By "neo-West," Brin first of all means "all the world's constitutional democracies, at least those where freedom of expression and
information are accepted norms [and those that have] a shared cultural
outlook based on individuality, eccentricity and suspicion of authority."
But he also pushes this definition into a more delinked, spatialized one,
insofar as, for example, "even large portions of the U.S population exclude
themselves from the *neo-West*" (336). That is, the *shared cultural outlook*
is not necessarily articulated geographically—thus, Brin sees the term
"not as having national boundaries, but rather fluid zones where cultural
assumptions about diversity and openness are strong or weak" (336). A
problem to be noted right away is the assumption that "Plato(nism)" is
somehow not "of" the neo-West, rather than being another foundational
polemic that serves to set up the neo-West in relation to its outside.

Brin is interested in recovering this fragile polemic and putting it to
work or, more specifically, testing it and its now more thoroughly institutionalized forms against contemporary information and surveillance technologies. He argues that the proliferation of such technologies in private
and state hands is now irreversible, and his argument challenges all of the
following claims about this development: the anarchist utopia of cyber-
punk libertarians who see the emergence of information technologies beyond the control of the state as heralding the (welcome) demise of the
state itself; the totalitarian dystopias of civil libertarians and privacy advocates who see these technologies primarily as instrumental in increasing
state and corporate domination of and interference in the lives of their citizens and workers; and, more implicitly, the "cyborgian" tendencies
within cultural studies that see the onset of a new posthuman era in
which the boundaries between the human and technological become
porous and undecidable, producing a world where hybridity reigns
(which "therefore" means that the more hybridity the better).

Brin begins not by deconstructing the privacy/freedom binary of his
book's title but by firmly hierarchizing the pair: Freedom comes first because political freedom can enable the protection of some form of privacy
but privacy by itself provides no guarantee of freedom (tyrannies can
maintain a substantial zone of privacy for their subjects). From there, he
goes on to reunderstand any future conception of privacy as an effect of
efforts to expand freedom and openness: The way to resist unwarranted
state and corporate intrusions into the lives of citizens is not to set (necessarily arbitrary and largely ineffectual) limits to the use of—cameras on
streets (linked, of course, to the local police station) and in the workplace,
the collection of DNA information by medical institutions and insurance
companies, etc.—but rather to employ these same means against state

and corporate concentrations of power (for example, by having cameras recording in the police station and accessible to anyone). To put it simply, everyone should be prepared to watch everyone else.

Brin is well aware that this can easily lead to various outcomes—such as a trivialization of free speech in an *America's Funniest Home Videos* type of society—and he doesn't exclude the more "dystopian" possibilities either. What this ultimately depends upon, he argues, is whether the openness gives rise to political forms in which democratic power is apparent and a force and whether such forms structure transparency in such a way that in-built limits develop in more or less commonly agreed upon ways. It is essential, according to Brin, that people develop a public-spiritedness so that they no longer seek to exempt themselves from the means of exposure that they nevertheless demand access to. Furthermore, a now self-reflexive interest in maintaining a space of privacy—a space no longer naturalized but explicitly a product of emerging practices—will make each individual less likely to disrupt without cause others' privacy. And much of Brin's book is taken up in examining the different forms of accountability transparency will require, along with the transformations in subjectivity it is likely to entail.

Brin's argument also provides him with a focus on contemporary cultural phenomena, the most important of which is what he considers to be the pervasive prorebellion propaganda of the neo-West. As he writes, "We could stay here all night listing famous novels, movies, and TV shows revolving around a single idea: that it is admirable to be independent-minded, eccentric, even defiant" (1998, 128). Brin never answers his own question (although he returns several times to express his puzzlement over it) about how "such a bizarre propaganda campaign come about in the first place," but he does thereby highlight the social and constructed character of autonomy—"we individuals were *taught* to believe in ourselves, and in our powers as free-thinking, autonomous beings" (128). He also champions the age of amateurs, self-taught citizens who check up on and challenge expert authority by shedding a light (via Web pages, camcorders, etc.) on abuses of power on the part of governments, professionals, corporations, and other institutions, none of whom will be able to keep many secrets anymore.

Now, there is much to critique in Brin's Popperian, empiricist, pragmatic liberalism. To follow up on my earlier point, his positing of Platonism as essentially an alien growth on the neo-West makes it impossible for him to notice the articulation of "Pericles" and "Plato" in the "democratic experiment . . . of Locke, Jefferson and Madison" (1998, 17) and reproduced in his own assumption of an immediate link between open inquiry, scientific method (which he proposes universalizing throughout the public sphere) and democratic political power. This assumption is manifested in his paradigm of political power, which still involves citizens speaking back to the state, exposing it, and making demands upon it, rather than a reduction of the state to the mere protector of the conditions under which citizens, through independently managed political forms, make the decisions, establish the priorities, and set the precedents that present them before an "outside."

Brin's liberal utopianism especially shows up in his critique of the notion of "virulent ideas," which could productively be situated as a polemic against Waite's concept of Nietzsche(anism). He does not deny the toxicity of certain ideas—"history is rife with novel ideas that seemed to spread like pandemic fevers, sweeping older creeds aside and creating new priestly castes" (1998, 123,) but he places any concern with this issue that would justify interference with freedom and transparency on the side of Plato and the elite management of mass consciousness. For Brin, the open discussion that provides for the perpetual self-education of citizens is antidote enough. But here, he falls prey to an ideological distinction that he addresses more effectively in his discussion of "privacy vs. Freedom," for he fails to ask whether the triumph of the neo-West doesn't place this question on a new terrain: More specifically, might it be getting increasingly difficult to distinguish "many" Platos from Pericles, especially since Platonic propaganda has itself always been carried out in the name of free thought and conscience? Here, symptomatically, the paradox Brin can't seem to get over returns: "If we citizens are becoming more independent and open-minded, that change only came about after some of the most persistent propaganda in history! Propaganda that so romanticized individualism and idiosyncrasy that many citizens now base their self-worth on how different they are from everybody else" (127).

The poststructuralist critique of this dilemma, exemplified by Tom Cohen, is that ideas only seem toxic because this is how all ideas appear against the assumption that they should have a coherent form and a regulated relation to reality; remove that assumption and there is nothing but "installed referential models," and it's a good thing, too! All that is left is to enter this fully Nietzscheanized environment and, if one wants to maintain his or her Left credentials, gesture to the fact that these models are of course contested, implicated in various power relations, etc. Brin, that is, is easy prey to various Left-Nietzscheanisms, and he is able to dismiss ("contain") the threat of toxicity because of his own production by toxic forces: We have a "pharmakon" here. But it might be more productive to take the question of toxicity (ideology) seriously, precisely insofar as it is capable of producing critiques on the margins while reserving for itself the right to decide on exceptions, where the very conditions of "romanticized individualism" are seen to be at stake.

What Brin cannot see is that the "open society" does not address the question of eso/exotericism, i.e., ideology. If the best formula for exoteri-

cism is still Kant's "All maxims which *stand in need* of publicity in order
not to fail their end agree with politics and right combined" (and this
more or less agrees with Brin's approach), we can point to the limits of
that approach. Exotericism today requires a more radical publicness than
either Brin or Cohen can account for. Rather than the "absolute" exterior-
ization demanded by Cohen (the collapse via cannibalization of the in-
side/outside boundary), some notion of the "inside," but as an effect of
the outside, is needed. The constitution of political action as presentation
before an outside means foregrounding one position and withholding and
rejecting other positions, thereby setting action in motion by establishing
priorities, focusing and crystallizing concepts and principles, and
strengthening the grounding of actions, principles, and knowledge in their
co-constitution—or, to put it another way, polemically separating accountability from subjectivity. This further means that the exposures enthusias-
tically described by Brin will be implicated in Platonism as long as they
are not instituted by an ideology critique (a point I return to throughout
this book[6]), which accounts for/causes such a grounding or, in other
words maintains an *outside* where the top/bottom binary (*class*) can *appear* as (concealed) efforts to destroy that outside.

At any rate, what we can see more easily in Brin's book than in most of
cultural studies is that there is no subjectivity that is not always already,
in an a priori manner, presented before an outside—not an outside to be
internalized as a superego or resisted as totalitarian "gaze" or as a
(Deleuzean) contextualized field of forces but an outside that can never
be incorporated because the exchange of polemics that constitutes not the
subject but accountable theory and action is what accounts for the in-
side/outside relation in the first place. Or at least this is the case if the relation is grasped politically, if cultural studies ("culture" in the sense of
the constitution of inside/outside formations) is practiced as the instantia-
tion of pedagogical space: that is, a space that is open because the actions
it enables and the accountabilities it requires presuppose an outside, a
space of judgment where those actions can be theorized by the foundational polemic that their limits have enabled and "caused."

✦◯

In this book, I defend and deploy the foundational polemic of Marxism
against postmodern cultural studies. Perhaps the increasingly strained
and defensive nature of attacks on anything resembling Marxism will
make it possible for such a polemic to be addressed responsibly.[7] In my
view, Marxism's foundational polemic is directed at liberalism—more
specifically, at liberalism's concealing of violence behind necessity (e.g.,
exploitation behind the neutral workings of the market) and, equally important, necessity behind violence (what appears as violence in the bourgeois imaginary are the anomalies, displacements, transitions, and dise-

quilibria intrinsic to capitalist production relations). The specific ordering of Marxist concepts and theoretical interests—including the dissection of the logic of capital, which brings exploitation out into the open along with the contradiction between the forces and relations of production; the precise forms of proletarian political practice (the dictatorship of the proletariat, the Soviets, the specific forms of political accountability manifested in Lenin's theory of the party, which have far more often been denounced than explored); and the notions of ideology and ideological struggle—are all, I would contend, "caused" by this polemic.

I therefore bring Marxism into confrontation with postmodern cultural studies as a new and increasingly dominant form of liberalism, one that reworks and restores the classical liberal categories of free subjectivity, experience as the source of truth and legitimacy, the nontotalizability of society, and politics as dialogue. It reworks and restores them under specifically late-capitalist conditions, in which the public regulation of the reproduction of labor power has placed the possibility for a political form outside of capitalism directly on the logics of socialization and public formalizations and in which the unprecedentedly rapid and aggressive globalization of the commodity form and wage labor have both undermined previous bases for internationalism while making it an immediate necessity. It will be noticed that I don't refer to the "explosion" of culture and its infiltration into economics and politics as a defining feature of late capitalism (or postmodernism). This is because part of my interest in this book is to open some distance from the notion of culture as a cause—precisely because, as I point out throughout the book, culture generally functions in contemporary Left discourses and in cultural studies in particular as the sign for the very absence of cause.

This effort also requires setting historical materialism to work on new terrain, in relation to the questions and problems raised by postmodern cultural studies and, ultimately, the changing forms of global capitalism. My analyses point in this direction through a symptomatic reading of the texts of postmodern cultural studies (especially in Chapters 2 and 3) that posits the public regulation of the reproduction of labor power—in contradiction to the necessarily private status of labor power required for capitalist relations of production—as the dominant form taken by the contradiction between the forces and relations of production in late capitalism. As I suggest in my discussion of the public and global consequences of this transformation (especially in Chapters 4 and 5), this places class struggle squarely within the theoretical struggles concealed by postclass alliances on the pragmatic Left. This means, in my view, that the open(ed) space of theoretical polemics and/as accountability today coincides with the defense of the categories of class, totality, and critique. This is the form, I am arguing, in which Marxism today engages the universal (the modes of world-historical accountability established by the state of the productive forces) and confronts its other (liberal democracy) across the institutions of global capitalism. To put it more simply, I consider the defense of these concepts, including the "asceticism" they imply, to be far more important for theory interested in the long term than the search for utopian modes of consciousness and narratives of desire and identity, i.e., Left strategies that presuppose an immanent radical core to subaltern modes of subjectivity. This further implies a mode of cultural analyses, which I can only indicate in this book, that examines the suppression of the productive forces as ideological violence against the forms of accountability materially possible and politically necessary—a mode uniting global explanations, a grounded normativity, and the conditions of theoretical collectivity.

I proceed primarily through close readings of texts "in" and "around" cultural studies in the narrow sense: the "line" that leads from Stuart Hall and the Birmingham School through to contemporary practitioners such as Andrew Ross, Henry Giroux, Angela McRobbie, and others. My focus in Chapter 1 is on this trajectory, in particular on the history of the displacement of categories such as class, totality, and theory in cultural studies. I also address other discourses, both broader philosophical ones that provide the underpinnings for cultural studies and parallel Left discourses that have followed a similar trajectory. So, in Chapter 2, I address developments within feminism, in particular its responses to postmodern theory, and in Chapter 3, I deal with some of the major trends in theories of postmodernity.

I also try to address those points where external developments lead to reworkings in cultural studies: So, in Chapter 1, I discuss what I consider one such point, Cary Wolfe's introduction of systems theory into cultural studies in his attempt to theorize the question of the outside in order to provide an adequate notion of critique for a post-Marxist, postrepresentational cultural studies. Similarly, in Chapter 4, I critique Nancy Fraser's reworking of Foucault and Habermas in her influential essay on counterpublics, published in a special issue of *Social Text* at the very beginning of still ongoing concerns about cultural studies and the public intellectual. And in Chapter 5, I look at how the issue of globalization is intersecting with efforts to found an international cultural studies.

I have written this book as an introduction to (as critique of) cultural studies, but I should say that I am not primarily interested in offering an "accurate or "comprehensive" portrayal of cultural studies as a field or discipline: I take cultural studies at its word that this can't be done in any traditional sense, so I think it is more important to identify the political-economic logic of this impossibility. I am thus more interested in tracing the fate of some concepts and issues central to Left or progressive politics in cultural studies—the primacy of the economic, the possibility of political responsibility, the space of theory, etc. This is why, for example, I interrupt my discussion of feminism in Chapter 2 with a brief theoretical inquiry into the concept of ideology or, later in the same chapter, stage a theoretical confrontation between Laura Kipnis and Judith Butler, on one side, and Catharine MacKinnon, on the other, regarding the question of pornography—here, I hope to bring out some connections between ideology, violence, and political accountability.

This brings me back to the question of close reading, which I don't see as a matter of fidelity to texts but rather as an attempt to surface the contradictions and struggles with which they are marked—in this case, again, the long and still ongoing struggle that today's liberalistic discourses conduct against historical materialism and scientific socialism. In the process, perhaps I can introduce some discord in the pervasive desire for reconciliation that is stifling thought—reconciliation between class politics and cultural libertarianism, between Marxism and poststructuralism, between redistribution and recognition, between globalization and local culture, and so forth. Any unity between these binaries will be a simulation—the best service intellectuals can render to those struggling for global social change is to highlight, clarify, and sharpen these and other antagonisms submitted to cultural mediation.

Notes

1. See *Minnesota Review* 1998.

2. See *Cultural Studies* 1998.

3. See the two special issues of *Social Text* dealing with academic labor: One is reprinted with additional essays in Nelson, ed., 1997, and the other is listed under the journal name in the Works Cited section at the end of this volume.

4. I am referring here to Etienne Balibar's arguments regarding neo-racism.

5. See Althusser's essay "Philosophy and the Spontaneous Philosophy of the Scientists" in Althusser 1990, especially pp. 85–100.

6. I will discuss this in particular in Chapter 2 but also in some detail in Chapters 4 and 5.

7. See Morley 1998 for a good example of how Grossberg's stereotyped attacks on Marxism (borrowed, in turn, from Stuart Hall) have become a virtual "meme" that circulates without question within cultural studies.

1

POSTMODERNISM AND CULTURAL STUDIES

Cultural Studies and the Academy

Cultural studies has been a sustained effort to transform the object of studies in the humanities. For example, in English departments, cultural studies has challenged the predominance of the governing categories of literary studies (the canon, the homogeneous period, the formal properties of genre, the literary object as autonomous and self-contained) in the interest of producing readings of all texts of culture and inquiring into the reproduction of subjectivities. To this end, pressure has been placed on disciplinary boundaries and the methods that police these boundaries, and modes of interpretation and critique have been developed that bring, for example, economics and politics to bear on the formal properties of texts. In addition, the lines between "high culture" and "mass culture" have been relativized, making it possible to address texts in terms of their social effectivity rather than their "inherent" literary, philosophical, or other values.

The two most significant categories supporting these institutional changes have been ideology and theory. Althusserian and post-Althusserian understandings of ideology, which defined ideology not in terms of a system of ideas or worldview but in terms of the production of subjects who recognize the existing social world as the only possible and reasonable one, made possible the reading of texts in light of the ways in which the workings of ideology determined their structure and uses. Marxist and poststructuralist theories, meanwhile, focused critical attention on the conditions of possibility of discourses and upon the exclusions and inclusions that enable their articulation. In both cases, critique becomes possible insofar as reading is directed at uncovering the "invisible" possibilities of understanding that are suppressed as a condition of the text's intelligibility.

Any critical intellectual and political project must support these struggles to transform the humanities into a site of cultural critique. At stake in these changes are the uses of pedagogical institutions and practices in late-capitalist society. If pedagogy is understood, as I would argue it should be, as the intervention in intelligibilities, then the outcome of struggles over culture and cultural studies will determine whether the humanities will become a site enabling polemics on the shape of emancipatory theory. Historically, the humanities has been a site at which the contradictions of the subjectivities required by late-capitalist culture have been addressed and managed. The introduction of theory has made it impossible to go back to that depoliticized problematic.

So far, I will argue, cultural studies has in the last instance updated and reinforced the traditional function of the humanities, rather than transforming it. Cultural studies has accommodated itself to existing practices, by producing new modes of fetishizing texts and preserving conservative modes of subjectivity. In this way, it continues to advance the ideological function of the modern humanities in a changed social environment. In particular, cultural studies has maintained the primacy of experience as the limit to critique, thus reworking rather than displacing the liberal subject.

The right wing attacks the changes introduced by cultural studies, charging—as in the ongoing "PC" scare and the "culture wars"—that the humanities are abandoning their commitment to objectivity and the universal values of Western culture. These commitments and values have, of course, been undermined by social developments that have socialized subjects in new ways while concentrating global socioeconomic power within an ever shrinking number of transnational corporations. The intellectual and political tendencies coordinated by cultural studies, meanwhile, are responding to these transformations by providing updated and therefore more useful modes of legitimation for capitalist society. At the same time, regardless of the explicit opposition on the part of many leading figures within cultural studies to privatization and the assaults on culture critique within the academy (which I will discuss in Chapter 4), the most fundamental concepts of cultural studies (such as "destabilization," "articulation," "interdisciplinarity," and so forth) provide ideological justifications for institutional streamlining and downsizing along with the suppression of critique.

These developments in the mode of knowledge production must be understood within the framework of the needs of the late-capitalist social order. The emergence of theory and (post)Althusserian understandings of ideology reflected and contributed strongly to the undermining of liberal humanism (in both its classical and its social-democratic versions) as the legitimating ideology of capitalism. The discrediting of liberal humanism, first under the pressures of anticolonialist revolts and then as a result of the antihegemonic struggles in the advanced capitalist heartlands, revealed a deep crisis in authority and hegemony in late-capitalist society. This discrediting also revealed the need for new ideologies of legitimation, free from what could now be seen as the naïveté of liberal humanist universalism, which has come to be widely viewed as a cover for racist, sexist, and antidemocratic institutions.

The institutional tendencies producing the constellation of practices that have emerged as cultural studies have, then, participated both in the attack on liberal understandings and in the development of new discourses of legitimation. The liberal humanism predominant in the academy has increasingly been seen as illegitimate because it depends upon an outmoded notion of private individuality—that is, the modern notion of the immediacy with which the privileged text is apprehended by the knowing subject. In this understanding, literature is taken to be in opposition to science and technology, as a site where what is essential to our human nature can be preserved or recovered in the face of a social reality where this human essence (freedom) is perpetually at risk. However, the more "scientific" methods (such as narratology) that initially undermined the hegemony of "new criticism" in the American academy, largely through the use of modes of analysis borrowed from structuralist anthropology and linguistics, were themselves discredited by postmodern theories as largely conservative discourses interested in resecuring disciplinary boundaries (for example, through the classification of genres) and protecting an empiricist notion of textuality.

Cultural studies, then, is the result of the combination of the introduction of theory and the politicization of theory enabled by these social and institutional changes. However, the postmodern assault on master narratives (theory) has responded to the discrediting of both structuralism and Marxism in a conservative political environment by redefining the term *politics* to mean the resistance of the individual subject to modes of domination located in the discursive and disciplinary forms that constitute the subject. This has opened up the possibility of a new line of development for cultural studies—one in which the local supplants the global as the framework of analysis and description or one in which "redescription" replaces explanation as the purpose of theoretical investigations. I will argue that the set of discourses that have congealed into what I will call postmodern cultural studies represents the definitive subordination of cultural studies to this line of development. That is, the ideological struggles carried out throughout the 1970s in such sites as the Birmingham Center for Cultural Studies in England and the French journal *Tel Quel* have now been stabilized into a different type of project: the full-scale reconstruction of liberalism on terms appropriate to late-capitalist social relations.

The Problematic of Cultural Studies

These opposing tendencies—on the one hand, cultural studies understood as the explanation of the conditions of possibility for the production and reproduction of subjectivities and, on the other hand, cultural studies understood as the description of experience—have been inscribed in the logic of cultural studies from the start. Stuart Hall, in his "Cultural Studies: Two Paradigms," distinguishes between a "culturalist" paradigm, which he associates with the work of Raymond Williams and E. P. Thompson, and a "structuralist" paradigm, which he associates with the work of structuralists such as Claude Levi-Strauss and the Marxism of Louis Althusser. The significance of the culturalist paradigm, according to Hall, is that it insists on an understanding of culture not as a set of privileged texts but rather as the systems of meanings embodied in all social practices. The strength of the structuralist paradigm, meanwhile, is that it critiques the humanism and experientialism of the culturalist paradigm. The structuralist paradigm decenters experience by showing it to be an effect of social structures that cannot be reduced to the "materials" of experience: "The great strength of the structuralisms is their stress on 'determinate conditions'" (1980, 67).

At stake in the distinction between culturalism and structuralism is the significance of theory. What the structuralist paradigm defends, in contradistinction to the culturalist one, is the necessity of providing explanations of social and cultural phenomena in relation to the determinations that produce them. Theory requires some notion of totality that can enable the understanding of the specificity of social phenomena as effects of that totality: In this case, experience does not contain within itself the conditions of its own intelligibility; rather, experience is what needs to be explained. The culturalist paradigm, meanwhile, undermines the possibility of establishing a hierarchy between determinations by taking as its starting point the activity of subjects in which social conditions and social consciousness are mixed in an indeterminate way. At the same time, Hall argues that culturalism's strength corresponds to the weakness of structuralism. That is, structuralism is unable to account for precisely those phenomena that culturalism privileges. "It has insisted, correctly," he says, "on the affirmative moment of the development of conscious struggle and organization as a necessary element in the analysis of history, ideology and consciousness: against its persistent down-grading in the structuralist paradigm" (1980, 69).

Hall's discussion of these contesting paradigms is part of a historical narrative of the emergence and development of cultural studies. According to Hall, cultural studies emerged as a distinct problematic through the interventions in literary studies of, especially, Richard Hoggart and Raymond Williams. The structuralist intervention, meanwhile, constituted a powerful challenge to this paradigm, making work along similar lines impossible. Hall is thus attempting to chart a course for the future of cultural studies, one that would appropriate the strengths and avoid the weaknesses of each approach and go beyond both paradigms in "trying to think both the specificity of different practices and the forms of the articulated unity they constitute" (1980, 72).

Given that cultural studies is constituted by opposing theoretical discourses that, taken separately, are both necessary but limited, some kind of conceptual transformation or epistemological break is clearly needed. If, as I suggested earlier, the problem facing cultural studies is that of theorizing determination, the resolution of this difficulty cannot be a question of combining the strengths and weaknesses of two incompatible theories but must instead entail starting from one set of premises and developing a new theoretical paradigm "by way of criticism" (Marx and Engels 1942, 105). The attempt to combine the results of incompatible premises is, in practice, a capitulation to the culturalist paradigm, the problems and contradictions of which Hall has already noted. This is because the consequence of such an attempt would be a theoretical eclecticism, unable to comprehend social phenomena as effects of more abstract determinations in a consistent way. This means, finally, that the categories privileged by the structuralist paradigm—theory, different levels of abstraction, conditions of possibility, and so on—must be the starting point if cultural studies is to be adequate to the tasks Hall sets for it in his essay.

Hall's response to this crisis in cultural studies—merely adumbrated in "Cultural Studies: Two Paradigms" but more fully developed in *The Hard Road to Renewal* and elsewhere—is to turn to Antonio Gramsci, especially his notion of hegemony. The usefulness of Gramsci is, according to Hall, twofold: first, in terms of his understanding of the "conjuncture" as a specific combination of a variety of determinations; second, in his critique of a kind of "economic reductionism" that sees cultural and ideological phenomena as direct expressions of some class position while still connecting these phenomena to social struggles between contesting groups. That is, the category of hegemony enables us to see political domination both as contested and uncertain and as encompassing the whole domain of social and cultural life (as opposed to being restricted to struggles articulated in relation to the state).

However, Hall's use of the categories of hegemony and articulation does not, in and of itself, solve the problem of determination or even provide the elements of such a solution. It still leaves the two sides of the equation—class domination, on the one hand, and the reproduction of the conditions of that domination, on the other—unarticulated. If the dominant ideology and culture are instrumental in securing class domination in however indirect or mediated a manner, then the analysis and critique of ideology and culture must proceed from a theoretical understanding of the needs, capacities, and problems faced by the ruling class in some specific relation to other classes with opposing and/or aligned interests. In this case, the significance or content of ideological struggles, or struggles over representations and meanings, cannot exist "in" those struggles themselves but must lie in the contradiction between the forces and relations of production and the class struggles they determine. In other words, one is still working within the framework of determination by the economic (but not necessarily an economic reductionism).

If, however, ideological struggles cannot be read back (or subordinated) to class interests and class struggles but are actually the site of the construction of these interests and struggles, then one is left with another, discursive kind of reductionism: That is, social positions are the results of positions constructed through discursive articulations and ideological struggles (in which case, of course, the issue of who is struggling and over what becomes highly problematic). Even though Hall, in the essays I am discussing, explicitly rejects this kind of position, which he associates with poststructuralist and especially Lacanian and Foucauldian approaches, he is left with what is ultimately an eclectic position, encompassing both a specific form of social domination from which nothing necessarily follows as well as struggles over meaning and representations whose outcome or significance cannot be determined by structures external to the struggles themselves.

An example of how this tension determines Hall's work can be seen in his discussion of the kinds of questions a Gramscian approach poses for the Left in Thatcherite England. Hall argues as follows in *The Hard Road to Renewal*:

> Gramsci always insisted that hegemony is not exclusively an ideological phenomenon. There can be no hegemony without "the decisive nucleus of the economic." On the other hand, do not fall into the trap of the old mechanical economism and believe that if you can only get hold of the economy, you can move the rest of life. The nature of power in the modern world is that it is also constructed in relation to political, moral, intellectual, cultural, ideological, and sexual questions. The question of hegemony is always the question of a new cultural order. The question which faced Gramsci in relation to Italy faces us now in relation to Britain: what is the nature of this new civilization? Hegemony is not a state of grace which is installed forever. It's not a formation which incorporates everybody. The notion of a "historical bloc" is precisely different from that of a pacified, homogeneous, ruling class.
>
> It entails a quite different conception of how social forces and movements, in their diversity, can be articulated into strategic alliances. To construct a

new cultural order, you need not to reflect an already-formed collective will, but to fashion a new one, to inaugurate a new historical project (1988, 170).

Both the economic and the cultural-ideological aspects of social domination are recognized here but in a way that separates them in an absolute manner and makes it impossible to theorize the relations between them. The two possible courses of action posited by this passage are either to reflect an already existing collective will that is to be found in the economy or to fashion a new collective will. The very notion of the economy as something that one could "get a hold of" presupposes the economic reductionism that Hall is presumably contesting: That is, it accepts the notion of the economic as something self-contained and independent. In this case, as soon as the contending classes step outside of the economy, they are no longer classes in any meaningful sense but rather positions struggling for power in relation to political, moral, intellectual, cultural, ideological, and sexual questions. This rigid antinomy is reproduced in the choice between reflecting an already formed collective will and fashioning a new one. The possibility of constructing a new collective will out of the contradictions situated in the economic structure, contradictions that are articulated in relation to other cultural structures where the elements of such a will are emerging as a result of differentiated arenas of struggle, is excluded here. Instead, the collective will can be fashioned through a synthesis of positions immanent in these specific struggles themselves.

This becomes more evident in Hall's concluding chapters to *The Hard Road to Renewal.* There, he argues that

electoral politics—in fact, every kind of politics—depends on political identities and identifications. People make identifications symbolically: through social imagery, in their political imaginations. They "see themselves" as one sort of person or another. They "imagine their future" within this scenario or that. They don't just think about voting in terms of how much they have, their so-called "material interests." Material interests matter profoundly. But they are always ideologically defined (1988, 261).

Once again, there is a reference to the importance of material, ultimately class interests, and Hall also mentions that people have conflicting interests as well as conflicting identities.

However, the claim that both the economic and the ideological are important—by itself, a commonplace observation—can lead in one of two fundamentally opposed directions. One possibility is to theorize the material interests of social classes and engage in an ideological struggle to clarify the contradictions that structure the ideologies and identities of oppressed groups, thereby making the production of oppositional class consciousness possible. The other possibility is to construct images and identities that are immediately accessible and intelligible within the framework of those contradictions, thereby resecuring subordinated subjects' consent for the social order that produces them. This latter possibility becomes the unavoidable consequence if politics is defined as "a struggle for popular identities" (Hall 1988, 282). In addition, this possibility is inevitable given Hall's reductive understanding of material interests as little more than income levels ("how much they have"), rather than in terms of the reproduction of all of the social and institutional conditions of the production of effective subjects.

The way in which these contradictions have been resolved in contemporary cultural studies can be seen in John Fiske's *Understanding Popular Culture*. Fiske is critical of radical understandings of culture that focus on the way capitalist culture functions to reproduce ruling-class domination, at the expense of trying to understand the multifarious ways subordinated groups appropriate the resources available within the dominant culture in order to gain more power relative to their oppressors. He distinguishes between the radical and the progressive, and he claims that critics of culture who measure cultural practices according to the standard of "radicality" (systemic transformation) are unable to comprehend or support the wide variety of oppositional practices that undermine or limit the power of dominant groups without necessarily challenging their dominance. Such critics therefore lose the opportunity—at this historical moment, for Fiske, the only opportunity that actually exists—for intervening in progressive articulations of the "popular," in order to enable them to take on more radical forms in the future.

At the same time, Fiske acknowledges that the popular is only potentially progressive, not necessarily so. In addition, many practices of the popular have both a progressive and a reactionary dimension. He also recognizes that the relation between progressive popular articulations and radical politics are often distant, difficult to produce or analyze, or nonexistent. However, the problems these reservations point to can be put even more strongly. If the popular is defined in terms of a kind of "guerrilla warfare" or "poaching" of the texts of the dominant culture that increases the power of the subordinated subject in relation to a specific articulation of power relations, then it is impossible to theorize the connections between progressivity and radicality. And beyond that, the entire distinction between progressive and reactionary loses its meaning. This is because one cannot move, either conceptually or politically, from reversals in local power relations to systemic transformations. If one takes such reversals as a starting point, it will be impossible to account for their structural consequences: They could either strengthen or weaken power relations elsewhere, and there is no way of theorizing this from the interior of the local reversal. Thus, when Fiske associates the progressive with the popular and understands it as at least a potential stage in the movement toward radicalization, his notion of progressiveness is necessarily external to his theoretical position. In other words, it is borrowed either from the cultural common sense or from those "radical" theories that Fiske critiques and that would themselves arrive at a substantially different assessment of the practices he includes in his notion of the popular. (For example, radical theories would argue that it is precisely by conceding local power reversals that global domination is maintained.[1])

Graeme Turner, in his *British Cultural Studies,* specifically refers to Fiske's work as an example of the way in which the increasingly powerful tendency within cultural studies (influenced by Michel de Certeau) to focus on popular, bottom-up resistance to domination may have gone too far. With the now prevalent use of the category of pleasure to refer to a space outside of ideological domination, Turner argues, cultural studies is in danger of celebrating rather than critiquing the dominant ideology and culture. He claims that "it is important to acknowledge that the pleasure of popular culture cannot lie outside hegemonic ideological formations; pleasure must be implicated in the ways in which hegemony is secured and maintained" (1990, 221).

However, Turner's own account of the positive effects of "the turn to Gramsci" in cultural studies supports the same theoretical incoherencies that lead to Fiske's conclusions. Turner contends that

> hegemony offers a more subtle and flexible explanation than previous formulations because it aims to account for domination as something that is won, not automatically delivered by way of the class structure. Where Althusser's assessment of ideology could be accused of a rigidity that discounted any possibility of change, Gramsci's version is able to concentrate precisely on explaining the process of change. It is consequently a much more optimistic theory, implying a gradual historical alignment of bourgeois hegemony with working class interests (1990, 212).

Leaving aside the question of why an alignment of bourgeois hegemony with working-class interests provides an optimistic outlook, this more optimistic theory is possible because, like Hall, Turner establishes a rigid and caricatured dichotomy between domination as "automatically delivered" and domination as "won." However, with what weapons is domination won? If it is won by the ruling class or the hegemonic bloc as a result of the advantageous position its control over the means of production grants it, then we are still left with the problem of theorizing the perpetuation of domination as a result of processes determined by the class structure, as domination that is won from the dominant positions already occupied. In this case, it is possible to understand "popular culture as the field upon which political power is negotiated and legitimated" (1990, 213), as long as it is clear which agents are engaging in the negotiations and under what conditions. However, once the theory of popular culture "dispos[es] of a class essentialism that linked all cultural expression to a class basis" (213), one can only understand the winning of domination as a victory on an indeterminate terrain that is constituted so that the contestants cannot be identified in advance and the conditions for any particular outcome cannot be specified. In other words, it is impossible to maintain a notion of systemic domination without an understanding of determination that views cultural practices as effects of the general system of domination, rather than as inherently indeterminate and reversible entities.

The turn to Gramsci in contemporary cultural studies, then, is a turn away from Marxism due to its insistence on abstracting from the specific and positing the specific as an effect of more general structures. This assessment is confirmed in a more recent text by Stuart Hall, entitled "Cultural Studies and Its Theoretical Legacies." In this contribution to *Cultural Studies,* Hall argues that Gramsci is important to cultural studies because he "radically *displaced*" (1992, 281) the entire Marxist problematic. This turn from theory is also the significance of Turner's optimistic representation of the progress made since the replacement of Althusser's more rigid and deterministic one by Gramsci's more flexible and subtle one. Turner argues that the emphasis on the "creative power of the 'popular'" has led to a "pendulum's swing . . . from containment to resistance . . . leading to a retreat from the category and effectivity of ideology altogether" (1990, 224), and he is mildly critical of this. However, this swing is a necessary consequence of the evacuation of the category of domination of any content, so that in Turner's discourse, as well, it (like Fiske's notion of progressiveness) is little more than an untheorized background to an understanding of "indeterminate" ideological struggles that would otherwise appear (as Turner fears) completely apologetic.

The (Post)Discipline of Postmodern Cultural Studies

This resolution of the contradictions constitutive of cultural studies has enabled the articulation of cultural studies within a post-Marxist, postmodern problematic. This is not to say that postmodern cultural studies is a completely homogeneous field of ideology production. It is precisely through its tensions and antagonisms that it is constituted. These tensions and antagonisms may involve the articulation of postmodern categories or even the viability or usefulness of the notion of postmodernism itself. However, the field of postmodern cultural studies is not therefore inherently plural and nontotalizable. The struggles and conflicts within the mainstream of today's postmodern humanities involve the relative force of competing claims to possess legitimate knowledge—legitimate, that is, in terms of the institutional resources a given project can attract. The struggles and conflicts are therefore necessary to the circulation and validation of ideological discourses; in global terms, then, it is possible to speak of a unified field of ideological production in which the differences are only apparent.

So, for example, Angela McRobbie, in her narrative of the development of cultural studies, celebrates the flexibility of the new tendency in this arena, which seeks to distance itself from "fixed" theoretical models: "There is a greater degree of openness in most of the contributions [to the volume *Cultural Studies*, in which McRobbie's essay appears as the conclusion] than would have been the case some years ago, when the pressure to bring the chosen object of study firmly into the conceptual landmarks, provided first by Althusser and then by Gramsci, imposed on cultural studies a degree of rigidity" (1992, 724).

However, McRobbie's celebration of this new openness is an ambivalent one. Earlier in the same essay, she expresses concern that "what has now gone, with Marxism, and partly in response to the political bewilderment and disempowerment of the left, is that sense of urgency [which, according to McRobbie, had characterized culture studies at an earlier historical moment]" (1992, 720). However, McRobbie does not theorize the relations between the new openness and this loss of urgency. Rather, she sees the changes she is describing as an "undecidable" mixture of "benefits" and "dangers": "This new discursiveness allows or permits a speculative 'writerly' approach, the dangers of which I have already outlined, but the advantages of which can be seen in the broader, reflective and insightful mode which the absence of the tyranny of theory, as it was once understood, makes possible" (724).

At the same time, the "bewilderment" and "disempowerment" of the Left, which figured into McRobbie's explanation of the disappearance of Marxism, itself disappears in her assessment of the new openness in culture studies. This she attributes to the replacement of one discourse by another: Ernesto Laclau's displacement of the unified class subject by an understanding of identities as contingent and inherently plural. This, apparently, has nothing to do with the weakness of the Left. On the contrary, McRobbie argues that the "collapse of Marxism need not be construed as signaling the end of socialist politics; indeed the beginning of a new era, where the opportunities for a pluralist democracy are strengthened rather than weakened, is now within reach" (1992, 724).

Therefore, according to McRobbie, the strength of Laclau's discourse is simply an effect of its greater insight into social mechanisms than Marxism. She cites with approval Laclau's claim to be going "beyond" Marxism. By thus positing the greater explanatory power of Laclau's discourse, McRobbie is able not only to equate socialism with pluralist democracy but also to affirm the ultimately beneficial effects of the new openness in culture studies. Put another way, if pluralism is equivalent to progress toward socialism, this must also hold true for the greater pluralism within cultural studies.

Two problems remain for McRobbie: the loss of political urgency in contemporary cultural studies and some "obfuscation" in Laclau's own account of subject formation. In particular, she finds that Laclau is not able to account for the "actual processes of acquiring identity." In fact,

> [it] is his commitment to the historically specific which allows Laclau to not be specific. He cannot spell out the practices of, or the mechanics of, identity formation, for the very reason that they are, like their subjects, produced within particular social and historical conditions. This permits a consistently high level of abstraction in his political philosophy. But the work of transformation which is implicit in his analysis is exactly concurrent with the kind of critical work found in the contributions on race in this volume (1992, 725).

Thus, the problem with Laclau's discourse is its level of abstraction. The solution to this problem, for McRobbie, is to produce concrete and specific analyses, which will be concurrent with Laclau's claims. She clarifies this claim at the end of her essay, which calls for more detailed ethnographic studies of everyday life. "This, then, is where I want to end," she writes, "with a plea for identity ethnography in cultural studies, with a plea for carrying out interactive research on groups and individuals who are more than just audiences for texts" (1992, 730). Although she does not say so explicitly, it would follow from her argument that such concrete, detailed studies would also resist the decline in the political effectivity of cultural studies, since they would then be more directly connected with the actual processes of identity formation that take place in the "fleeting, fluid, and volatile formations" (730) of everyday life (and, presumably, cannot therefore be grasped with an abstract theoretical discourse).

In the context of McRobbie's absolute privileging of Laclau's discourse and her acceptance of his claim that we now live in a post-Marxist universe, it is impossible to take seriously her rhetoric regarding the openness of contemporary cultural studies. Instead, what she is describing is the replacement of one set of limits by another: The sense of openness is simply the privileging of the new set of limits by those who benefit from it, whose relative power is supported and increased by this set of limits. That is, McRobbie's assessment of the strengths and weaknesses of contemporary discourses in cultural studies reflects a transformation in the political economy of discourses, and it is carried out from the standpoint of the most valued discourse within that political economy.

The problem of the legitimation of these valuable discourses explains the panic that McRobbie says she was "gripped by" on her first reading of the papers in the volume. She began "to lose a sense of why the object of study is constituted as the object of study in the first place. Why do it? What is the point? Who is it for?" (1992, 721). I would suggest that this anxiety over the loss of the object is a professionalist anxiety over the impossibility of maintaining both the institutional legitimation of cultural studies as a (non)field of study and its radical character (which constitutes the only legitimation of its existence as a critique of dominant forms of knowledge).

In this sense, the narrative McRobbie constructs, like the volume *Cultural Studies* itself, produces an identity out of the various kinds of work being done in cultural studies. This need for identification accounts for the uncritical valorization of pluralism (as opposed to contestation and critique). An instance of this is revealed in the fact that, despite her broad criticism and apparently deep anxiety over the present state of cultural studies, McRobbie can find no particular contribution to the volume that she considers deserving of criticism. In fact, she takes great pains to assure us that the general criticism she makes regarding the effects of the introduction of deconstruction into cultural studies is not applicable to any of the specific texts in the volume (or elsewhere) that actually make use of deconstruction. She explicitly exempts, for example, Gayatri Spivak and Homi Bhabha from the "formalism" to which deconstruction tends. This, of course, undermines her apparent criticism of deconstruction as an ideological discourse because the problem would therefore be not with its political effects but with its misuses by individuals.

Contrary to McRobbie's claims about openness, then, the purpose of her "criticism" of deconstruction, like her participation in the removal of Marxism from the theoretical and political landscape, is to establish a set of inclusions and exclusions that will support the current constitution of the political economy of institutional values—not too much formalism, not too much abstraction, no Marxism, and so on. However, as opposed to the "tyrannical" regime of theory that McRobbie is glad to be rid of, these inclusions and exclusions are measured not against determinations of political effectivity that are rigorously theorized but rather against an untheorized notion of their proximity to the actual processes of identity formation. Those who are presently excluded from the pluralist institution of cultural studies could then, at some point, be included—not on the condition that they account for their project by proposing some critical rearticulation of the general project of cultural studies but rather by moving a bit closer to the details of everyday life, by uncovering some previously neglected aspect of the processes of identity formation.

Consequently, I would refer to McRobbie's discourse as an appreciative one, in the sense that it attempts to assess the relative values represented by discourses within a political economy of discourses that remains itself unquestioned. Discourses of this type, such as the ones presently dominant in the field of cultural studies, are appreciative in the sense that they are assessments of the various objects they account for (the details of everyday life), and they are also self-reflexively appreciative because they are interested less in the theoretical and political effectivity of their own discourse than in their institutional value. Of course, one type of appreciation supports the other: The most valuable institutional discourse will be the one with the investment in some field of inquiry that can yield the highest return. As I suggested before, this will take the form of the discovery of some interesting object or tradition of texts that had previously been neglected or undervalued. These operations preserve the newness and importance of the field and therefore legitimate it according to current academic standards.

Likewise, discourses that are too formalistic are deemed embarrassing because they are too much like traditional literary studies. And Marxism is problematic because it excludes too much and therefore disenables the constitution of a unified political economy of discourses by threatening the coherence of the field and its acceptability within liberal academic discourse. Finally, this eclectic pluralism requires a reunderstanding of political effectivity as intervention in local processes of identity formation, such as that provided by Laclau, since without some claim to be doing urgent work, culture studies will appear too close to traditional humanistic studies (too formalist) and therefore irrelevant.

The use of the category of culture, as it is understood in contemporary discourses, and the displacement of the category of ideology have enabled the reconstitution of cultural studies on the terms McRobbie describes. In Marxist understandings, ideology refers to those discourses that contribute to the reproduction of capitalist social relations by "educating" individuals in the inevitability or desirability of those relations; ideology works by producing the subjects required by capitalist social relations. This assumes a relation of determination between production relations and class rule, on one side, and the mechanisms that guarantee or reproduce those relations and that rule, on the other.

The advocates of a postmodern cultural studies, meanwhile, privilege the category of culture precisely because it undermines this relation of determination. As Michael Ryan argues in *Politics and Culture,*

> another name for that boundary between reason and materiality that I have described as form might be culture, since culture is generally applied to everything that falls on the social and historical side of materiality, and it can also be a name for everything that falls on the rhetorical and representational side of reason. Culture includes the domains of rhetoric and representation,

as well as the domains of lived experience, of institutions, and of social life patterns (1989, 8).

For Ryan, the usefulness of the category of culture is that it breaks down boundaries between ideality and materiality, between "rhetoric" and "reality," between "culture" and "extracultural" (for example, social) relations. It then becomes impossible to critique any cultural process for its role in reproducing existing relations of exploitation: "The point, therefore, of emphasizing the culturality or rhetoricity of such things as trade and dwelling is to underscore both their role in the elaboration of political power and their plasticity as social forms that can change shape and acquire new contents" (1989, 17). In this case, any particular cultural form can be equally important in supporting some power relation and therefore as a site of intervention, but at the same time, any cultural form is equally open to being filled with some new content. So, for example, the existing state could just as easily become an instrument for emancipating oppressed classes rather than oppressing them as it does now.

Ryan arrives at his "poststructuralist approach to culture" in part through a critique of the Birmingham School's model of hegemony, which "still implies that the primary agent of cultural activity is the ruling class" (1989, 18). By contrast,

> [the] post-structuralist approach to culture thus places a much more positive emphasis on popular forces and on the potential of popular struggles. And it can be extended to the cultural sphere. Rather than being understood simply as an instrument of hegemony, cultural forms can be read as sites of political difference, where domination and resistance, the resistance to the positive power of the dispossessed that is domination and the counter-power, the threat of reversed domination, that is the potential force of the dispossessed, meet (1989, 19).

In other words, any form of domination contains within it some mode of potentially effective resistance. In fact, the domination is itself nothing more than the resistance to that resistance. Since, according to this argument, domination is not domination for some purpose or in defense of some interest, no priority can be established between one mode of resistance and another, nor can we account for the consequences of any mode of resistance.

According to appreciative cultural studies, the meanings of identities and the struggles over them are immanent to those identities themselves. In this case, as McRobbie argues, "when contingency is combined with equivalence and when no social group is granted a privileged place as an emancipatory agent, then a form of relational hegemony can extend the

sequence of democratic antagonisms through a series of social displacements" (1992, 724). If no group or practice can be privileged over any
other, then the problem of the site and effectivity of critique must be
raised: Critique in the name of what? To address this question, it is necessary to take sides, to enter into conflicts over the conditions of emancipatory politics. However, if emancipatory politics amounts to nothing more
than ad hoc arrangements between "popular forces" that emerge contin-
gently, then the moment of critique and contestation can be evaded. Put
another way, any practice that one might be engaged in is potentially as
important and useful as that of anyone else (or at least, there would be no
grounds for denying this assertion). In this case, if various practices are
combined, there is always the possibility that they will add up to emancipatory results. Or not. At any rate, there are no grounds for critique as a
central element of political struggle.

In this context, the indeterminacy of cultural studies can be valorized.
As Lawrence Grossberg, Cary Nelson, and Paula Treichler write, "Cultural
studies needs to remain open to unexpected, unimagined, even uninvited
possibilities. No one can hope to control these developments" (1992, 2).
"Its methodology, ambiguous from the beginning, could best be seen as
bricolage" (2), they contend. They then go on to define cultural studies as
follows:

> Cultural studies is an interdisciplinary, transdisciplinary and sometimes
> counter-disciplinary field that operates in the tension between its tendencies
> to embrace both a broad, anthropological and a more narrowly humanistic
> conception of culture. Unlike traditional anthropology, however, it has grown
> out of analyses of modern industrial societies. It is typically interpretative
> and evaluative in its methodologies, but unlike traditional humanism it re-
> jects the exclusive equation of culture with high culture and argues that all
> forms of cultural production need to be studied in relation to other cultural
> practices and to social and historical structures. Cultural studies is thus com-
> mitted to the study of the entire range of a society's arts, beliefs, institutions,
> and communicative practices (1992, 4).

By establishing that cultural studies operates in the tensions between
incompatible understandings ("broad, anthropological," which is to say
structural and historical, ones and "more narrowly humanistic," that is,
experiential, ones), Grossberg, Nelson, and Treichler interpret the eclecticism of contemporary cultural studies as a form of diversity abstracted
from rigorous contestations over the meaning of culture or cultural studies. Furthermore, they agree with Raymond Williams that the word *culture*
"simultaneously invokes symbolic and material domains and that the
study of culture involves not privileging one over the other but interrogat-

ing the relation between the two" (1992, 4). Therefore, the indeterminacy of culture studies merely reflects the indeterminacy of culture itself: In both cases, one is only able to produce specific articulations with no necessary relation to a broader field of economic and political relations. Like McRobbie, they argue that investigators in the field of culture studies are free to explore their own specific area of knowledge (in other words, to accumulate intellectual capital in the various disciplines and the interstices between them) without the productive tensions between different knowledges ever becoming contestation or being directed at the transformation of the disciplines, much less the entire structure of disciplinary knowledge.

Postmodern philosophical and theoretical categories and presuppositions have been essential to the constitution of what I will call "mainstream" or "appreciative" cultural studies. I understand postmodernism as consisting of all those discourses and practices governed by the assumption that reality is constituted by an unbounded plurality of heterogeneous forms. As with cultural studies, though, I do not limit the field of postmodernism to those discourses that openly support this assumption or refer to themselves as "postmodernist." Rather, I understand postmodernism as being constituted by a political economy of competing positions that reproduce the legitimacy of those areas of knowledge and practice governed by the presupposition and privileging of heterogeneity. I would include within the category of postmodernism, then, discourses that consider themselves indifferent to or even hostile to postmodernism. I would cite, for example, Jurgen Habermas's attacks on postmodernism, which are based on his understanding of communicative rationality and the project of modernity. By situating these attacks within the framework of how one adjudicates between different forms of established knowledge and discourse, Habermas simply reproduces the terms of the debate as constituted by postmodernism—a debate, that is, that is actually a struggle over the terms of a new mode of liberalism adequate for a late-capitalist global order in crisis (and over who will "possess" those terms). Habermas's discourses fulfill this function by understanding the conditions of possibility of communication as immanent to specific and autonomous communicative situations and forms themselves. In fact, the legitimation and hegemony of postmodern culture studies within the arena of culture critique depend upon the existence of a range of competing positions that, as in the logic of the market as studied by Marx, "average out" in "the long run."

The discourses of postmodern cultural studies are unable to theorize in a rigorous way the politics of the institutions in which they are situated. Therefore, the incoherencies and contradictions of these discourses are most evident in relation to the question of devising a politics of resistance to these institutions, in particular the academy. So, for example, Grossberg, Nelson, and Treichler acknowledge from the start of their introduction that the volume they are presenting emerges at the height of a "cultural studies boom" (1992, 1) of international dimensions. Later, they contend that "it is the future of cultural studies in the United States that seems to us to present the greatest need for reflection and debate" (10). This is understandable because, as they argue earlier, the "boom is especially strong" in the United States and has "created significant investment opportunities" (1).

However, they go on to contend, the "threat is not from institutionalization per se, for cultural studies has always had its institutionalized forms within and outside the academy" (Grossberg, Nelson, and Treichler 1992, 10). Rather, the "issue for U.S. practitioners is what kind of work will be identified with cultural studies and what social effects it will have. . . . Too many people simply rename what they were already doing to take advantage of the cultural studies boom" (10–11). Thus, it is not the institutional situation—with its limits and possibilities—that is at stake but policing the intellectual property and copyright of the new (non)discipline. The "multi-," "non-," and even "anti-" disciplinary character of cultural studies, on this account, enables the formation of a site of accumulation of institutional capital whose "unfixity" also frees it from accountability to critiques of its institutional positioning. As far as its social effects go, we have already seen that these are wholly contingent and therefore cannot be theorized or critiqued in any systematic way.

Grossberg, Nelson, and Treichler do not consider the possible uses to the institution of the free-floating, unfixed character of culture studies. They do not see that the "extra-" and "cross-" disciplinary location of culture studies they celebrate actually allows the academy to provide a space for radical discourses, without exerting any pressure to transform the existing disciplinary structure. The question that needs to be raised here is not, of course, in regard to the legitimacy and necessity of working within late-capitalist institutions (such as the university). Rather, the issue is the identification of institutionalization with institutionality in postmodern cultural studies, along with the institutional and ideological forms that support and naturalize this conflation. Put another way, there is a difference between working within and against dominant institutions and becoming an integral part of the functioning of those institutions. Working against dominant institutions from within requires the contestation of the various institutional forms that reproduce institutional power and authority; becoming institutionalized entails fulfilling the need of the institutions for new ways of reproducing their power and authority. The relation between cultural studies and the existing disciplines proposed by Grossberg, Nelson, and Treichler is inadequate in this context because of its ultimately laissez-faire approach to institutional forms and their uses. In contrast, I would argue it is necessary to occupy positions within the disciplines and exploit the contradiction between their claims to universality and their specialist partiality in order to challenge their very separateness and legitimacy. (For a more extended discussion of this issue, see Chapter 4.)

These contemporary discourses of the local and specific find their theoretical and ideological support in the founding texts of postmodernism, in particular those of Jean Baudrillard, Gilles Deleuze and Felix Guattari, Jacques Derrida, Michel Foucault, Jacques Lacan, and Jean-Francois Lyotard. Despite the local differences among their texts, all of these theorists develop justifications for the privileging of the local and specific—whatever is irreducible or incommensurable to global structures and processes. For example, in Derrida's notion of the *bricoleur* (which is, according to Grossberg, Nelson, and Treichler, a prototype of the practitioner of cultural studies), practice is understood as the piecing together of elements that have been left unarticulated by dominant institutions and knowledges, forming new combinations. Two aspects of this conception are most urgent for my discussion here: first, the resistance to totalizing abstraction, which can identify the structure of dominant institutions and their mode of operation, and second, the privileging of the immanence of local constructs and "unique" combinations of heterogeneous elements that could not have been anticipated or the result of a plan.

Articulation and the Politics of Identity

Postmodern discourses, by displacing Marxism along with the hegemonic liberal humanism, provide the necessary legitimation for the extradisciplinary spaces and institutional interstices privileged by postmodern cultural studies. In other words, the categories of heterogeneity and difference operate in postmodern cultural studies in the interest of institutional reformism and the establishment of a political economy of institutional values capable of legitimating and protecting the work already being done. By combining the critique of liberalism with that of Marxism, postmodern cultural studies has been able to establish a theoretical space in which it can make a claim to have superseded existing discourses on society and culture and therefore legitimate its institutional independence. (Angela McRobbie, for example, notes that the "debate about the future of Marxism in cultural studies has not yet taken place. Instead, the great debate around modernity and postmodernity has quite conveniently leapt in and filled that space" [1992, 719].)

The critique of Marxism by cultural studies has, by now, become a series of unthinking reflexes and slogans that are mobilized to dismiss historical materialist critique as quickly as possible. It has been replaced by what is generally agreed to be Stuart Hall's articulation of the concept of articulation, which leads directly to the depoliticization of cultural studies that so many of its practitioners decry even as they recirculate that very concept. Articulation is taken to be a solution to the problem of determination in cultural studies, but it actually is the liquidation of the problem itself. Articulation is taken to be a nonreductive way of accounting for the relation between different social and cultural fields and tendencies that is itself a mode of theoretical and cultural intervention in that it imposes an "arbitrary closure" (as Jennifer Daryl Slack puts it [1996, 115]), a "unity within differences," and so on. However, without a hierarchy of instances and contradictions, articulation becomes nothing more than contextualization tied to voluntaristic political claims. Furthermore (despite the insistent denials of Hall and others), it leads to a pantextualism or panrepresentationalism, since textualization and representation will turn out to be what all practices have in common.

But closure is not arbitrary, and causal hierarchies and political priorities (and not merely "decisions") are possible. So, for example, with a materialist understanding of articulation, one has to give politics and theory priority over culture—this is implicit even in one of the most widely circulated definitions of cultural studies as "politicizing theory and theorizing politics." In this case, we can begin by asking how the economic appears within politics and how this appearance itself appears within theory. The economic is determined by the laws of motion of capital; the primary mode of violence constitutive of that sphere is the invisible mode of exploitation exercised by the capital-labor relation; and the main countertendency to the laws of motion of capital is the socialization of the productive forces. As I suggested in the introduction to this volume, politics should be understood, in the last instance, as being constituted by a space of openness and accountability, where doers can be associated with deeds and actions can be presented before an outside (i.e., a space of judgment). The principal form of violence possible here would be the assault on or even destruction of the possibility of such a space, as performed, for instance, by Nietzsche(anism) in Geoff Waite's account.

Here, then, we might have some helpful questions. Where and in what forms does economic violence appear as (anti)political violence? What new modes of accountability are opened by the socialization of the productive forces or by attempts to suppress, contain, and direct those forces? These are, to be sure, theoretical questions, which arise where theory (most broadly, the inquiry into what lies behind appearances) finds its condition of possibility in politics, in the continual self-clarification from the outside required by properly political action. And the main question about culture for cultural studies in this case would be this: Where do cultural articulations (distinguished, let's say, by the justification through repetition, replication, appropriation, and imitation characteristic of cultural as opposed to economic, political, and theoretical practices) collude with the economic in producing "insiders" for whom the constitutive modes of violence remain invisible? Beyond that, where do they lay the groundwork for emancipatory politics by instituting the mutual constitution of theory and politics? The obvious and banal objections that the cultural constitutes the economic and that everything, in fact, constitutes everything else can be easily dismissed—if a particular analysis is ultimately interested in the question of where politics and theory are most interested in each other.

The concept of articulation, as it has become fixed in cultural studies, does not lead to an inquiry into where global economic contradictions take shape in political antagonisms and produce new questions on the boundary of theoretical inquiry itself. Instead, the concept leads to the privileging of the destabilization of the discursive categories—such as essentialized forms of identity or self-present consciousness upon which a given form of subjectivity depends. In this way, the discourses take credit for this destabilization, and they are able to evade their complicity with the attempts of late-capitalist crisis management to develop modes of subjectivity appropriate for changed historical conditions. I would argue that the emergence of collective modes of practice and public mechanisms for reproducing labor power have produced a crisis in the liberal humanist subject. In other words, the target and model of cultural categories under late capitalism is no longer the individual property owner presupposed by classical liberalism. Rather, it is the subject charged with circulating within and managing late-capitalist institutions that involve extensive divisions of labor and therefore an objectification of tasks and subjective capacities. Consequently, the valued subject under such conditions is no longer the autonomous individual capable of tending to his or her own property, which presumably bears his or her own personal imprint. It is, instead, the individual who can situate himself or herself into a wide variety of essentially interchangeable collective practices that are indifferent to the personal qualities of the individual (except insofar as individual differences correspond to some classification determined by the needs of the institutions and the stability of the system).

Thus, the destabilization of the liberal subject is one aspect of a process that also involves the restabilization of the private individual on the terms set by the collectivized structures of late capitalism. The category of the bricoleur, for example, enables the privileging of individualist modes of "free" praxis that take into account the institutional limitations of late capitalism. That is why this category is so useful for legitimating the creation of islands of extradisciplinary practice for the subject of postmodern cultural studies (the petit bourgeois intellectual attempting to make use of his or her monopoly on the production and legitimation of valued knowledges to position himself or herself advantageously within late-capitalist institutions). Within this framework, it is also possible to see that the differences or pluralized identities privileged by postmodern cultural studies aid in the segmentation of heterogeneous sections of the global workforce—heterogeneous, that is, in relation to the varied needs of a global capitalist order. I would therefore argue that postmodernism's universalizing critique of universals simply takes one historical form of universality as absolute in the interest of resisting the possibilities of producing new modes of universality on the basis of a conscious realization of the collectivization of social relations.

Some of the implications of the critique of universalism based upon antiessentialist discourses, developed in particular by Ernesto Laclau and Chantal Mouffe in their *Hegemony and Socialist Strategy,* can be seen in Kobena Mercer's discussion of transformations in the signs articulating categories of race in the post–World War II world. Mercer argues that the establishment of democratic identities is a result, on the one hand, of struggles over signs or the "social relations of representation" (1992, 429) and, on the other hand, the construction of new chains of equivalence in accord with a new term introduced by a reversal or shift in the valence of some term.

For Mercer, the category of identity replaces that of class in the theorization of agencies in contemporary postconsensus or postmodern society:

> The relativization of the oppositional aura of Marxism and modernism actually enables us to appreciate the diversity of social and political agency among actors whose antagonistic practices have also contributed to the sense of fragmentation and plurality that is said to characterize the postmodern condition. Over the past decade, developments in black politics, in lesbian and gay communities, among women and numerous feminist movements, and across a range of struggles around social justice, nuclear power, and ecology have pluralized the domain of political antagonism. There is no satisfactory common noun that designates what these so-called "new social movements" represent and it's my impression that "identity" is currently invoked as a way of acknowledging the transformations in public and private life associated with the historical presence of new social actors (1992, 424).

This substitution of identity for class is the logical consequence of the tendency in cultural studies that I already noted in the work of Stuart Hall. Rather than a transcendence of class politics, identity, as the product of an identification produced by affiliations grounded in common conditions and struggles, marks the site of a contradiction. The social identities Mercer is referring to (in particular those articulated around the categories of race, gender, and sexuality) are the products of the representation of new forms of collective labor power that take shape in late capitalism. With the entrance of previously excluded groups or classes into the economic and cultural institutions of the capitalist order and with the more favorable conditions of struggle this provides, categories such as "women" and "blacks" cease to be merely the signs marking the subordination of groups designated as inferior or external to the social order. Rather, these categories take on a new meaning, representing the demand that outmoded forms of authority be eliminated in the interest of democratizing all social relations. However, this reversal or revaluation of terms, if it is not resituated within a global analysis, tends to reproduce those very categories that these struggles have problematized and to do so in abstraction from the overall development of the relations and forces of production.

Within cultural studies, meanwhile, the production of discourses on culture by Hoggart, Thompson, and Williams resulted from a similar set of contradictions. On the one hand, it was the attempt to preserve and appreciate working-class cultures that were being eroded by the institutions and practices of mass culture. On the other hand, this attempt was itself the result of the entrance of members of the working class into the university. As the university was being transformed into a site of mass (or collectivized) cultural production, it was becoming a site that would make these very discourses accessible by integrating at least sections of the working class into institutions of knowledge production. Thus, cultural studies has come into being as the result of (and is constituted by) the very contradiction that is articulated by the categories of experience and identity. Put differently, cultural studies and related political and intellectual tendencies articulate the contradictory situation of subordinated classes, intellectual work, and emancipatory politics under the conditions established by the regime of private property as it becomes dependent upon the publicly organized reproduction of labor power. Cultural studies has never superseded this contradiction. And this is why, as is evident in Stuart Hall's narratives of cultural studies, each new identity or problem that has confronted cultural studies (feminism, race, the linguistic turn, etc.) has induced a crisis that brings this contradiction to the fore (see, for example, the discussion in Hall's "Cultural Studies and Its Theoretical Legacies"). Furthermore, each such crisis, while undermining some of the liberalistic elements of cultural studies, in the end reinforces the hegemony of the culturalist or experiential pole of cultural studies. Thus, McRobbie's celebration of a cultural studies that is in the process of becoming an ethnography of identities, with which the investigator identifies in an appreciative way, in a sense returns cultural studies to the practices initiated by Richard Hoggart in *The Uses of Literacy* and *Speaking to Each Other*. In both of these works, a working-class individual destabilizes academic discourse by analyzing the working-class culture with which he identifies from a distance.

Within this framework, it becomes possible to account for Mercer's argument that "throughout the modern period, the semiotic stability of this

nodal system in racist ideology [i.e., the logic of absolute difference between "black" and "white"] has been undermined and thrown into a state
of dialectical flux as a result of the reappropriation and rearticulation of
signs brought about by the subaltern subjects themselves" (1992, 428).
Categories such as instability and flux only take on meaning if they are
measured against some standard of stability, i.e., against the subordination
of the term to meanings required by the ruling class. If the production of
new representations and identities results from "symbolic displacements of
the 'proper name'" (428), then these new representations, even if they are
the result of reappropriations and rearticulations of oppressed groups, can
only, in themselves, be ways of proposing new stabilities that would still
accept the general equivalent of ruling-class control. Mercer cannot avoid
this consequence of his argument, since he understands these reappropriations of the materials of subject formation as ends in themselves, as opposed to ways of mobilizing struggles at a particular stage in their development, with specific and historically limited materials.

The same problems arise with Mercer's argument that the struggles
over the categories of race enabled the construction of a whole series of
democratic equivalents by other groups and movements and therefore a
deepening of democratic struggles. As opposed to pedagogical relations
between political agents in which critiques and countercritiques emerge
out of the differential situations occupied, strategies employed, and ends
pursued, Mercer advances an understanding of the connections between
political agents based on the extension of radical democratic equivalences
through imitation and alliance. "On the one hand," he writes, "there is a
mode of appropriation that results in a form of *imitation,* based on a
mimetic strategy of self-representation through which the white subject
identifies with the de-valorized term of the black/white metaphor" (1992,
432). "On the other hand," he continues, "the question of political appropriations that result in forms of democratic *alliance,* entails analysis of the
way white subjects dis-identify with the position ascribed to them in
racist ideologies" (433). The adoption of political identities through a
mimetic strategy of appropriation precludes the possibility of a theoretical
accounting of the relative usefulness of one mode of political practice as
opposed to others. In fact, Mercer's notion of imitation here is based on a
concept of a similarity that can be strong enough to ground an alliance
and yet indeterminate enough to ensure that no partner in this alliance
has any claims on the others; in this scenario, there will be no emergence
of a general will establishing a new logic of commensuration and priorities that would subordinate the various partners. For this reason, such an
alliance, grounded in a post-Marxist politics, can be nothing more than an
attempt to acquire more value by establishing new sites of circulation
within the existing system of value production.

And so, in Mercer's discourse (as with Fiske's), the very possibility of establishing criteria according to which one kind of social change could be considered more "desirable" than some other kind is undermined because class has been replaced by identity. Contrary to the economistic understandings of class that writers such as Hall accept in order to dismiss, Marxism understands class not only as a position within an economic system but as a set of possibilities regarding the arrangement of the entire social and cultural order. The primacy of working-class power in Marxist theory and practice is not a result of the exceptional degree of suffering experienced by the working class or of any moral virtues they possess. Instead, that primacy derives from the fact that the proletariat "organized as the ruling class" represents the potential for exploiting the socialization of the forces of production created by capitalism in the interests of freer, more democratic, and egalitarian social relations. However, this criterion regarding the possibilities represented by any struggle or agent is excluded from the category of identity, which can only reverse the criteria or values contained in the dominant system. This idealizes those agents in the form in which the dominant culture has produced them, leading to a utopian or moralizing politics. In this case, it is easy to understand Mercer's claim that "the vocabulary of left, right, and center is no longer adequate to the terrain of post-consensus politics" (1992, 424). Destabilization, which opens the possibility of local reversals and revaluations in the interest of a more favorable insertion within the existing order, becomes the limit of oppositional politics. This does not mean that the social identities imposed upon subjects due to their imbrication within a culture based on exploitation do not have a (secondary) role in political struggles: Their significance lies in the necessity to indicate, analyze, and oppose the reproduction of reactionary forms of authority in myriad ways within all practices, including oppositional ones.

The Question of the Outside

Since the issue I am addressing here is ultimately the relation between postmodern theory and the possibility of an outside, as a theoretical space unimplicated in local identities and affiliations, it will be helpful to examine Cary Wolfe's *Critical Environments: Postmodern Theory and the Pragmatics of the "Outside."* Wolfe brings together pragmatism, systems theory, and the "thought of the outside" proposed by Foucault and Deleuze to account for the possibility of progressive theory and political critique without the representational premises of Enlightenment modernity. As I will explain more carefully in a moment, systems theory actually bears most of the burden of Wolfe's argument. Wolfe uses pragmatism—Richard Rorty in particular—to defend postmodern theory against the charges, first, that it is self-refuting (that its critiques of universalizing, totalizing, realism, etc., are themselves universalistic, totalizing, and realist) and, second, that postmodern theory is unable to account for causality and social transformation. Foucault and Deleuze, meanwhile, serve primarily as a "radical" antidote for the liberal stances of Rorty and Niklas Luhmann (Deleuze in particular provides the "ontology" to Luhmann's "epistemology" [1998, 140]).

Wolfe explicitly critiques most of the postmodern Left for failing to engage the relations between theory and politics—for wanting to hold on to an often tacit or "strategic" essentialism along with a therefore compromised commitment to postmodern theory: "Most contemporary critics have settled for an uneasy compromise somewhere between these two poles, out of the line of fire, as it were, believing (if only tacitly) that there is indeed a pre-existent, finite reality with its own independent nature, but which is viewed differently by different observers according to the cultural and social determinations that shape their vision of things" (1998, xii). To accept such compromises is to reduce theory to a strictly instrumentalist relation to a pregiven political position that is hence free from interrogation. Rejecting this approach, Wolfe contends that "my guiding conviction here, then, is that theoretically and politically, the only way out is through" (xii)—i.e., through to the logical conclusion of postmodern theory.

I say that Luhmann's systems theory carries the main burden of Wolfe's argument because it is Luhmann whom Wolfe draws upon to dismantle the single most important claim at which his book takes aim—the claim that one can be "outside of that outside" (that is, the outside of a pragmatic self-reflexivity), which would, in turn, be seen as "expressive of a unitary cause: global capitalism" (1998, xxi). Wolfe associates this claim with Fredric Jameson (using Jameson, as he does again in his conclusion, as a synecdoche for Marxism). Luhmann's theory of self-observation provides, for Wolfe, the definitive refutation of a Marxist view of the outside via a demonstration of a necessary "blind spot" that renders any observation contingent and partial. Foucault and Deleuze essentially bypass this issue, and Rorty's pragmatism refutes representationalism (and, by implication, Marxism) but without providing an adequate alternative. Only Luhmann, in Wolfe's opinion, enables not merely "a well-meaning commitment to open-mindedness and self-critique" but also "*a rigorous and coherent theoretical account of that desirability's necessity*" (143).

According to Luhmann, there is a paradox intrinsic to self-observation, which is itself a product of the self-reproduction of autopoietic systems (modern systems whose only source of legitimacy is immanent to their own functioning): In reproducing themselves, systems also necessarily produce regulatory observations of their own functioning (e.g., to prevent or overcome blockages and other dysfunctions). Hence, the external position of the observer is the product of the inside of the system itself, making the inside/outside distinction internal to both system and observer. So, in the example Wolfe takes from Luhmann, determining the legality of an action presupposes the legal/illegal distinction internal to both the functioning of the system and the observation; supposedly, since this distinction makes the observation possible in the first place, it is necessarily invisible (the distinction itself cannot be seen). For Wolfe, this guarantees both sociality and epistemology—insofar as "the process of 'deparadoxicalization' [the constant need to resolve tautologies such as 'this is legal because in corresponds to the law,' etc.] requires that a system's constitutive paradox remain invisible to it, then the only way that this fact can be known as such is by an observation made by *another* observing system" (1998, 68). So, the epistemological rigor that seems to be lost with the discrediting of representationalism and realism and that pragmatism can only supply at the cost of suppressing the plurality of standpoints is here recovered. One's claim to knowledge would meet the criterion of being outside the observed system in that it constitutes itself as the outside of the other observer(s), pointing out the blind spot or constitutive paradox necessarily invisible to other positions.

This is, in fact, how Wolfe's own book is structured. So, Luhmann enters the book as Rorty's outside, showing the necessity of plurality and hence of challenges to the complacent we that Rorty can't account for:

> In the end, then, representationalism is undone on the *philosophical* level in Rorty's pragmatism, but only to reemerge in more powerful and insidious form on the plane of the *political.* . . . Rorty finds himself in this position because of his "evasion" of theory and epistemology-centered philosophy—an evasion that prevents him from exploring how the necessity of other beliefs, observations, or points of view *outside* of the *ethnos* in question might be generated by confronting, with renewed *commitment* to theory, the contingency of his own (1998, 19).

Donna Haraway, to take another example, enters as Luhmann's outside: Her notion of "embodiment" pressures Luhmann's inability to account for power and other differentials between observers (1998, 74). Deleuze and Foucault's theorization of the outside as the "fold" (the way in which life continually produces excesses, doublings, and resistances) is outside of both Luhmann and Rorty; Luhmann later returns as Deleuze's outside, observing Deleuze's inability to break thoroughly with unity and identity. Finally, pragmatism itself returns as the outside of Luhmann and Deleuze, relating their thinking to concrete political issues. Thus, the analyses of these discourses "unfolds"; Wolfe doesn't simply pick and choose eclectically among the various systems he observes.

The eclecticism, though, returns at another level. In the conclusion of Wolfe's book, Fredric Jameson (as Marxism) returns as Luhmann's outside but, more importantly, as Wolfe's own outside (and Wolfe adopts the same position vis-à-vis Jameson). Wolfe needs to engage his own outside because his book has been unable to account for not only the desirability but also the necessity of a "common anti-capitalist politics" (1998, 139), which he claims to support. If such a politics must be argued for on pragmatic rather than foundational grounds, it would seem that the entire theoretical apparatus Wolfe has constructed is ultimately irrelevant to the question of an anti- or procapitalist politics: He could claim little more than to be a bit to Rorty's left. However, if pragmatism provides the form of the argument, Deleuze and Luhmann come back to provide the content. From Deleuze (and Foucault), Wolfe takes an "analysis of the microdynamics of power and resistance, including the outside of capitalism that resonates in the concrete practices and spaces on which it is dependent for reproduction—as a reservoir of complexity and difference, a space of relatively 'free' or 'unbound' points, to use Deleuze's terminology" (1998, 150–151). But this claim collapses immediately. A nontotalizable capitalism produces elements that it is unable to totalize, which is, in turn, to provide the elements of political opposition to something that can't be totalized anyway (and so what, exactly, is one opposing?).

If, as I have suggested, Jameson is brought into the book to serve as Wolfe's "bad conscience" (1998, 142), that conscience only gets worse or at least more muddled in the conclusion. Insofar as Wolfe's Jameson observes his "constitutive blind spot," the author is unable to incorporate this observation into his theory's inside: Wolfe's call for "strategic totalization" (142) leaves him in exactly the same position as those critics he rejected at the beginning, who want to be foundationalists and antirepresentationalists at the same time. (In this case, presumably, one could totalize as long as we all agree that we don't really mean it.) Wolfe's blending of systems theory with Jameson's theory of postmodernism doesn't help matters. As noted, Wolfe uses Jameson as Luhmann's outside: "In the world of late capitalism, do we find persuasive or even plausible Luhmann's contention that the world we live in is one of horizontally functionally differentiated systems in which no system—most conspicuously in light of Jameson, of course, the economic—exerts a centrifugal force on the others?" (146). But at the same time, Wolfe (now introducing Raymond Williams) proposes that we see Luhmann's horizontal system as an emergent postmodern phenomenon, still subordinated to the dominant modern (hierarchical and stratified) system. He contends that "such a hybrid account would present a more persuasive and compelling picture of our current situation than either Jameson's Marxist Utopian totalization in the name of the economic or Luhmann's liberal Utopian view of functional differentiation taken singly" (148). Yet he doesn't seem to notice that, on this account, an anticapitalist politics is certain to become less and less relevant all the time (whether it succeeds or fails), since we are well on the way (considering the speed of contemporary transformations) to Luhmann's utopia anyway—and the only objection that Wolfe seems to have to it is that it doesn't actually exist (yet). In other words, the eclecticism he resists on the theoretical level returns with a vengeance on the political level, where the support for an anticapitalist politics collapses back into the localist pluralism he seeks to distinguish it from.

Because Wolfe's book implicitly invites the reader to read him from the outside, I want to propose that a good place to begin might be to ask what if, contrary to Wolfe's comfortable reconciliation of Luhmann and Jameson, the modern, hierarchical system actually works through, deepens, and reproduces itself precisely by differentiating itself horizontally? After all, it's impossible to see why the articulation of the vertical through its concealment behind proliferating horizontal differentiations (the history of capitalism as generalized commodity production) doesn't create the conditions for an outside observer just as intrinsically as the autopoietic system does; the only difference here is that we would have to account for an intrinsic antagonism between different categories of observers. In this connection, it is useful to note that the relations between the different observers in the model Wolfe takes from Luhmann constitute an allegory of the self-understanding of today's "progressive intellectuals" as articulated by cultural studies. The first observer is a functionary, interested in regulating the system; the second observer is a critic, a more or less marginal dissident who challenges the impartiality of the first observer. The relation between these two observers is therefore political. To take this a step further, the first observer must, at some point, get around to observing the second observer and attempting to suppress, blunt, and finally co-opt that transformative observation (though Wolfe claims that the second observer is necessary, this doesn't mean that the first observer knows about, much less acknowledges, this necessity until left with no choice).

More precisely, that first observer must struggle against the insights of the second by appropriating the blind spot of that second observer and articulating the entire critical discourse around that blind spot. He and his fellow first observers must produce a space organized around the visibility of that blind spot. And, ultimately, the most irreparable and incriminating blind spot is the insistence on the possibility of another system—the polemic that can, in fact, "see" the legal/illegal distinction and therefore make judgments not only about the legality but also about the legitimacy of the system and can do so only as the "outside of the outside." This outside can only be opened by piercing the successive layers of insiders, which becomes more difficult as the distinction between first and second observers grows increasingly undecidable. The blind spot upon which first and second observers come to agree is the assumption that revolutionary transformation is impossible. This is because "our" knowledges, which were produced by the system, would no longer be (our) knowledges if the system ceased to exist. The critical labor of dismantling this assumption, though, is itself only possible if one allows for the presupposition that the inside was set up and set in motion by an external principle that the system doesn't grasp precisely because it has become an internal, "functional" one (for example, the contradictory unity of use value and exchange value in the commodity). Furthermore, these "third observers" (because they discern the link between the first two sets and hence that the legitimacy of the dissident principles doesn't reside in the principles themselves) must act so as to bring precisely such distinctions as legal/illegal into view before other observers interested in questioning their legitimacy.

Consequently, Wolfe's argument only holds if we presuppose the unspeakability of a polemic that is exclusively interested in the founding binaries of society (legitimate/illegitimate, theory/common sense, just/unjust, etc.), which functional differentiation serves to conceal. The relation between functionally differentiated spheres, where Lyotard's differends emerge, are, today, the inside masquerading as the outside. The point of my own allegory is that Marxism does serve as a foundation by articulating (in the sense I indicated earlier) labor, politics, and theory in a polemical relation to liberal mystifications. The proof of this lies in Wolfe's own discourse, which, like all such mystifications, must introduce the question of class exploitation from the *outside* of his own discourse and at the same time establish an *internal* mechanism for excluding it even there.

In sum, postmodern mainstream or appreciative cultural studies is an emergent institutional and cultural form that facilitates the required (post)liberal modifications of pedagogical and other institutions. Its post-disciplinarity corresponds to the postmodern liberal politics of identity, which requires modes of knowledge flexible enough to manage the contradictions of post–welfare state capitalism. This argument, however, should not be read as supporting the existing disciplines, which is to say the existing intellectual division of labor and segmentation of knowledges. Rather, it is a critique of the evasion of the accountability that is associated with a collective project of knowledge production directed at advancing a theorized and therefore contestable purpose. If explanation or theory only extends to the point at which identities are affirmed unproblematically, thereby allowing the category of experience to be introduced, then it becomes possible to produce flexible institutional sites that can reconcile opposition with the needs of dominant institutions in a populist manner, leading to merely local changes (and changes, moreover, that enable the institution to develop more up-to-date forms of authority). The project of a critical cultural studies interested in making visible new (polemical) boundaries of emancipatory theory must today take on two tasks: first, analyzing, in all its horizontal differentiations, the increasingly closed space of cultural studies insiders, and second, reopening the space of Marxist theory, upon whose closure the consolidation of postmodern cultural studies depends.

Notes

1. For a useful critique of the "cultural populism" constitutive of cultural studies, see McGuigan 1992. McGuigan traces effectively the links between the culturalist turn in British cultural studies, the contradictions of Gramscian hegemony, and the privileging of consumption over production. He ends, however, with an affirmation of "critical utopia" (248), itself a populist notion, as a basis for cultural analysis. My view is that cultural analysis needs to be located where theoretical struggles become political and political struggles become theoretical: Culture is the site where this location is either suppressed or made visible against the background of political economic violence. Also see Beasley Murray 1998 for a useful analysis and critique of the foundational populism of cultural studies.

2

CULTURAL STUDIES AND THE POLITICS OF (NON)IDENTITY

Feminism and the Critique of Experience

The strength of postmodern discourses, as I suggested in the previous chapter, is in the effectivity with which they have undermined the basis of liberal humanism: the free and rational individual as the subject of a democratic and pluralist order. To a great extent, this effectivity depended upon a dismantling of the dominant, empiricist understandings of knowledge. That is, postmodern theories made it possible to see that truth claims based on experience in fact simply reproduced the privileged epistemological and political position of those who control and benefit from the production of the conditions of experience.

The displacement of the category of individual by that of subject and of those of ideas or consciousness by sign or signification is extremely important here. Subjects and signs as theoretical categories are the results of an abstraction from the immediacies of experience and everyday life. They enable an understanding of practices as the results of a process of production, a system of differences that precedes and conditions the formation of any particular identity. In other words, if the subject is not originary, then the content or meaning of subjectivity must be understood as an effect of systemic interrelations. Experience and interpretations of experience can, in this case, no longer be seen as either legitimating existing social relations due to their obviousness or naturalness (their conformity to experience) or as providing the kinds of knowledges necessary for emancipatory movements seeking structural transformations (since the experience of the oppressed is also constructed by the dominant ideology and culture).

It is necessary to inquire into how the categories of experience and identity, which have been so severely and even definitively problematized by the strongest aspects of postmodern theory, have, in recent years, returned to ground cultural studies within the very theoretical framework designed to repudiate them. In this chapter, I will interrogate the function of the categories of experience and (especially) identity in stabilizing postmodern cultural studies along the lines I analyzed in the Chapter 1. I will address these questions through an engagement with some of the most provoking and problematic questions raised by some (I would argue, dominant) contemporary feminisms, in particular those whose problematic is determined by postmodern theory. I am interested in the symptomatic significance of certain forms of feminism that have the power to determine the types of discourses that will be possible and legitimate within the institutions of knowledge production. (In this context, I am especially interested academic feminism—a characterization that I take to be a description of its institutional location and not, as is often the case, a term of abuse or a suggestion of a lack of political engagement.) Furthermore, this engagement will presuppose the urgency of the question of women's emancipation and the centrality of that question to any project of systemic social transformation.

In this chapter, I argue that contemporary feminist theorists whose work is informed by postmodern theory have distanced the predominant forms of academic feminism from the more radical political positions of an earlier generation of radical and socialist feminists. This critique is shared by other (dissident) feminists within the academy. For example, Teresa Ebert critiques the dominant "ludic feminism" and argues for a revolutionary, "red feminist" agenda. Such revolutionary feminist projects have nevertheless been significantly displaced and downgraded. As a consequence, the conditions of possibility for feminism and the production of gender as a site of self-consciously political antagonism, which lie in the contradiction between sexist structures and the specific ways in which women have been integrated into the working and middle classes within late-capitalist society, are increasingly unexamined. What remains, a politics based upon the negotiations between a "stable" identity or a destabilized "nonidentity," will be unable to grasp the significance for the various contending social forces (including women) of the antagonisms articulated by the category of gender.

I take this detour through some of the discourses of contemporary feminism to clarify a parallel trajectory in cultural studies. Feminism, like cultural studies, inquires into the connections between power and subjectivity, and it does so from the standpoint of the dominated. In addition, feminism shares with postmodernism a critique of the abstract and universalistic modes of knowledge and subjectivity associated with liberalism—a critique that, in both cases, is advanced from the standpoint of marginality, or those subjectivities and interests excluded as heterogeneous to (and yet necessary for) the constitution of the dominant order and dominant representations. Furthermore, I will argue that the discourses of postmodernism, cultural studies, and feminism are also related in that they are produced by the contradictions between the categories of private and public that are introduced by the publicly organized reproduction of collective labor power characteristic of late capitalism. Finally, I will argue that these discourses have been reciprocally useful in enabling one another to resolve, in imaginary ways, the contradictions that constitute them: Postmodernism enables cultural studies and feminism to distance themselves from totalizing discourses, and feminism serves this same purpose for cultural studies in relation to Marxism in particular and, in addition, provides postmodernism with a "radical" legitimating appearance. This is why, I would argue, the contestations over the categories of identity and difference have taken on such developed and intense form within and in relation to feminism.

Toward a Postmodern Feminism?

In her introduction to *Feminism/Postmodernism,* Linda Nicholson argues that

> on the one hand, there are many points of overlap between a postmodern stance and positions long held by feminists. Feminists, too, have uncovered the political power of the academy and of knowledge claims. In general, they have argued against the supposed neutrality and objectivity of the academy, asserting that claims put forth as universally applicable have invariably been valid only for men of a particular culture, class, and race. They have further alleged that even the ideals that have given backing to those claims, such as "objectivity" and "reason," have reflected the values of masculinity at a particular point in history. Feminists have criticized other Enlightenment ideals, such as the autonomous and self-legislating self, as reflective of masculinity in the modern West. On such grounds, postmodernism would appear to be a natural ally of feminism (1992, 5).

The grounds for such an alliance, furthermore, are situated in relation to a critique of earlier versions of feminism, which Nicholson regards as too closely aligned to Enlightenment assumptions (for example, claims of transhistorical determinants of gender oppression or attempts "to describe a woman's distinct perspective" [6]). However, in this narrative of feminism's overcoming of its ties to Enlightenment rationality, very different kinds of modern feminisms are contrasted to the postmodern one Nancy Fraser and Nicholson support in "Social Criticism Without Philosophy." The critique of metanarratives they support includes Marxist class reductionism, Shulamith Firestone's biological essentialism, Nancy Chodorow's theory of mothering, and Catharine MacKinnon's understanding of sexuality, among others. What unites all of these metanarratives is that they are attempts to explain domination, to subordinate one set of determinations to another.

According to Fraser and Nicholson, the problem with metanarratives is that they "are insufficiently attentive to historical and cultural diversity, and they falsely universalize features of the theorist's own era, society, culture, class, sexual orientation, and ethnic, or racial group" (1992, 27). This means that any attempt at totalizing generalizations can only reflect the experiences or standpoint of the subject doing the theorizing, and it must do so at the expense of some other subject. However, this can only be the case if all theorizing necessarily reflects the experiences of the subject of theory; therefore, the same would be true of "small" and particular narratives, the only advantage of the latter being that this particularity would be recognized as such and no "false universality" would be imposed upon others. That is, while critiquing an empiricist and universalist humanism, Fraser and Nicholson ultimately introduce experientialist understandings in another form.

In this context, it is easy to see on what grounds Fraser and Nicholson argue for the usefulness of postmodernism in relation to contemporary feminist theory and practice, which they see as "increasingly a matter of alliances rather than one of unity around a universal or shared interest or identity" (1992, 35). In this sense, contemporary feminism is "already implicitly postmodern" (35). The purpose of introducing postmodern theory, then, would be to bring about a greater self-consciousness of the existing realities of contemporary feminism. This critique of Enlightenment ideals actually only qualifies traditional forms of empiricism by specifying the conditions that make particular and limited cognitive appropriations of reality possible; however, the notion of knowledge as a direct reflection of the immediate reality of the subject remains intact. In this case, the effect is to exclude inquiries into the ways in which the various determinants of gender oppression are unified in their effects and their systemic articulation within a global capitalist system. The immediacy with which the subject of knowledge reflects reality and therefore has a privileged access to the real through experience is resecured by incorporating new subjects into the system of knowledge and power supported by empiricist discourses.

Arguments such as Fraser and Nicholson's for the need to deconstruct and contextualize rigid (totalizing) notions of gender identity are generally made in the context of a critique of earlier (and still prominent) modes of feminism that claimed to speak on behalf of all women but in fact represented primarily First World, white, middle-class women. However, the postmodern framework Fraser and Nicholson establish merely accommodates these critiques by diversifying the field of feminism without really transforming it. In other words, the recording of the diverse experiences of different groups of women can in no way add up to more general emancipatory theories or practices; only a structural approach can aid in this attempt. The political effect of the substitution of description (empiricism) for explanation is twofold. First, principled discussions over competing (and not only different) strategic perspectives become impossible, since the only universal criteria for the postmodern feminism Fraser and Nicholson propose is the inclusion of more descriptions. Second, the mode of theorizing Fraser and Nicholson support takes existing realities and existing differences as given and thus makes it impossible to examine the contradictions and opposed potentialities of the forces constituting those realities; it thereby becomes impossible to intervene in the formation of these forces or the realization of these potentialities. What I termed in the previous chapter the *political economy* of the field of knowledges and positions remains intact, and, therefore, so do the advantages that accrue to the most valued position. All that changes is the mode of distributing values in such a way as to incorporate new identities that are required for the functioning of the general political economy. This politics of inclusiveness in effect excludes two key questions: "Inclusion" in what? And for what purpose?

In their historical narrative of the development of feminist theory, Fraser and Nicholson argue that in the late 1960s and early 1970s, feminists needed to produce essentializing metanarratives in order to have the question of women's liberation placed on the agenda, alongside the questions of class and race, in particular. However, through the 1980s, the use and legitimacy of metanarratives sharply declined, for two reasons. First, there were the intrinsic problems of discovering a single main or universal cause or form of women's oppression. Second, metanarratives tended to construct a unity among all women that, by excluding differences and inequalities between (and within) women, tended to identify this unity with the standpoint of more privileged (white, middle-class) women. In other words, both intellectual developments and the challenge to a dominant, ultimately liberal feminism produced a self-reflexivity and self-criticism among feminist theorists and placed the question of differences on the agenda.

However, the shift away from generalizing metanarratives to the specific, local, and concrete has another component. As Fraser and Nicholson argue,

> since around 1980, many feminist scholars have come to abandon the project
> of grand social theory. They have stopped looking for *the* cause of sexism

and have turned to more concrete inquiries with more limited aims. One reason for this shift is the growing legitimacy of feminist scholarship. The institutionalization of women's studies in the United States has meant a dramatic
increase in the size of the community of feminist inquirers, a much greater
division of scholarly labor, and a large and growing fund of concrete information. As a result, feminist scholars have come to regard their enterprise
more collectively, more like a puzzle whose various pieces are being filled in
by many different people than like a construction to be completed by a single
grand theoretical stroke. In short feminist scholarship has attained its maturity (1992, 31–32).

At the same time, the existence of quasi metanarratives continues to be
prevalent in feminist theory. Thus, there is a conflict between the "de-
creasing interest in grand social theory" and "essentialist vestiges" (Fraser
and Nicholson 1992, 33). The authors account for this by arguing that
"feminist scholarship has remained insufficiently attentive to the *theoretical* prerequisites of dealing with diversity, despite widespread commitment to accepting it politically" (33). Their proposals for a postmodern
mode of feminist inquiry involve a focus on the genealogies of terms such
as *sexuality* and *mothering,* rather than simply using these types of terms
to produce metanarratives (unified explanations), as well as a focus on
differences and contrasts insofar as connections are made across various
cultures, historical periods, and so forth.
   In other words, a political and scholarly maturity needs to be supple-
mented by a theoretical maturity or a theoretical understanding that can
reflect the maturity already attained in other areas. However, in this narrative of maturation, the connection between the two aspects of development (political and scholarly) has been severed. Fraser and Nicholson do
not explain why conflicts within feminism, even if they produce different
and opposing modes of feminist practice, necessarily lead to the kind of
fragmented and piecemeal inquiry that they describe. Why would conflicts
over constructs such as woman or gender not have led to opposing metanarratives or totalizing forms of explanation? Even more, how can such
conflicts be accounted for and clarified without taking on such a form, in
which the consequences of contesting approaches can be investigated?
Fraser and Nicholson's concern with theoretical prerequisites represents an
interest not in theorizing the conditions of possibility of the current feminist enterprise but rather in legitimating it by showing that it corresponds
to contemporary theories of knowledge and politics. In the process, contestations and conflicts necessarily get reduced to different areas of interest,
different pieces of the (same?) puzzle. Thus, the theoretical maturation
they call for will have the effect of sanctioning a particular way of resolving the (political and institutional) crisis of feminism and excluding other
possible resolutions by presenting this one as an unproblematic reality.

Thus, the turn toward postmodernism in contemporary academic feminism suppresses the conflict between two modes of theorizing gender and feminism in relation to other social categories and struggles: first, the theorization of gender in relation to class and capitalist social structures, which was the project of many feminists who emerged out of the New Left in the late 1960s and early 1970s (as in the case of those advancing a socialist feminism) and second, a theorization of gender in relation to the categories of sign, discourse, and identity. Dominant tendencies within contemporary feminism have moved decisively in the latter direction, and this requires that explanations of gender in relation to class structures and the social totality be represented as obsolete, naive, and oppressive. For example, Fraser and Nicholson argue that Lyotard's version of postmodernism "throws out the baby of large historical narrative with the bathwater of philosophical metanarrative and the baby of social-theoretical analysis of large-scale inequalities with the bathwater of reductive Marxian class theory" (1992, 25). However, by "large historical narrative," Fraser and Nicholson mean genealogies of historically specific institutions (such as "the modern, restricted, male-headed, nuclear family" [34]) and not transformations in the mode of production (which would enable us to theorize changes in subordinate modes of production—such as the family—in relation to the global division of labor). As a result, their assessment of Marxism and a social theory grounded in the mode of production and class struggle is essentially the same as Lyotard's. Such theory, for Fraser and Nicholson, is necessarily reductive and universalizing, and therefore it ultimately reflects the interests and experience of privileged Western groups.[1]

Postmodern theories have been useful, since their critique of metanarratives relieves one of the necessity to theorize particular social categories in relation to the social structure as a whole. In this way, postmodernism enables dominant forms of feminism to distance themselves from Marxism; in turn, as I suggested before, feminism has added to the legitimacy of postmodern theory by giving it the necessary radical credentials. At the same time, postmodernism, in its own way, undermines the unity of the category of gender, if taken to its logical conclusion. This is because postmodernism requires that the self-identity of all categories be deconstructed in relation to the internal differences that both constitute them and enable their dismantling. Thus, feminism is different from itself as a result of its relations to categories (such as class and race) that are both external and internal to the categories required to ground feminism. So, if there can be no feminist politics as such, what actually unites all the different feminisms and thereby justifies the use of the category in the first place? Or, more important, how, within a postmodern framework, can this question even be formulated?

This difficulty makes the relation between postmodernism and feminism highly problematic, and it requires a solution that entails its own contradictions: The differences constituting the category of woman can be recognized through the use of postmodernism; however, the limits of difference are imposed through an untheorized notion of what is good or necessary for feminism. To phrase it differently, the category grounding feminism (gender) is left outside of the theory, as the criterion governing the uses of one or another theory, leaving the negotiation of these internal differences, the distance between feminism and postmodernism, and external differences between feminism and other politics based on similarly untheorized categories the central problem for feminist theory. Therefore, what is presented as an investigation into the problematic status of the category of gender turns out to be a deployment of postmodern theoretical discourses for the purpose of protecting from theoretical inquiry a notion of gender that implicitly presupposes its autonomy from contradictions situated at the level of the mode of production. However, this strategy begs the very questions that necessitated the turn toward postmodernism (and that is placed off limits by postmodernism): What are the interests of feminism? What would the emancipation of women entail and how can it be achieved? And how can these questions be theorized? The tendency now dominant in academic feminism can only insist on an abstract unity in difference (reflected in the category of experience), which must exclude rigorous contestation over the content of this unity as well as the social basis and political effects of these differences.

This observation holds true for those feminisms that are critical of postmodernism as well as for those that embrace it. For example, Nancy Hartsock, in her contribution to *Feminism/Postmodernism* ("Foucault on Power: A Theory for Women?") argues that discourses—such as postmodernism—that claim that generalizing, systematic, and accurate knowledge of social structures is impossible cannot be of any use to marginalized and oppressed groups. Furthermore, she questions the motivations behind postmodernism's problematization of categories such as agency and progress, precisely at the historical moment when oppressed groups are claiming subjectivity and agency for themselves. In short, Hartsock suggests that postmodernism is merely the self-questioning of dominant Enlightenment values and categories and not a critique from an oppositional standpoint. And this, she claims, is the case even for figures such as Foucault and others who claim (and whose discourses have been alleged) to support struggles for change. Hartsock asserts that Foucault occupies the position of the colonizer who resists his position but is unable to ally himself in any meaningful way with social transformation; in the end, in fact, she argues that Foucault's prescriptions regarding legitimate and effective means of resisting domination place him in opposition to struggles for emancipation.

However, according to the standpoint theory of knowledge Hartsock defends (and has helped to develop), knowledge of social conditions is ultimately the self-knowledge of marginalized groups, to which their marginalization gives them special access. She argues that oppositional struggles have "two fundamental intellectual theoretical tasks—one of critique and the other of construction" (1992, 163). For her, critique involves dismantling the categories and representations that have enabled the production of the oppressed as Other; construction, by contrast, involves the claiming and constitution of the subjectivities of the other(s). Despite Hartsock's call for "systematic knowledge about our world and ourselves" (171), the source of knowledge according to her understanding is the self-constituting marginalized subject, which she also claims needs to be understood as multiple and diverse (171). She does not explain how this multiplicity and diversity can enable the construction of "*an* account which can expose the falseness at the top and can transform the margins as well as the center" (171, emphasis added). Furthermore, it is impossible to address this issue within the framework of standpoint theory, which sees knowledge as a result of subjectivity, not contradictions in the social structure, and which therefore cannot ever be anything more than a reflection of the experience of specific subjects. The construction of new subjectivities can, then, only be a remaking of materials already given within the dominant culture and ideology, which is to say a reversal of the dominant terms. However, since a series of reversals does not add up to systematic knowledge, Hartsock is left with prescriptions that are no different from those of the postmodernism she critiques: describing and respecting multiplicities and differences.

In other words, even in its "strong" versions that make a claim for a certain ground for knowledges that can transform reality, standpoint theory is, in the end, situated within the same political economy of (postmodern) knowledges it professes to oppose. The significance of standpoint theory for my argument is that its claims are paradigmatic of the claims made within postmodern cultural studies for identity as the basis of knowledge and politics. The assumption here is that experience and capacities acquired under oppressive conditions are, a priori, those that are necessary to struggles for emancipation. However, the category of women gets placed (or imposed) upon the public and political agenda precisely when the sexual division of labor has been outmoded from the standpoint of the forces of production—when the integration of women into the public and economic institutions of a highly organized capitalist order makes that division of labor (and the subjects it produces) increasingly irrational and produces the conditions under which it can be contested. Thus, categories that are the products of oppressive relations become visible when those relations conflict with new social needs and practices. This process of becoming outmoded, though, is not an even or uncontested one, nor is it exempt from reversals; it is an overall tendency that becomes the site of political struggle. This is where one must theorize the contradictions that enabled a critical reflection on that experience in the first place and that provide the necessary materials of transformative practices.

This is the case even though Hartsock is careful not to derive emancipatory knowledge immediately from women's experience. As she argues in *Money, Sex and Power: Toward a Feminist Historical Materialism*, the feminist standpoint is both "achieved" and "liberatory" (1983, 232) (hence being a "feminist" and not a "women's" standpoint), and it is also developed out of those conditions that make women's lives qualitatively different from those of men (those differences, that is, that follow from the sexual division of labor). She sees the feminist standpoint as a critique of "abstract masculinity" (240), which "can be seen to have structured Western social relations and the modes of thought to which they give rise" (241). By contrast, women's experience leads toward "an opposition to dualisms of any sort; valuation of concrete, everyday life; a sense of a variety of connectednesses and continuities both with other persons and with the natural world" (242). The feminist standpoint does not merely reflect this experience; rather, it advances a critique of abstract masculinity by reversing the valuation of these respective modes of thought and practice. Nevertheless, the immanent link between experience and knowledge remains: The feminist standpoint expands, develops, and raises to consciousness the qualitative differences of women's lives, rather than feminist theory theorizing the production of those differences and hence laying the basis for feminist politics.

So, standpoint theory and the politics it advances simply reproduce and update the very liberal categories they wish to critique. Such understandings proceed in the same way as liberalism: They construct a model subject based upon a fetishized abstraction from relations between individuals (such as those produced by gender psychology) and then transform this abstraction into a regulatory principle for evaluating social relations. This fetishized abstraction, just like the abstraction classical liberal theory makes from the exchange of commodities between individual producers, corresponds to outmoded private relations (the domestic servitude of women) that have been made visible as oppressive and unnecessary as new social relations have become possible. The liberal ideal of contractual agreements between equal and free individuals provides capitalist society with a way of managing contradictions and crises by making them appear remediable without fundamental transformation: That is, capitalism simply needs to be freed from distortions and returned to its own standards of fairness and equality.

In the same way, the ideals posited by standpoint theory provide new cultural and ideological resources for capitalist society to claim that social problems can be solved by local feminist reorganizations without addressing the foundations of private property. Whether or not Hartsock or other standpoint theorists intend such a conclusion is beside the point; it is an unavoidable consequence following the assumption that one's preferred set of values (and the agents who bear them) are internal to the present order. This assumption itself is necessary if one presupposes an essential continuity between experience and practice. Such a utopian understanding excludes a theory of conflict that sees social change as the result of confrontations between collective material forces representing opposed interests and produced by global social structures and contradictions; in this case, the realization of the values represented by one of the opposing agencies would include their radical transformation (as a result of the transformations in the social structure), not their implementation or privileging in an unchanged form. According to the assumptions of standpoint theory, the values in question can be realized in a piecemeal, peaceful, and cumulative manner—in which case, material confrontations between collective agencies should be avoided and, if necessary, suppressed.

Thus, I see the relation between postmodernism and feminism differently than Sara Ahmed does in her *Differences That Matter: Feminist Theory and Postmodernism*. Ahmed makes the important move of insisting upon and establishing a critical distance from postmodernism. She questions the kind of strategy used by Fraser and Nicholson, among others, whereby postmodernism is taken to be always already at least implicitly feminist and feminism always already implicitly postmodern, contending that an apparently "dialogical model of the relationship" "gives way to an asymmetrical power relationship whereby feminism is placed as an instance of, and hence derivative of, the postmodern" (1998, 3). She proposes a close reading of the very texts that construct the "obviousness" of postmodernism and hence facilitate its remaking of institutional space: "Close readings may serve to demonstrate how postmodern texts establish their own limits and boundaries, as well as how this process of delimitation does not (and cannot) fix postmodernism into an object" (9).

By analyzing the gendered assumptions and elisions in the dominant postmodern discourses, as well as challenging claims on the part of its adherents and opponents alike that it is fixed, "feminism's role in the debate" can be "transformative" (Ahmed 1998, 9). In this case, feminism can "speak back" to postmodernism, showing, for example, how the feminist critique of rights, with its focus on difference concealed beneath a homogenizing equality, cannot be reduced to a generic postmodern concern with difference as such. In fact, through an inquiry into the way in which postmodern critiques of rights tend to erase the concrete political practices that have called the universality of rights into question (while also deploying it in new ways), the feminist critique is renewed and deepened through the encounter with postmodernism. In addition, this polemical and distanced relation to postmodernism, for Ahmed, enables feminism to clarify its own internal differences, as well as its constitution by categories such as class and race.

However, to claim that postmodernism is itself unstable and open to challenge is already to take postmodernism at its word and hence remain enclosed within its problematic. This is confirmed by Ahmed's reading of the relation between "woman" and "women" in terms that are essentially identical to those canonical within postmodern feminism and cultural studies: "Theorizing the over-determined relation between signifier and subject-effect enables us to consider how the meanings of 'woman' become stabilized or fixed in time and space in a way which constitutes the boundaries of women as embodied subjects. So while the instability of the category may be a condition of possibility for feminism, so too is the stabilisation of the category" (1998, 91). The problematic of stabilization/destabilization remains in place, even if one side is privileged over the other. In fact, the specifically stabilized place from which feminism speaks back to postmodernism is, overwhelmingly in Ahmed's discussions, tied to local practices and specific embodiments. This means that not only is feminism's theoretical constitution (that is, its implication), from the beginning in theoretical struggles, elided but also that the question of what institutional spaces feminist texts have constructed, maintained, and stabilized is not addressed. In other words, feminism is still standing outside of postmodernism not as an instance of global critique but as an experiential remainder that can't be accounted for. Hence, the central problem of Ahmed's book turns out to be very similar to that of Fraser and Nicholson's work: how to establish acceptable terms for dialogue between postmodernism and feminism and within feminism. This accounts for Ahmed's very autobiographical conclusion, which focuses on ethics rather than politics, on unilaterally postmodernist terms: "An ethical reading must admit that the differences that matter between us or within us are never simply in the present as such, but open up a radically uncertain future. The deferral of justice is here the condition of possibility for the judgements I have made about postmodernism and its narratives of difference" (197). What are ultimately institutional negotiations defer the necessity of speaking back to postmodernism by using it to stage the irreconcilable theoretical and political projects constitutive of feminism, along what are ultimately class lines.

The De/Reconstruction of Identity

Of course, as I suggested before, postmodern understandings also presuppose the primacy or necessity of nonidentity as a mode of radical theory and practice—this move is necessary for the regulation of the field of postmodern feminism due to the contradictions inherent in the attempt to (re)ground feminism in postmodern theory. As I pointed out earlier, postmodernism is a critique of identity, of homogeneity and self-sameness; however, this critique presupposes the continued existence and even stability of that which is, in turn, to be destabilized or to enact its own destabilization. That is, just as the poststructuralist critique of empiricism produces the conditions under which experience can be reinstated by another means, the postmodern critique of identities, which appears to dissolve all identities into a chain of signification constituted by their differences, actually provides a new basis for the category of identity as a political and theoretical category.

Teresa de Lauretis proposes such a politics of nonidentity in her "Eccentric Subjects: Feminist Theory and Historical Consciousness." She argues that feminist theory came into its own, or became possible as such—that is, became identifiable as feminist theory rather than a feminist critique of some other theory or object-theory in a postcolonial mode. By this I mean it came into its own with the understanding of the interrelatedness of discourses and social practices, and of the multiplicity of positionalities concurrently available in the social field seen as a field of forces: not a single system of power dominating the powerless but a tangle of distinct and variable relations of power and points of resistance (1990, 131).

De Lauretis sees feminist theory as having achieved its autonomy in the postmodern moment, when social reality could be understood as a nontotalizable series of differences. Furthermore, according to de Lauretis, this understanding of the social as a "diversified field of power relations" (1990, 131) was a result of the intervention of women of color and lesbians into a "feminist discourse that was anchored to the single axis of sexual difference (or rather, heterosexual difference, however minutely articulated in its many instances) and that was finding itself stalemated once again in the paradox of woman" (131). A postcolonial feminist theory, by contrast, understands differences as constitutive and as a condition of possibility of agency.

However, this postcolonial feminism, which becomes possible when "the feminist critique of sociocultural formations (discourses, forms of representation, ideologies) becomes conscious of itself and turns inward, as MacKinnon suggests, in pursuit of consciousness" (de Lauretis 1990, 138), also leads to a transfer of the locus of feminist practice to consciousness and discourse. De Lauretis proclaims the necessity for what she calls the "eccentric subject," a mode of subjectivity that begins by inquiring into its location and situatedness, but to "sustain the subject's capacity for movement and displacement" (139), it is necessary to effect a dislocation and disidentification with that very location and the assumptions and conditions it takes for granted. This dislocation and disidentification, as the term *eccentric* would suggest, is directed less against any structures or practices of male domination (which would, in fact, be impossible, since de Lauretis has located this type of practice in the interior of feminist theory, as a mode of articulating differences within/between women) than against identities held together by exclusions and representations "that enable any ideology of the same" (139). "It is a position of resistance and agency," she writes, "conceptually and experientially apprehended outside or in excess of the sociocultural apparatuses of heterosexuality, through a process of 'unusual knowing' or a 'cognitive practice' that is not only personal but also textual, a practice of language in the larger sense" (139).

De Lauretis makes use of materialist and Marxist terms (often by way of materialist feminist analyses, such as those of Catharine MacKinnon and Monique Wittig)—for example, supporting Wittig's formulation of the goal of feminism as the disappearance of women (understood as an oppressed class). Yet her theory of subjectivity is, in fact, grounded in a notion of identity as articulated discursively (through signifying orders) and that can therefore be most effectively transformed in the same way. For instance, she rewrites Wittig's understanding of lesbian society not as a mode of collective resistance to structures of oppression "but rather [as] the term for a conceptual and experiential space carved out of the social field, a space of contradictions, in the here and now, that need to be affirmed but not resolved" (1990, 144). Feminist consciousness, in this case, can "only exist historically, in the here and now, as the consciousness of a 'something else'" (144). Finally, this eccentric subjectivity or consciousness of something else, which undermines articulations of sameness and otherness, is "a position attained through practices of political and personal displacement across boundaries between sociosexual identities and communities, between bodies and discourses" (145). Put another way, not only the feminist movement is to be saved by the eccentric subject proposed by de Lauretis; so, too, will be the categories of experience and identity, which are not so much transformed by practices of eccentricity as rearticulated along a series of differences that preserves their specificity and autonomy.

Thus, the differences between and constitutive of women are to be articulated through the tension between identity and nonidentity (developed through the eccentric subject's displacements and critiques of ideologies of the same), in addition to being displaced onto language and consciousness. Both formulations are necessary for the understanding of feminist subjectivity that de Lauretis supports, one that is abstracted from (in excess of) the social totality and any kind of theoretical knowledge with explanatory power. De Lauretis argues for an "excessive critical position" (1990, 145) that is located in a "conceptual and experiential space carved out of the social field, a space of contradictions, in the here and now, that needs to be affirmed but not resolved" (144). However, this assertion of an autonomous conceptual and experiential space renders problematic the need to employ social contradictions in the interest of contesting dominant institutional structures, for it produces an understanding of critique and opposition as immanent to a "space carved out of the social field" rather than in relation to their global effects. Therefore, the struggle de Lauretis proposes will ultimately resist the totalization of the social space (which would exclude the possibility of carving out an eccentric position), not transform in a systemic way the current (totalizing) organization of social relations.

At the same time, there is a difference implicit in these formulations that de Lauretis does not address: the difference between those practices and subjects who reproduce the identities required for a feminist politics and those who are able to produce practices of displacement across those boundaries. That is, the relative continuity and stability of those identities that de Lauretis can presuppose as a condition of border crossing and eccentricity are only possible on the condition that the participation in a variety of identities in which one is equally not at home is not equally available to all those inhabiting or practicing those identities. De Lauretis, then, is able to negotiate the differences constitutive of feminism and to abstract those differences from any material effectivity, but in doing so, she must reproduce internal to the series of differences the very inequalities this series was charged with managing (by representing them as differences).

The eccentric subject as theorized by de Lauretis is the deconstructive bricoleur who, unlike the engineer who presupposes the homogeneity of his or her means of production, recognizes the intrinsic heterogeneity of those means and the ad hoc nature of any practice. Since bricolage, as I noted in the previous chapter, has become exemplary of a properly postmodern practice within the postmodern common sense, it is useful to return to Jacques Derrida's theorization of this mode of practice. In his "Structure, Sign and Play in the Discourse of the Human Sciences," Derrida elaborates on Claude Levi-Strauss's problematization of the subject of science. He deconstructs the binary opposition constructed by Levi-Strauss between the engineer and the bricoleur.

The engineer, in this conception, begins with a set of a priori categories, which are already commensurate and homogeneous and designed and destined for a specific and precisely delimited use. Furthermore, the engineer is not himself implicated in these categories; rather, he manipulates them from without from an ahistorical position of plenitude. The bricoleur, meanwhile, does not approach a given task with an abstract schema that simply needs to be applied. The bricoleur, an enlightened, pragmatic subject, is aware that while he is starting from a prior arrangement of categories and techniques that determine his field of possibilities, this arrangement is itself derived from a nontotalizable series of arrangements that are themselves given a merely contingent organization in the given instance. The arrangement of categories, then, is elaborated by the bricoleur not systematically and in advance but under the pressures of unforeseeable requirements and possibilities that only take shape in accord with the immanent process of engaging in the activity itself. Rather than standing outside of the means in question and determining those means in accord with an end comprehended by a conscious, sovereign subject, the bricoleur is herself determined by the differential logics and ends embodied and deferred by the means and categories articulated.

In reality, argues Derrida, there is only bricolage: "If one calls *bricolage* the necessity of borrowing one's concepts from the text of a heritage which is more or less ruined, it must be said that every discourse is *bricoleur*" (1978, 285). The engineer is a myth, produced by the myth-making activity of the bricoleur. However, once the opposition between the two terms has been deconstructed, the very notion of bricolage is "menaced" (285), with the system of differences it constructs losing its meaning. In this case, if the engineer is, in fact, a myth produced by the bricoleur, then it must be a myth that is required so as to legitimate some types of practices as opposed to others on the basis of their claim to be the absolute origin of their own discourse (insofar as the distinction works to include some forms of practice and exclude others). In other words, the more powerful and privileged bricoleurs require the myth of the engineer and the entire engineer/bricoleur distinction as a fiction supporting their own authority.

The consequence of this, though, is that no absolute or pure bricolage, one that does not require some fiction of authority, could be possible. Derrida raises the question of whether the dismantling of the engineer/bricoleur binary reduces all discourses to epistemological equivalence. That is, could there be an absolute bricolage, an ontological plurality of discourses arranged nonhierarchically, each engaged with nothing more than the pragmatics of its own local effectivity and articulation? His text does not answer this question, and, I would argue, the question cannot be answered without confronting the contradiction between the claims that can indeed be made for such an equivalence and the fact that such claims would always be undermined by the unequal social and political effectivities of different discourses, including these claims. This is because the very claim to this kind of equivalence presupposes access to a mode of commensurability that would supersede or oppose differences based on claims to truth or coherence; this claim itself would have to be read as a fiction of authority or self-authorship that would also have the function of self-legitimation. In this case, the more powerful discourses and practices could recognize that they have no inherent or nonarbitrary claim to their power, but this recognition could only be a more sophisticated and self-reflexive device for relegitimating that power by pointing to its effectivity.

For deconstruction, this fictive character of authority opens up a space for indeterminacy that produces a kind of freedom for the subject: the freedom to reinvent these categories perpetually in a pragmatic and playful way without the constraints of any governing structure or end of practice. However, this discussion makes it possible to see that, while posing as a critique of authority and its modes of self-legitimation, deconstruction maintains the categories and assumptions required to support existing modes of authority precisely by relegating them in a cynical manner to the status of a necessary fiction that simply allows the work to proceed. The opportunistic character of this logic lies in the fact that if the bricoleur employs the means and materials at his disposal, he must also utilize and reproduce whatever modes of institutional authority are closest at hand and simultaneously make them impervious to a critique of their legitimacy (not merely their processes of legitimation), by positing "legitimacy" (the justification of the ends or purposes served) as a naive and meaningless question.

I have focused on this aspect of Derrida's text because it enables us to see the political dimension of his claim that the thought of the structurality of structure (the necessity arbitrarily to stop the free play of the elements that have combined to produce the structure) has led to a decentering of structure that makes totalizing discourses impossible. That is, the decentering of structure and the authority of the engineer through the activity of deconstruction in the end enables the engineer to resecure his control over the material sources of social power. The power of the engineer is the effect not of an illusion of presence but of his possession of the mechanisms—knowledge and institutional authority—through which materials are procured and arranged (and declared appropriate for a given task), and his control over those mechanisms determines the lack of public access to them. This question is excluded and mystified by deconstruction's renunciation of those modes of legitimation most vulnerable to critique and adoption of more up-to-date ones.

Furthermore, Derrida's account excludes a highly significant point: the class position of the engineer. The engineer is a member of the new petite bourgeoisie, that class that abstracts the determination of its income from the workings of the law of value. In addition, it thereby appropriates a portion of the total surplus value by maintaining a relative monopoly on certain skills and knowledges and the means of certification and accreditation of the "owners" of those skills and knowledges required by the political economy of (late) monopoly capitalism. The engineer's ultimate lack of control over the determination of the means and ends of his activity—the lack of control that makes a deconstruction of his transcendental claims possible—is an effect of his lack of control over the means of production, owned by the capitalist class. This very claim to control, though, is one of the mechanisms by which this relative monopoly is secured. The central contradiction of this class position, then, is that its position of domination and the logic of its subordination are intrinsically connected—a contradiction that finds ideological expression in its claim to carry out its class function in the interests of "technical neutrality" but also, in periods of crisis, in the deconstruction of this claim.

Ideology

The theory of ideology now dominant in cultural studies has been proposed (in slightly different forms) by the post-Marxism of figures such as Ernesto Laclau and Slavoj Zizek. For post-Marxism, the social has no center, no single organizing logic. Rather, the positing of any such center or logic is the product of a specific antagonism. So, for example, the bourgeoisie did not struggle against feudalism in the name of or as a result of the development of the productive forces or the principles of freedom and equality. Instead, the very concepts of development, equality, and so on, at least as we understand them today, are both constituted by and constitutive of the bourgeois/feudal antagonism. Thus, the only real mystification is the illusion that the constitutive antagonism necessary for subjectivization is *the* antagonism, and it can impose closure on the social. In this view, ideology involves the assumption that the norm can account for the exception, the universal for the particular—i.e., the norm or universal is grounded in nature or necessity. The critique of ideology in this case involves pointing out and performatively instituting the contingency of any closure, insofar as any closure simply produces new antagonisms and new constitutive closures. So, the truth of the universal lies precisely in its need to represent itself via some particular content, in its excess over itself; the truth of the norm lies precisely in the exception, in the fact that the norm doesn't stand above and regulate the decision—on the contrary, the (ultimately ungrounded and arbitrary) decision itself retroactively installs the norm by which it justifies itself.

My argument is that this understanding of ideology is an apology for the dominant form of ideology today, what I would refer to as "exceptionalizing the norm." The view of theorists such as Laclau and Zizek acquires its plausibility because ideology *is* closely connected to the question of universality, in particular those universals of modern politics (democracy, subjectivity, equality, etc.) that anchor politics in prepolitical principles and relations and thereby neutralize politics. Ideology is antipolitical politics, the subversion and cannibalizing of politics from within through the use of the exception to ground norms immanently in existing social conditions: The exception is invariably invoked in the name of the protection of the basis of subjectivity. And the assumption, underlying both Laclau's and Zizek's accounts, of a fundamental violence (of desire) constituting the political realm is simply the rationalization of the dominant ideology, which seeks to discredit revolution as nothing more than the attempt to impose a permanent closure.[2]

The argument I am proposing presupposes that ideology critique has an intrinsic connection to liberal democracy: The transformation of the Enlightenment polemic against religion (the priests manipulate the fears and desires of the people and thereby obscure their natural view of reality) involves accounting for how the secularized categories underlying that critique (reason, subjectivity, consent, natural right, etc.) became antirevolutionary, i.e., came to justify revolution in general and yet deny its possibility in every particular case. The reification of reason in-itself, subjectivity in-itself, and so forth comes not only to mystify but also to actively oppose, among other things, the political labor of clarifying the interests of reason in relation to this unreasonableness, the space and modes of free action in relation to this violent process of objectification, and the conditions and manifestations of consent in relation to this expropriation of legitimate power and this range of possible dissent. This doesn't mean, though, that an adequate critique of Enlightenment reifications is to reify, in turn, the excess to reason and subjectivity, for example, by locating the irrational foundation of reason or the irreducible alterity constituting subjectivity. An adequate critique is made possible only by clarifying the mutual constitution of these categories in changing historical conditions.

The most useful theorization of ideology under contemporary conditions will account for both the "critical" and the "neutral" versions of ideology, as Jorge Larrain has termed them,[3] within the Marxist tradition. The neutral theory, expressed most forcefully by Lenin, sees ideology as the discursive form taken by contending class interests; the critical view sees ideology as mystification and false consciousness. What needs to be preserved in Lenin's account is the assumption that ideology reflects (ratifies and contests) the circumscription of the field of politics. Ideology is the discursive form of class interests, which also means that the pertinent and urgent stake in ideological struggle, where ideological struggle appears as such, is the point at which class struggle enters theory and hence becomes political (i.e., engages common ground unifying and dividing all of the classes and institutions of capitalist society). In other words, Lenin's conception of bourgeois versus socialist ideology as the line running through all theoretical and practical possibilities places the question

of ideology on the boundary of the constitution of politics: The engagement of ideological struggle establishes the "line of demarcation"
whereby something can appear as political that wouldn't otherwise. Ideological struggle contests the violence of closing off politics to struggles for
emancipation.

The critical account of ideology, meanwhile, explains why, within ideological discourse, the foundational political-economic categories and
boundaries (necessity/violence/legitimacy) systematically appear in one
another's place: The quintessential ideological locution is "yes, but . . . ,"
indicating, for example, the justice of a claim that ("unfortunately") contradicts necessity, the necessity of an action regardless of its illegitimacy,
and hence the contamination of legitimacy with violence. The mystification of the wage-labor relation is exemplary in this regard. The wage contract establishes a relation that is fair on its own terms (labor power is ex-
changed at its value for money); at the same time, it generalizes the
contract as the definitive form of fairness, further justified by the necessity of maintaining the institutions of social production. The mystification
here involves both the invisibility of the exploitation effected by the difference between the value of labor power and the value created by labor as
well as the way in which insight into this fundamental relation is blocked:
Any struggle against the violence of exploitation as such is confronted by
claims to necessity (this is the only way things can be done) and legitimacy (you freely chose this relation), which are both conflated (this is the
most just order) and serve as alibis for each other (it's unfair, but we have
no choice; life is hard but it is a product of our own choices). The questioning of the terms of fairness itself, one of the most significant preliminary political acts, is thus stigmatized a priori as violent and unthinkable.
The critical or negative view of ideology, that is, engages ideological obfuscations insofar as they interfere with emancipatory theory and action
against the background of a (contradictory) economic necessity mediated
by (anti)political (ideological) violence. A slight modification of Lenin's
view is therefore necessary: There is no proletarian ideology, but there is
proletarian ideological struggle, i.e., the struggle to open up the articulation of theory and politics suppressed by bourgeois ideology.

In this case, Althusserian and post-Althusserian understandings of ideology as the production of subjects can be taken as attempts to address
these interlocking problematics on the terrain of late capitalism, driven by
the competing regimes of the public regulation of the reproduction of labor power and the reprivatization of labor-power via the massive global
extension of the wage-labor relation in its simplest form. Interpellation
calls for ideology *critique* (the problematic of the critical view) to the extent that it opens for inspection the mechanisms of subjective (re)produc-
tion: The *legitimacy* of the subject loses its basis in *necessity,* and the sub-

ject can be rearticulated as an effect or symptom. It also calls for ideological *struggle* (the problematic of the neutral view) in that the production of subjectivities now appears as an instance of violence against which the exoteric exposure of neutralized categories acquires its legitimacy. The dismantling of the Althusserian theory of ideology, brought about in particular by arguments such as those of Laclau that interpellation (ideologically) presupposes a fixed identity prior to interpellation and a social center where interpellation issues from, can be resisted on the following grounds. Far from instituting the political (the field of antagonistic subjects, according to Laclau), ideology forecloses politics by neutralizing that space where the question of the articulation of necessity, violence, and legitimacy appears. And this space does preexist the subject and does presuppose a social center—the reciprocal implication and accumulation of economic and political violence. (I will return to these questions in Chapter 5 in particular.)

A rigorous concept of ideology is more necessary now than ever because there is no other way to grasp the central contradiction of contemporary politics: that the more fields of social life that undergo politicization, the more politics is reduced to culture, that is, the problematics and adventures of subjectivities. This is a result of pervasive ideological violence as interpellation, a trade-off between local sites of empowerment and withdrawal from accountability for the world. The dominant ideology allows the subject to return its "Yes, but . . . ": It is antinormative and impossible, but precisely for that reason, I am going to go ahead and do it anyway. The exemplary subject is the exception who proves the rule and does the rule another favor: It conceals the necessary violence of class rule behind an appearance of contingency. The point of ideological struggle, then, is to clear the ground for power to unite with accountability to the world; the point of ideology critique is to expose the career of subjectivity (of subjectivity splitting into subjectivities) as an always ironic inversion of necessity (appearing as freedom).

Historicizing the Politics of (Non)Identity

The postmodern politics of (non)identity privileged in contemporary cultural studies and academic feminism alike is a result of those class practices or those class struggles of the post–World War II period that I discussed earlier. As in Fraser and Nicholson's narrative of maturation, what conditions de Lauretis's understanding of the relation between feminism's independence and its postcolonial condition is the institutionalization of feminist struggles and discourses. To put it another way, due to the reactionary structure of the institution, drawing upon external political resources is essential to gaining the power to represent; however, in the process, these resources are also deployed in the interest of preserving this institutional power, regardless of its uses or effects. That is, one's experience or identity is necessary in order to legitimate one's position; however, the subject's use and protection of that position also requires the recognition of a nonidentical relation to that experience or identity.

The deconstruction of the category of identity, then, like all deconstructions, keeps that category in place but posits it as different from or nonidentical with itself, as one on a long chain of significations that cannot be totalized. To put it another way, this process entails the production of the type of (petit bourgeois) class position I discussed earlier within the collective agency "women," a transformation reflected in the growing predominance of postmodern feminisms of difference that, according to this argument, situate feminists of the new petite bourgeoisie as the crisis managers of inequality. This position requires both the claim of identity (being feminists—tied to a larger collectivity—within, say, the academy) and the claim of nonidentity (being only a nonauthoritative member of that collective within a specific institutional site, one articulation among many others that are implicitly equivalent).

We can see this in one essay that directly addresses the institutional implications of the poststructuralist turn in thinking about identity, Pamela Caughie's "Let It Pass: Changing the Subject, Once Again." Caughie is interested in the problem of the political necessity, constitutive of what she calls "culture studies",[4] of identifying oneself politically with certain groups and agendas, while being unable to provide any foundations for that identification: "The practitioners of culture studies experience a double bind in which the desire—indeed the imperative—to speak as or for members of a particular social group conflicts with the anxieties such a practice evokes. The writer who deliberately assumes another's position risks being accused of unconsciously doing so" (1997, 27). Caughie attempts to resolve this double bind with a pedagogy based on the notion of *passing*, shifting the term from its common signification of "representing oneself—for social, economic, or political reasons—as a member of a particular group not considered one's own" (27) to a more general structure of subjectivity as such. Passing, in this case, is a result of the "slippage between the volitional and performative subject" (28): "Passing happens," i.e., it is not a question of choice, in which case the question becomes whether one will suppress this constitutive structure or deploy it responsibly.

Deploying it responsibly involves "coming to terms with the precariousness of one's identity" (Caughie 1997, 36), which is to say one takes the impossibility of identity as one's pedagogical object. This, though, is not the most productive way of thinking through the "double bind created by the discrepancy between what we profess and how we are positioned, between the demands of a critical pedagogy and the constraints of postmodern culture" (36). In fact, the possibility of a rigorous depersonalization that would make the institutional circulation of categories of identity visible is thereby foreclosed. Addressing, along with Caughie, institutional modes of pedagogy, this means establishing a pedagogical space wherein the concepts central to the classroom structure the relations between texts, student, and teacher and, more broadly, the institutional and social conditions that are both cleared away and set up as the boundary of the pedagogical space. Insofar as the project of the class is to transform given concepts (e.g., identity) into boundary concepts (in other words, to situate them via the reciprocal constitution of politics and theory), then questions of identity or the positionality of students and teachers can enter the space of the classroom, either as sites of theoretical struggle implicated in contending problematics or, symptomatically, as cynically and violently disposed toward that space.

In this way, there is room for, say, explicitly feminist, antiracist, and socialist polemics, including those that attend to the visible identity of the enunciator(s)—or target(s)—of the polemic by situating it in relation to theoretical polemics displayed and unfolded in the classroom. This mode of pedagogy avoids the most obvious problem with passing, which is that it is closed off as a possibility to anyone without access to several institutional locations: It consolidates petit bourgeois class privileges by reproducing a fantasy of upward mobility. Even more important, the pedagogy of passing excludes any theoretical position that relies not upon a foundational identity but upon the foundational assumption that there is nothing at all natural about "the discrepancy between what we profess and how we are positioned"—i.e., that a theoretical act can and should open a space wherein professions and positions are exoterically examined and performed consistently.

The necessary outcome of the politics of (non)identity, in sum, is that power differentials, which are seen as constitutive of individuals, seem to disappear in relation to the problem of articulating identities through contingent discursive links. In other words, the proponents of the progressiveness of recognizing and respecting differences (as opposed to explaining and transforming them) are unable to account for how inclusiveness and diversity actually contest the differentials in power that are reproduced in both oppositional practices and the dominant culture. A theoretically determined politics based upon the category of totality can account for this in terms of the category of pedagogy, which works to make theoretical knowledges public property and hence to open them up to struggles over their uses and effectivity. The experiential politics of nonidentity, though, enables the subject of cultural studies to fabricate or discover an identity that links him or her to the object of cultural studies differentially without recognizing the responsibility to advance some modes of knowledge at the expense of others. The politics of (non)identity, then, supports a postmodern liberalism that continues to protect the experiential basis of the subject from critique.

Feminism as Totalizing Theory and Ideology Critique

As my discussion of Fraser and Nicholson's essay showed, the postmodern politics of (non)identity defines itself, to a great extent, against totalizing feminisms that seek to explain gender in terms of more abstract determinations. An important instance of such a feminism is that articulated by Catharine MacKinnon. MacKinnon is indicted by Fraser and Nicholson for "monocausality" due to her understanding of gender oppression in relation to the category of sexuality (1992, 31). In an even more antagonistic account, Donna Haraway characterizes MacKinnon's version of radical feminism as "a caricature of the appropriating, incorporating, totalizing tendencies of Western theories of identity grounding action" (1992, 200). According to Haraway, "MacKinnon's radical theory of experience is totalizing in the extreme; it does not so much marginalize as obliterate the authority of any other women's political speech and action. It is a totalization producing what Western patriarchy itself never succeeded in doing—feminists' consciousness of the non-existence of women, except as products of men's desire" (201).Thus, MacKinnon's feminism is deemed "authoritarian."

To clarify what I consider to be at stake in my discussion of MacKinnon, I will address two of her critics. Laura Kipnis's defense of pornography in *Bound and Gagged: Pornography and the Politics of Fantasy in America* is symptomatic of the larger antinomies of cultural studies. Kipnis contends that pornography "is both a legitimate form of culture and a fictional, fantastical, even allegorical realm; it neither simply reflects the real world nor is some hypnotizing call to action . . . it does—and this is part of its politics—insist on a sanctioned space for fantasy" (1996, 163). As a legitimate form, pornography is to be seen as a Bahktinian "counteraesthetic" (166) that undermines the class distinctions reproduced through aestheticism and even a form of "civil disobedience" (206). As with any object of cultural studies, to analyze it is to enter into a more or less qualified alliance with it. The legitimacy of a politics based on preserving a space of fantasy presupposes a notion of freedom grounded in desire: "the freedom, displaced from the social world of limits and proprieties, to indulge in a range of longings and desires without regard to the appropriateness and propriety of those desires, and without regard to social limits on resources, object choices, perversity, or on the anarchy of the imagination" (202–203). Kipnis elevates this desire to the level of a kind of natural freedom, which an older form of liberalism found to reside in property: "Or perhaps the abundance of pornography . . . resonates with a primary desire for plenitude, a desire for counter-scarcity economies in any number of registers: economic, emotional, or sexual. Pornography proposes an economy of pleasure in which not only is there always enough, there's even more than you could possibly want" (202).

At the same time, by linking pornography to masturbation (in particular via their common function in right-wing discourses interested in infantalizing the "lower" classes and by implication discrediting an expanded democracy), Kipnis ties pornography to the question of need: "What masturbation implies, then, thematically, is the simple possibility of a need met" (1996, 187). We could have the elements here of an ideology critique that accounts for how both the Right and pornography collude in displacing questions of need, freedom, and democracy onto questions of desire, fantasy, and transgression. But part of pornography's value for Kipnis is precisely that it resists this type of analysis: It undermines critical and rational public discourse, or, to stay within the terms of Kipnis's analysis, it disrupts the elitist fantasies that pass as such discourse by "exposing the culture to itself," displaying its "inner tensions and unconscious conflicts" (162), making the exemplary public figure one who is "determined to parade the contents of his private obsessions as public psychodrama" (158).

The problem with pornography's opponents in this case (and, of course, MacKinnon is constantly attacked on these grounds) is that "they seem universally overcome by a leaden, stultifying literalness" (Kipnis 1996, 163). MacKinnon, in fact, is one of the very few intellectuals writing today who is willing to be "literal"—to connect causes and consequences, political intents and acts with the global structures of violence. This, I am arguing, is necessary if one is to conceptualize politics otherwise than as the disruption and exposure of fractured identities. Another type of exposure is made possible by MacKinnon's polemic, that of interlocking—political, juridical, technological, ideological—modes of violence, an exposure that is aimed at opening up the possibility of theoretical and political accountability. The weakness of her polemic, as I will argue in a moment, is not her hostility to fantasy and desire but the fact that it is insufficiently political-economic.

Judith Butler's critique of MacKinnon is also concerned with her literalness—in this case, with MacKinnon's assumption that "perlocutionary" speech acts can be felicitous. In critiquing Butler's position, I want to begin with a brief, unelaborated, and anomalous passage in her *Excitable Speech: A Politics of the Performative*. While analyzing a couple of Supreme Court cases dealing with the application of hate crime laws, Butler says the following about (presumably) the specificity of the violence constitutive of state power: "It will be necessary to distinguish between those kinds of violence that are the necessary conditions of the binding character of legal language, and those kinds which exploit that very necessity in order to redouble that injury in the service of injustice" (1997, 62). In fact, this distinction between legitimate and illegitimate uses of state power and violence, although required in order for Butler to critique the Supreme Court decision she is discussing as unjust, never returns to play any role in her text. On the contrary, her critique of proponents of hate crime legislation, including MacKinnon and, more important, her broader "politics of the performative" aim precisely at rendering determinations of legitimacy impossible. More specifically, violence that is the "necessary condition of the binding character of legal language" is a necessary referent that cannot be accounted for within Butler's discourse.

The necessity and impossibility of this distinction points to a crucial aporia in Butler's thought. She speaks of the "arbitrary use of this [state] power to promote conservative goals" (1997, 62), implying the possibility of a nonarbitrary, progressive application of state power. Meanwhile, her critique of the Court's decision protecting cross burning as a form of free speech charges the decision with being "a paranoid inversion of the original cross burning narrative. . . . The fire which initially constituted the threat against the black family becomes metaphorically transfigured as the threat that blacks in trauma now wield against high officials" (59). The injustice in the Court's decision lies in the way in which the justices identify with, but then "substitute themselves for" the victimized black family and, in effect, resignify their narrative by appropriating it for what Butler consistently refers to as the fiction of sovereignty that supports state power. What makes their narrative "paranoid" is that they take the identification of their role as defenders of a neutral constitution and public order literally; the violence of their speech lies in the elision of the authoritative space that they produce and that is simultaneously the condition of possibility for their self-representation as neutral. In this case, a nonarbitrary, nonparanoid (i.e., legitimate) use of state power would be one that refused the ground of "literalness" and "normativity"—that refused to situate its decision within the space of the "necessary condition of the binding character of legal language" (62). The legitimate use of power is one that recognizes its own nonbinding (or actually antibinding) character, which means it must, in the name of justice, refuse all claims to legitimacy or the protection or defense of anything at all.

The same aporia shows up in Butler's remarks, scattered throughout her book, on the status of the state in contemporary politics. On the one hand, the importance and power of the state is systematically minimized. Drawing on Foucault, Butler contends that "power is no longer constrained by models of sovereignty . . . it emanates from any number of 'centers'" and that the "constitution of subjects" (1997, 78) represents a more basic and important instance of subjugation. This claim is, of course, central to the broader argument of the book for a politics of resignification, which finds the "futural form of politics" (161) in the "potential incommensurability between intention and utterance . . . utterance and action . . . and intention and action" (92). Demystifying the state as just another (albeit powerful) instance of the fiction that doer can correspond to deed would seem to point to a democratic postmodernity.

At the same time, Butler's critique of efforts such as MacKinnon's to criminalize hate speech is based on the claim that they fail to recognize the dangers of relying upon the state and thereby giving it more power. Perhaps the problem is just with propping up an outmoded institution that we are (thankfully) almost rid of, but in that case, it is not clear why state speech cannot be resignified, precisely by drawing it more explicitly onto the terrain of postsovereign discourse. For some reason, it seems too dangerous, too essentially "arbitrary"; it apparently *necessarily* believes in its own fictional foundations. Even more important, she notes—again, briefly, but her entire discussion of the military regulation of "homosexual speech" depends on this claim—that the military "suspends certain rights for its own personnel that are accorded to citizens," that this "overlap[s] with other retractable zones of citizenship for immigrants," *and* that "such comparisons might well be considered in relation to Giorgio Agamben's recent thesis that the state itself has become a protracted 'state of emergency,' one in which the claims of citizenship are more or less permanently suspended" (1997, 105). Here, via a series of comparisons whereby the exception becomes the (normless) norm, the state appears to be increasingly violent, entrenched, and overwhelming.

In Butler's discourse, we can see the cost of rejecting claims that "language itself can only act to the extent that it is 'backed' by existing social power" (1997, 158). Butler also goes on to ask, rhetorically, "Is the mimetic relationship ascribed to language and the prior institutions of social power not itself a relation of signification, that is, how language comes to signify social power?" (1997, 158). This understanding of the relation between language and social power enables us to read Butler's own discourse, which manages to install, without defending or explaining it, the following portrait of the contemporary state: It is increasingly desperate, paranoid, and dangerous, precisely because the postmodern politics of resignification is undermining the (discursive) basis of its power. Thus, Butler's position mimetically represents itself as both remarkably effective and urgently necessary.

Of course, the state is only dangerous if one believes in it: "The fantasy of sovereign action that structures the threat is that a certain kind of saying . . . would be an illocutionary performative, in [J. L.] Austin's view, one that immediately does what it says" (Butler 1997, 12). One can reinforce this fantasy in two ways. One can treat the state as a neutral institution that can be transformed so as to actually protect the universal values it proclaims, or one can share its fantasy by opposing it:

> The critical task is not simply to speak "against" the law, as if the law were external to speech, and speech the privileged venue for freedom. If speech depends upon censorship [i.e., a prior, constitutive censorship that produces speech in the first place], then the principle that one might seek to oppose is at once the formative principle of oppositional speech. There is no opposition to the lines drawn by foreclosure except through the redrawing of those very lines (Butler 1997, 140).

The fantasy of performative politics is that it is heroically undoing a form of politics that is increasingly destructive and that it performs this feat simply by "doing what comes naturally," merely exploiting the resources of language and action that are always already there (and that have been unnaturally held back, not so much by the state as by taking the state literally), the disjunction between intention, utterance, and action.

This contention can be substantiated by examining Butler's use (mediated significantly, of course, by Derrida) of Austin's distinction between illocutionary and perlocutionary speech acts, the main conceptual machinery of her book. Illocutionary acts immediately do what they say (as in "I sentence you to ten years in prison"), whereas perlocutionary acts disperse their effects across a wider field, thereby making their consequences more complex and difficult, if not impossible, to measure. Butler tends to equivocate, but she seems to think that genuine illocutionary acts are possible (here, she distances herself slightly from Derrida, as her claim to provide a viable theory of agency requires), but her point is that those who presuppose the sovereignty of the state (as a reality) and of subjects (as an ideal) systematically mistake perlocutionary acts for illocutionary acts. This is the way in which she undermines MacKinnon's claim that pornography "does" what it "says"; according to Butler, pornography is in fact performing the impossibility of doing what it says, i.e., the impossibility of "fixing" gender.

This is the real axis of politics for Butler: the liberation of the perlocutionary from the illocutionary. This liberation is accomplished through both the singularity of the body ("the body exceeds the speech it occasions; and speech remains irreducible to the bodily means of its enunciation" [1997, 156]) and the appropriation of both universalizing terms (*democracy, freedom,* etc.) and degrading terms (such as *queer*). Now, none of this works unless one shares Butler's teleological claim that things are moving in this direction already, that perlocutionary acts are more and more tending to undermine the fixity of illocutionary acts. But here, I want to return to that distinction between violence necessary to the "binding character of legal language" and violence that "exploits that necessity." How can Butler account for the necessity of a binding, presumably illocutionary act in order to issue judgments? Is the violence the illocutionary act itself, that is, is the viability of illocutionary felicity the necessary violence? Or is it another violence necessary for this viability— and if so, is it a prior, "originary" violence (this is Derrida's view) or a violence that follows and protects that viability? And how is this entire scene, however we resolve it, anything other than a fiction whereby perlocutionary acts posit illocutionary ones as their basis and legitimation— in which case, why isn't it always already exploited, with the only responsible approach therefore being to deconstruct the distinction between necessary and exploited violence?

The confusion over this fundamental point is necessary to the illocutionary and perlocutionary effects of Butler's discourse. She requires both a scene of originary violence and the sliver of sovereign neutrality that her discourse is ostensibly aimed at dismantling. After all, the more the sovereign state and subject insist upon the power of their illocutions, the greater the gap between intention, utterance, and act must be and hence the more space for "insurrectionary" speech acts. Butler contends that a "performative 'works' to the extent that *it draws on and covers over* the constitutive conventions by which it is mobilized. In this sense, no term or statement can function performatively without the accumulating and dissimulating historicity of force [or] ritualized practice[s]" (1997, 51). There is, again, a constitutive undecidability here. Butler makes this claim in the course of accounting for why the "injurious term injures" (52), i.e., to account for the violence of hate speech. But how could this not be true for effective performatives of the kind Butler proposes? Wouldn't they also need the accumulation of ritualized citations, that is, illocutionary acts? This would introduce foundations into Butler's performative politics and in an especially cynical way (one would have to know that one is concealing force, i.e., be doing it deliberately). Or is their effectivity of a totally other kind?

This is ultimately the case: The effectivity of properly Butlerian performatives would be the effectivity of singularity and dispersal. The point is, precisely, perlocution for its own sake, the continual highlighting of the disjunction between intention, utterance, and act; this, at the same time, requires for its background the very fixing and paranoid defense of foundations that Butler presents as the main adversary. This is the (highly contagious) fantasy she is promoting: a continual struggle against a sovereignty whose dangers can be constantly evoked and that is perpetually on the verge of defeat. Butler's real enemy is not what she, in a rather self-congratulatory manner, calls "dogmatism" and "anti-intellectualism"

(1997, 162). It is the theorization of the articulation of illocutionary acts (e.g., manifestos, programs) and perlocutionary acts (precedents, polemics) *outside* of the originary, neutralizing violence of sovereignty. The foundation here is produced as naive by poststructuralist discourses (this is their illocutionary effect): The work of ideology critique and ideological struggle, as a foundational mode of engagement, is both illocutionary and perlocutionary—that is, it names, surfaces, and literalizes the unity of illocution and perlocution in the ideological utterance aimed at dispersal and fictionalization, and it deploys this opening (not dissimulation) in acts of establishing public pedagogies that draw "lines of demarcation" across different arenas.

Reading MacKinnon as the "other" to the narratives of performativity and desire, then, will lead us to focus on her refusal both to view power relations as always already deconstructed and inherently reversible, and to see the possibilities for the emancipation of women as immanent to the category of women itself. MacKinnon's position on these questions is determined by her understanding of difference as an effect of inequality and domination:

> From this perspective, considering gender a matter of sameness and difference covers up the reality of gender as a system of social hierarchy, as an inequality. The differences attributed to sex become the lines that inequality draws, not any kind of basis for it. Social and political inequality begins indifferent to sameness and difference. Differences are inequality's post hoc excuse, its conclusory artifact, its outcome presented as its origin, its sentimentalization, its damage that is pointed to as the justification for doing the damage after the damage has been done, the distinctions that perception is socially organized to notice because inequality gives them consequences for social power. Gender might not even code as difference, might not mean distinction epistemologically, were it not for its consequences for social power. Distinctions of body or mind or behavior are pointed to as cause rather than effect, with no realization that they are so deeply effect rather than cause that pointing to them at all is an effect. Inequality comes first; difference comes after. Inequality is material and substantive and identifies a disparity; difference is ideational and abstract and falsely symmetrical. If this is so, a discourse and a law of gender that center on difference serve as ideology to neutralize, rationalize, and cover disparities of power, even as they appear to criticize or problematize them. Difference is the velvet glove on the iron fist of domination. The problem then is not that differences are not valued; the problem is that they are defined by power. This is as true when difference is affirmed as when it is denied, when its substance is applauded or disparaged, when women are punished or protected in its name (1989, 218–219).

In this totalizing understanding, there is clearly no place for a conception of difference as a problematization or destabilization of ideologies of the same, which are assumed to be either the cause or primary support of systems of domination. What is totalizing in MacKinnon's theory is the insistence on identifying the systemic internal logic of male domination as a precondition for theorizing its contradictions and the intersection of gender with other categories, instead of presupposing the inherent instability of that mode of domination. At this most general level of MacKinnon's argument, then, if women as a category are the products of a male-defined and male-controlled reality, there is no place for women's agency other than as adaptations to that reality that, in the end, confirm it; also, within this framework, there can be no affirmation of a specifically female or feminine subjectivity.

This understanding is grounded in MacKinnon's theory of sexuality as constitutive of male domination: "Sexuality, then, is a form of power. Gender, as socially constructed, embodies it, not the reverse. Women and men are divided by gender, made into the sexes as we know them, by the social requirements of its dominant form, heterosexuality, which institutionalizes male sexual dominance and female sexual submission. If this is true, sexuality is the linchpin of gender inequality" (1989, 113). In addition, feminism has a theory of power: Sexuality is gendered as gender is sexualized. Male and female are created through the eroticization of dominance and submission. The man/woman difference and the dominance/submission dynamic define each other. "This is the social meaning of sex and the distinctively feminist account of gender inequality," MacKinnon writes, and "sexual objectification, the central process within this dynamic, is at once epistemological and political. The feminist theory of knowledge is inextricable from the feminist critique of power because the male point of view forces itself upon the world as its way of apprehending it" (113–114). From this analysis, MacKinnon argues that "if women are socially defined such that female sexuality cannot be lived or spoken or felt or even somatically sensed apart from its enforced definition, so that it is its own lack, then there is no such thing as a woman as such; there are only walking embodiments of man's projected needs" (119).

This, of course, as MacKinnon recognizes, makes the existence of women's resistance (which, she suggests, is sometimes effective) and, indeed, of the feminist position from which she speaks problematic: "Feminism affirms women's point of view, in large part, by affirming its impossibility" (1989, 115). If a women's point of view were possible, it would no longer be necessary because there would be gender equality (and hence, no gender). Connected with this problem (which can be formulated as the question of how feminism is possible) is that of relations be-

tween women who are feminists and those who are not (or are even an-
tifeminist) and the relation between different and opposing versions of
feminism.

MacKinnon addresses this problem through the category of consciousness-raising, which she sees as the feminist method in theory and practice. Through consciousness-raising, women produce collectivities that
enable them to see the pervasive reality of male domination—which represents itself as universal—as a mode of domination. By transforming
women's experience into collective self-knowledge of that experience, by
situating the personal within the political, and by thus contesting the oppositions upon which male supremacy depends (i.e., subject and object,
sex and violence, private and public), the all-embracing imposition of
male supremacy can be opposed. However, the distinction between this
experience and knowledge of it that produces effective opposition still has
to be established.

To address this issue, it is necessary to have a theory of hegemony as
part of the theory of male domination. In fact, MacKinnon's theory does
understand the need for this, and it provides some of the materials for
constructing one. "Combining, like any form of power, legitimation with
force, male power extends beneath the representation of reality to its construction: it makes women (as it were) and so verifies (makes true) who
women 'are' in its view, simultaneously confirming its way of being and
its vision of truth, as it creates the social reality that supports both" (1989,
122). This would account for the necessity of the theory of objectivity that
MacKinnon associates with male domination and that it is therefore in-
cumbent upon feminism to overthrow. That is, the ideology of objectivity
would compel women to see their domination as a "fact" and as "desire"
rather than as the effect of power relations. It would also help to account
for the necessity of the "velvet glove" of ideologies of difference in addition to the "iron fist of domination." However, if male power unilaterally
produces women's reality, why is women's desire and women's sexuality,
in which they "choose" to be objects for the subject, necessary? MacKinnon writes: "Like the value of the commodity, women's sexual desirability
is fetishized: it is made to appear a quality of the object itself, spontaneous and inherent, independent of the social relation that creates it, uncontrolled by the force that requires it. It helps if the object cooperates:
hence, the vaginal orgasm; hence, faked orgasms altogether. Women's
sexualness, like male prowess, is no less real for being mythic" (123).

However, why does it help if the object cooperates, that is, if it acts as if
it were a subject? If sexuality is an expression of male domination, why
are practices that appear to make that domination dependent upon the
"cooperation" of those upon whom it is exercised "helpful"? It could be
answered that the reproduction of that domination, the constant enact-

ment of its enforcement and its overcoming of resistance, is essential to its realization. This would provide a useful foundation for the development of a theory of male hegemony and female desire. It would also be a way of analyzing the contradictions of male domination, which not only requires power over women but also needs—at least sometimes—to disguise this domination by assuming the autonomy of its object. But a theory of male domination as internally contradictory and therefore dependent upon external conditions of possibility would be a different theory than the one MacKinnon proposes.

In other words, her theory cannot solve the problem of the unity of power and hegemony, of force and consent in the mechanism of male domination, a problem, furthermore, that is raised by that theory itself and that is distinguished precisely by its insistence that material and ideal, objective and subjective, sex and violence are interconnected moments in the process of reproducing male supremacy. This difficulty has its effects in MacKinnon's understanding of pornography, which, as the consummate expression of the eroticization of domination and submission, appears in her theory both as the dominant form taken by male domination and as a system of practices required for the regulation and reproduction of that form of domination and therefore analytically separate from it.

The strength of MacKinnon's critique of pornography is that it undermines the liberal distinction between sex ("normal," "healthy," sex) and violence ("distorted" sex), which presupposes the possibility of some mode of sexuality outside of the relations of violence that constitute sexuality and gender, outside of ideology and culture. At the same time, there is a contradiction in MacKinnon's understanding of pornography. She argues that

> possession and use of women through the sexualization of intimate intrusion and access to them is a central feature of women's social definition as inferior and feminine. Visual and verbal intrusion, access, possession and use is predicated upon and produces physical and psychic intrusion, access, possession and use. In contemporary industrial society, pornography is an industry that mass produces sexual intrusion on, access to, possession and use of women by and for men for profit. It exploits women's sexual and economic inequality for gain. It sells women to men as and for sex. It is a technologically sophisticated traffic in women (1989, 195).

This passage articulates the distinction between physical and psychic modes of intrusion, access, possession, and use and visual and verbal modes, suggesting a relation of causality in which physical and psychic modes are predominant. It does the same with regard to women's sexual and economic inequality and the industry of pornography that exploits this inequality for gain (and therefore, presumably, contributes to the reproduction of this inequality). However, MacKinnon also argues that pornography is the dominant form taken by gender inequality:

> Pornography, in the feminist view, is a form of forced sex, a practice of sexual politics, and institution of gender inequality. In this perspective, pornography, with the rape and prostitution in which it participates, institutionalizes the sexuality of male supremacy, which fuses the eroticization of dominance and submission with the social construction of male and female. Gender is sexual. Pornography constitutes the meaning of that sexuality. Men treat women as whom they see women as being. Pornography constructs who that is. Men's power over women means that the way men see women defines who women can be. Pornography is that way (1989, 197).

According to this passage, it would have to be psychic and physical along with economic modes of inequality that are produced by visual and verbal modes or by men's way of seeing, which is, in turn, produced by pornography. However, in this case, what is the difference and relation between pornography and other (violently constructed) modes of sexuality? Why, for example, does it seem "essential to the kick of pornography that it be to some degree against the rules, but never truly unavailable or truly illegitimate" (1989, 214), whereas this is apparently not the case with other forms of sexuality?

The problem here is not one of distinguishing between sexual acts and sexual expressions or representations—MacKinnon sufficiently problematizes this distinction, showing its relativity to specific contexts and viewpoints and therefore its complicity in existing power relations. Rather, it is a question of understanding the structure of male domination and the determinations that produce and reproduce it. If pornography in fact constructs or determines sexual inequality, then it would be necessary to explain the relations between the more abstract (in the sense of an isolation of certain features—such as the eroticization of domination and submission—and the exclusion of other features—such as women's resistance and agency) representations prevalent in and even definitive of pornography and the more mediated forms of domination found in gender relations elsewhere. Also, it would be necessary to explain how and why pornography changes. MacKinnon argues that

> the old private rules have become the new public rules. Women were sex and are still sex. Greater efforts of brutality have become necessary to eroticize the taboo—each taboo being a hierarchy in disguise—since the frontier of the taboo keeps vanishing as one crosses it. Put another way, more and more vi-

olence has become necessary to keep the progressively desensitized consumer aroused to the illusion that sex (and he) is daring and dangerous. Making sex with the powerless "not allowed" is a way of keeping "getting it" defined as an act of power, an assertion of hierarchy, which keeps it sexy in a sexual system in which hierarchy is sexy (1989, 200–201).

Here, it would seem that there needs to be, according to the logic of pornography, a continual increase in the levels of brutality; however, this would not account for the transformation of the old private rules into the new public rules. MacKinnon continues:

In addition, pornography has become ubiquitous. Sexual terrorism has become democratized. Pornography has become truly available to women for the first time in history. Among other effects, this central mechanism of sexual subordination, this means of systematizing the definition of women as a sexual class, has now become available to its victims for scrutiny and analysis as an open public system, not just a private secret abuse. Hopefully, this was a mistake (1989, 201).

This analysis situates pornography in a different way than much of the rest of MacKinnon's discussion. First of all, MacKinnon claims that pornography has become ubiquitous: Presumably, she would not describe sexual inequality in the same way (since sexual inequality has been pervasive in all class societies). This assumes that rather than being the determinant of sexual inequality, pornography is one of the forms it takes, which is to say that it contributes to the reproduction of the system of inequality and is subordinated to the dynamics of that system. This would account for the term *sexual terrorism,* since terrorism is only intelligible as a type of force that takes on its significance in relation to more comprehensive (organized and hegemonic) systems of coercion. At the same time, this passage points to a contradiction in the effects of pornography, since it is both increasingly available to men and increasingly brutal while at the same time more vulnerable to the public scrutiny (and perhaps, MacKinnon's unease expressed in the final sentence suggests, even the use) of its victims, which furthermore seems to suggest that the conditions of possibility of consciousness-raising depend upon the development of social contradictions that publicize the ideological terms of domination. In other words, MacKinnon is describing here a complex and contradictory transformation in gender inequality that her understanding of pornography, as the script that determines male domination, cannot account for.

These (extremely productive) contradictions in MacKinnon's understanding of pornography are rooted in her problematic theory of (male) power. If male domination takes the form of direct and incessantly repeated violence against women, then the essence of that domination should indeed be sought in the most extreme, purified, and even vivid representation of that violence. (I say "representation" and not "instance" because, due to the contradictions in MacKinnon's theory of male hegemony, the kind of direct violence against women that she sees as essential to male domination can best be sought out in the systematically controlled environment that representation makes possible.) However, in this case, other representations and other forms taken by that domination, determined by the requirement that it at times be disguised, disavowed, or modified, remain inexplicable, on the terms of that mode of domination taken in isolation. It also follows that the most effective way of struggling against male domination is by directing all resources toward the abolition of pornography, on the assumption that the other, less direct and derivative forms of violence, due to their dependence upon the perpetuation of pornographic practices, would then lose their effectiveness. This is why pornography needs to be theorized as an instance of ideology, as producing a space of representation wherein the exception (direct, unmediated violence) undermines the norm (democracy, equality) precisely by esoterically producing itself as the truth of that norm—the originary violence-as-desire constitutive of the social.

MacKinnon's understanding of male domination is useful, in spite of and because of these difficulties, because she is attempting to theorize male domination under the conditions produced, as the latest passage I cited suggests, by its generalization or its transformation from a private system in which women are controlled by individual men (patriarchy) to a public system in which male domination enters into the construction of all social institutions, thereby contributing to the management of those institutions (sexism). Male hegemony (in addition to and as an aspect of male power) would then be necessary because women as subjects are no longer defined solely in terms of their articulation within gender inequality but as a result of the contradiction between their production within that system and their production as the subjects of other (economic, educational, etc.) institutions.[5]

In this way, MacKinnon produces at least the elements of a feminist theory of masculinist hegemony and feminine desire that would be based on the requirement that male domination be historically modified and qualified by women's partial and contradictory access to abstract and collective modes of subjectivity—modes that make the kind of total physical control implied by the slave relation impossible (while this still remains the telos of male domination). Within this framework, pornography would be a result of the need for an idealized or purified imaginary representation of an unhindered mode of male domination (which must incorporate representations of women's resistance as destined to be overcome) in order to regulate and reproduce the more complicated actual modes of domination (which themselves modify and qualify class exploitation); at the same time, it would also be the result of the need to have this absolutist mode of domination disavowed and relegated to the fringe. Thus, MacKinnon's critique of pornography opens up the possibility of a mode of ideology critique that can theorize the production of gendered subjectivities at all social sites.

In this case, women can resist and have agency precisely because they are "women" and because women's subjectivities are produced through their organization within a wide variety of social institutions that both provide them with access to the powers situated in those institutions and confront them with the contradictions between the social possibilities implicit in those institutions and sexist forms of authority. In other words, the resources for feminist struggles are not internal to women's subjectivity, whether this be understood in terms of their distinctive standpoint or their eccentricity with regard to homogenizing systems and ideologies that cannot contain the difference represented or enacted by women. These understandings can now be seen as regressive insofar as they preserve the gender abstraction by merely reversing or revaluing its terms and understanding this reversibility as symptomatic of its instability and indeterminacy, rather than theorizing its contradictions and the crises that pervade it. MacKinnon does not theorize a way out of the gender abstraction, but by refusing any form of consolation that its seeming intractability provides, she is able to foreground its contradictions and thereby produce the elements of a critique of it. It is precisely MacKinnon's theorization of the unity of the content and various forms of male domination that, despite her failure to theorize the hierarchical determinations that constitute this unity, enable her discourse to contribute to an understanding of gender that is systematic and that indicates where its contradictions are to be found. That is, it enables us to understand the conditions of possibility of contesting patriarchy not in the excessive unintelligibilities or experiential data of women's subjectivities but in the totality of social contradictions that become public and visible in a determinate way in the gender abstraction. (I would argue that the claim that, despite appearances, MacKinnon's work actually theorizes the masculinist dimension of ruling-class hegemony under conditions of late capitalism is supported by her approach, which in fact focuses on male domination as it is constructed through contemporary capitalist economic, political, ideological, and legal systems and on the contradictions of these constructions.) Again, this is possible because of the totalizing character of MacKinnon's feminism, which understands male domination in relation to a notion of social necessity (in the sense of the laws of motion of a social form) rather than in terms of contingent and unstable articulations.

And this, finally, is the deepest objection to her work on the part of many critics who are otherwise inexplicably hostile.

Notes

1. For a discussion of the history of the socialist feminist project, see Philipson and Hansen 1990. The authors also argue that the questions raised and aims advanced by socialist feminism have been downgraded in contemporary feminism. However, they generally support these developments, thereby aligning themselves with the tendencies I am critiquing here.

2. See Laclau 1990, especially p. 92, and Zizek 1989. I will address Zizek's more recent discussions of politics and revolution in Chapter 5.

3. See Larrain 1996.

4. Caughie distinguishes between cultural studies as "a distinct methodology and critical tradition" and culture studies as "the state of the humanities in the aftermath of the theoretical and social upheavals of the past two decades" (1997, 37), a distinction that is not very important for my discussion.

5. For a series of discussions central to debates concerning the relations between gender and class and Marxism and feminism, see Sargent 1981. For other useful accounts of the relation between gender and class from more consistently Marxist positions, see Dixon 1983 and Jenness 1972.

3

CULTURAL STUDIES AND POSTMODERNITY

Theory, Materialism, and Cultural Studies

Contemporary cultural studies emerged out of attempts to understand the new type of capitalism that followed World War II. The forerunners of cultural studies, such as the critical theorists of the Frankfurt School and investigators into the structures of everyday life such as Henri Lefebvre and Roland Barthes in France, were interested in new forms of social control, economic regulation, media, consumption, and subjectivity that distinguished postwar capitalism from its predecessors. Theoretical categories such as the society of bureaucratically controlled consumption and the totally administered society were developed, in particular, in order to produce critical understandings of the ways in which knowledges and forms of organization predominant within the workplace were extended beyond the workplace to transform and more thoroughly subordinate society as a whole.

Such critiques and investigations, actualized and deepened by the effects of the social struggles of the 1960s, were directed as much against bureaucratic and scientistic forms of social control, cultural modes of domination, the limits of traditional left-wing parties and politics, and the oppressive structures of everyday life as against economic exploitation and state power. The project of the New Left, that is, both confirmed the need for understandings of contemporary capitalist society and culture that went beyond the parameters of traditional Marxist theory and contributed in significant ways to the development of new theoretical frameworks. Despite its limitations and its ultimate failure to overthrow existing social relations in any advanced capitalist country, this project placed new questions and problems on the agenda for social and cultural theorists, in part by revealing the limitations and contradictions in the Western democracies, which had previously appeared to be immune to crisis and significant opposition.

Contemporary attempts to conceptualize these cultural shifts have generally broken with the Marxist and neo-Marxist assumptions of this earlier generation of theorists, especially those regarding the predominance of production and economic processes in determining these changes. At the same time, they have abandoned the project of the New Left, which, for all of its contradictions, remained committed to combining economic and cultural emancipation. Theories of postmodernity, as a general cultural condition reflecting a decisive break (assumed to have originated either in the wake of World War II or in the crisis of Western societies following the struggles of the 1960s and the economic instability of the 1970s) with an earlier condition of modernity, usually argue that distinctions between labor and signs, material and intellectual production, base and superstructure, production and consumption are no longer useful, since one of the defining characteristics of postmodernity is the reciprocal integration and (in)determination of the cultural and the economic. In this chapter, I will examine the relations between theories of postmodernity, postmodernism (as a set of ideological, cultural, and especially theoretical practices), and postmodern cultural studies. I will argue, in particular, that the move away from an understanding of culture in terms of its determination by the economic makes a radical cultural critique impossible. This is because the autonomy of culture removes any external standpoint from which one could theorize cultural products in relation to systemic contradictions. It follows, then, that one can only critique culture from within, which, I argue, reduces cultural critique to the function of pointing out the uselessness of outmoded cultural forms. This provides an important service for the ruling class, by updating dominant institutions and developing more subtle and sophisticated modes of domination.

As I argued in the previous chapter, postmodern cultural studies rejects the categories of theory and ideology in favor of those of experience and identity. This shifts the terrain of political struggle from the social processes that produce subjectivity to the destabilization of restrictive identities and their pluralization and empowerment (as I suggested, on the terms set by the dominant culture, not against that culture). In this chapter, I will argue that postmodern theories of postmodernity work to delegitimate the categories of materiality and production. This makes it possible to eliminate any social or critical theory that attempts to explain the products of culture in terms of a hierarchy of determinations or through an abstraction from the immediacy of those products. This means that critique is limited to immanent critique. Totalizing critiques need to be grounded in some outside of the structures producing the object of critique. However, postmodernism insists that there can be no such outside, thereby supporting the notion that any liberation must take place on the terrain of existing social relations themselves, that is, without transforming those relations. The dominant theories of postmodernity wish to claim *both* that the interpenetration of materiality and discursivity, production and reproduction makes systemic opposition aiming at structural transformation impossible *and* that this situation opens up the possibility of local forms of emancipation that escape systemic determinations. Postmodern theory, based on the notion of liberation through heterogeneity, thus follows from the understandings of postmodernity I will examine here. Furthermore, postmodern theory, as an immanent critique of postmodernity, is able to present itself as the most effective response to the condition of postmodernity. In this way, postmodernism attacks any notion of emancipation that results from the contestations between collective agencies produced through the contradictory processes of material production.

Postmodern cultural studies also rewrites the category of materiality to refer to local practices and, ultimately, the body. For example, postmodern cultural studies theorist John Fiske, while defining the material in terms of economic constraints, at the same time argues for an understanding of materiality as the absence of any possibility for abstraction, of any distancing from the products of culture. "Culture," he says, "is inescapably material: distantiation is an unattainable luxury. The culture of everyday life is concrete, contextualized, and lived, just as deprivation is concrete, contextualized and lived" (1992, 155). Since he identifies the material with the lived experience of everyday life in the face of oppression and with the construction of an individualized environment that makes survival and resistance possible, he goes on to locate materiality in the body: "The body and its specific behavior is where the power system stops being abstract and becomes material" (162). For this reason, he considers it important to develop a "bottom-up" (165) notion of subjectivity, as opposed to those theories in which contradictions in subjectivity "are traced back to the complex elaborations of late capitalist societies" (161). This, I argue, excludes the possibility of understanding materiality in terms of the systemic connections between specific practices. It reduces subjectivity to the local contexts in which individualized modes of life are constructed, and it refuses any theory that does not involve "the development of the ability to experience as far as possible from the inside other people's ways of living" (159). In this case, of course, it becomes impossible to theorize the world market or capitalist class domination, since these would be considered abstract categories that cannot be inside anyone's way of living.

Postmodern cultural studies therefore views subjectivities as the effects of local experiences, and it sees them as the result of individualized constructive processes that escape social determination. The argument that economic and cultural processes have interpenetrated one another to the point where the distinction itself is no longer useful therefore supports another argument that, on the surface, seems quite different but actually shares the same logic of indeterminacy—that the production of subjectivity is an exclusively cultural matter, which cannot really be explained but only described in a sympathetic and affirmative manner. Explanations can only go so far. In fact, the limits on explanation are set at that point where explanations threaten the free individuality of the subject. The dominated subject can then be recouped within what I will argue in the following chapter is the liberal coalitionist politics supported by postmodern cultural studies.

In contrast, I understand materiality as the systematic organization of practices within the social totality, which subordinates all practices to a single logic. This understanding of materiality thus requires both the notion of homogeneity (the interchangeability of practices and subjects as an aspect of transformations in the productive forces) and that of contradiction (between incompatible ways of controlling the productive forces). Put another way, I understand the objectivity of actuality in terms of both its structured and organizing processes and the opposition between antagonistic modes of organizing reality. A materialist theory begins with the global articulation of the economic, social, and cultural divisions of labor. A materialist understanding of subjectivity, then, views subjectivity as an effect of the global division of labor produced by the totalizing practices of capitalism, which reduces all practices and products to a single measure. Whereas postmodern cultural studies argues that liberation consists in resisting these processes of homogenization and commensuration, a materialist politics, as I understand it, contends that emancipation depends upon opposing another mode of organizing the global division of labor to the existing one. This means that instead of inquiring into the possibilities of coexistence between differentially situated subjectivities, it is necessary to locate, clarify, and exacerbate their antagonistic relations, their subordination to the contending modes of production. Theoretical knowledges, in this case, comprehend and advance some set of possibilities presupposed by a given organization of labor. Furthermore, they seek to reproduce one articulation of reality in opposition to another actual or potential one.

This mode of conceptualizing materiality also requires an argument for the necessity of theory. Although every discourse and practice is theoretically informed or presupposes theoretical understandings, the argument for theory entails an insistence upon the self-conscious and consistent deployment of theoretical assumptions and understandings (as opposed to eclectic combinations of various theoretical approaches that do not recognize the ideological oppositions that are always involved in theoretical differences and thus support the dominant ideology by occluding these oppositions).

The argument for theory is possible in part because of the emergence of the theoretical discourses of poststructuralism and other forms of antifoundationalism in the humanities in the 1970s. This set of developments was a response, as I suggested in the first chapter, to the crisis in liberal humanist modes of subjectivity that presupposed an unproblematic relation between subject and object, text and meaning. This crisis in private individuality generated inquiries into the conditions of possibility of subjectivity and of meaning. These inquiries generally focused on the discursive processes of meaning and subject production (rather than the material processes, in the sense in which I have defined the term *material*). Since these theoretical discourses were often aligned with radical politics (such as Marxism or feminism) and were creating new possibilities of understanding, they generally had a demystifying effect upon disciplinary assumptions. This was the case not least of all because of the very insistence upon the indispensability of theory itself, which served a critical function in relation both to the forms of everyday common sense in advanced capitalist societies and to the seeming obviousness of domains and objects of knowledge within specialized discourses. This critical function, I would argue, has been exhausted because the social and class interests they ultimately served (a resituation of private individuality along postcollectivist lines) has been achieved with the consolidation of postmodern cultural studies. This means that the argument for theory, which is necessary more than ever given the predominance of the neoexperientialist common sense of postmodern cultural studies, must now be directed at the production of historical materialist theorizations of culture and subjectivity.

Theories of Postmodernity

One line of investigation into the condition of postmodernity derives from Jean-Francois Lyotard's *The Postmodern Condition*. As is well known, Lyotard defines postmodernity as the end of the credibility of the "grand narratives" of modernity. According to Lyotard, modern societies legitimate the production of knowledge through one of two grand or universalizing narratives. The first is the narrative of "humanity as the hero of liberty" (1984, 31) or of "emancipation." The second is the narrative of the production of knowledge as an end in itself, which Lyotard acknowledges is often intertwined with the first in that knowledge is seen as a mode of universal emancipation.

Lyotard argues that the legitimation effect of these narratives has sharply declined "as an effect of the blossoming of techniques and technologies since the Second World War, which has shifted emphasis from the ends of action to its means" (1984, 37). Under such conditions, science (and more broadly knowledge) is legitimated by its performativity rather than its reference to some external end or ideal. Knowledges are true or correct insofar as they have effects or have the consequences of producing prescriptions. At the same time, Lyotard claims that it is not socioeconomic and technological conditions alone that have brought about this delegitimation of the grand narratives: "In order to understand how contemporary science could have been susceptible to those effects long before they took place, we must first locate the seeds of delegitimation and nihilism that were inherent in the grand narratives of the nineteenth century" (38). These seeds of delegitimation and nihilism, according to Lyotard, lie in the necessity that the grand narratives support themselves through the use of a priori assumptions that cannot be supported or proven according to the terms of proof established by scientific discourses themselves.

In this way, the grand narratives of modernity themselves lay the groundwork for the types of legitimation Lyotard considers characteristic of postmodernity. In accord with his use of Ludwig Wittgenstein's notion of language games (which reproduce themselves and the social bond by way of the fact that they are recognized as legitimate through their repeated use and that they enable effective articulations on the part of their participants rather than through any external reference), the unprovable presuppositions of modern language games can also be understood in a totally different sense, one that takes us in the direction of postmodern culture. As he puts it, "We could say, in keeping with the perspective we adopted earlier, that this presupposition defines the set of rules one must accept in order to play the speculative game" (1984, 39). In this sense, the delegitimation of the grand narratives can be seen as internal to those narratives themselves, to the extent that their claims to special status demonstrate that they are, in fact, one set of language games within a social field constituted by many such games, none of which can claim a privileged status. Lyotard's narrative displaces social relations and structures onto knowledge. Throughout *The Postmodern Condition*, Lyotard recognizes that knowledges and their relations to technology are organized within a capitalist framework, but by arguing that performativity in itself is the source of legitimation, he sets aside the question of economic relations. This becomes possible because Lyotard assumes that criteria for performativity are themselves internal to knowledges and technological apparatuses. So, on the one hand, he states that

> the State and/or company must abandon the idealist and humanist narratives of legitimation in order to justify the new goal: in the discourse of today's financial backers of research, the only credible goal is power. Scientists, technicians, and instruments are purchased not to find truth, but to augment power (46).

In this case, the logic or criterion of performativity is clearly subordinated to some externally determined social goal—the power of dominant groups. On the other hand, he notes that since "reality" is what provides the evidence used as proof in scientific argumentation, and also provides prescriptions and promises of a juridical, ethical and political nature, one can master all of these games by mastering "reality." That is precisely what technology can do. By reinforcing technology, one "reinforces" reality, and one's chances of being just and right accordingly. Reciprocally, technology is reinforced all the more effectively if one has access to scientific knowledge and decision making authority (47).

According to this argument, the very dependence of power upon technology and technology upon knowledge ultimately transfers to the possessors of knowledge an independence in that they are the ones shaping the reality within which struggles over power must be situated.

This reversal of relations between capital and state power and scientific knowledge makes it possible for Lyotard to propose what must ultimately be seen as a theory of hegemony. For him, legitimacy involves not eliminating any of the positions that a given language has articulated—it means an absence of terror. Technology, which is more directly related to power, is unable to guarantee this: "Force appears to belong exclusively to the last game, the game of technology" (1984, 46). However, the authority that must be delegated to a postpositivist science that cannot define the terms of truth and justice in advance means that potentially subversive or unproductive positions cannot be eliminated from the game, since counterexamples, paradoxes, and unintelligibilities (54) are precisely the means by which new (i.e., useful) knowledges are produced. The consequence of this would be that the dominant social forces have no power to control the play of experimentation intrinsic to the postmodern sciences, and this perpetual experimentation (the production of paralogies) can therefore become an arena of freedom that at least escapes from or even resists or challenges those forces.

I would contend that we can only understand some of the contradictions in Lyotard's argument in *The Postmodern Condition* if we read his analysis as a kind of sublimation of the Marxist understanding of the contradiction between the forces and relations of production and the notion of hegemony. For example, Lyotard does not explicitly account for how the postmodern science he valorizes is possible, given his own account of the social structures that determine its emergence; also, as has been noted, his proposal to open the data banks of information as a way of democratizing knowledge production (and, implicitly, society) directly contradicts his own claim that these banks are under the control of agents (corporations and the state) that clearly have little incentive to open them (and whose control would most likely survive and perhaps even be enhanced by any likely mode of transparency). According to the reading I have offered, these anomalies become intelligible as necessary elements of the legitimation of postmodern language games aimed at by Lyotard's text.

At the same time, though, this reading makes the questions regarding the consistency or truthfulness of Lyotard's own argument less urgent. That is, it is less important to point out that his descriptions of contemporary science bear little resemblance to actual scientific practices (see Conner 1989, 35) or that his proposals are unrealistic. What is more significant, I would argue, is the ideological character of Lyotard's reification of knowledge, his abstraction of knowledge from its social conditions of production. If his analysis in fact entails a sublimation of the Marxist understanding of social transformation, it also involves a transfer of the locus of resistance to existing social relations from the proletariat to the class produced by the independence of knowledge production, which I termed the "new petite bourgeoisie" in the previous chapter.

If we can read Lyotard as an ideologist of the new petite bourgeoisie, then we can inquire into what kind of subject position his argument is intended to produce, what interests his conception of the postmodern is concerned to articulate and reproduce. Thus, Lyotard's account of postmodern science and his location of freedom from terror in the potentially infinite proliferation of heteromorphous language games can be read not merely as utopian or as instances of flawed reasoning and incorrect analysis but also as required for the production of the necessary social imaginary for a class seeking to secure its place in hegemonic social relations.

To this end, the following should be noted. First, despite Lyotard's criticisms of the uses and structure of knowledge in contemporary postliberal capitalist society, his account of the autonomy of nonterroristic language games depends upon the autonomy of knowledge produced by that society. That is, the abstraction of the category of language games as a basis for the social bond depends upon the real abstraction of languages and knowledges from local communities that has characterized the history of capitalism. To put it another way, the autonomy of language games from terror posited by Lyotard is actually an effect of those terroristic power relations themselves. Thus, despite his references to precapitalist communities in which small narratives are self-legitimating, Lyotard's understanding presupposes communities that have been posited by capitalist relations. Second, then, the bearer of the language games Lyotard is interested in are themselves subjects produced within the universalizing and centralizing processes of capitalist production and reproduction. They are collectivized subjects, the results of a stage of capitalist development when the integration of individuals into capitalist production cannot be left to the workings of the labor market and the "labourer's instincts of self-preservation and of propagation," as in the model developed by Marx (1906, 627); instead, they must be the result of capitalism's intervention in the processes of subjective reproduction.

Lyotard's theory of the "differend," wherein "phrase-regimes" enter into a relation of incommensurability such that the claim of one cannot be articulated in the terms of the other (so that the litigant becomes a victim), rests upon the same assumptions. The heterogeneous phrase-regimes he privileges border each other because they are already abstract; hence, they are already open to each other, and each is equipped with its polemic against the other(s). The main purpose of the concept of the differend is to identify the central mode of modern violence and thereby develop a postmodern ethical discourse. But the main form of modern political violence is not directed against discourses resistant to performativity or totalization but against the conditions of possibility for specific kinds of totalization, which would articulate (anti)political with economic violence.

The notion of the differend, with its reliance upon the primacy of functional differentiation over homogeneous class relations, on the one hand, and the pervasiveness of potentially totalitarian obliteration of difference, on the other, obscures the real structure of ideological violence. Liberal democracy can always be more or less open to new politicizations, paralogies, micropolitics, intensities, etc. In fact, all this is what keeps it going, as Lyotard himself came to acknowledge.[1] What liberal democracy is not open to is what Marx called (in his discussion of the Paris Commune) "expansive political forms"—in which doers can actually be connected with deeds (hence the provision for the immediate revocation of delegates in the Paris Commune), in which part of the deed is the establishment of polemical "lines of demarcation" emerging from the limits of previous deeds, and in which power appears as actions that unfold the logic concealed behind and operationalizing ideological violence. As I will explain soon in my discussion of sensationalism as the ideological form of late capitalism, ideological violence is directed at breaking up any hint of expansive politicality.

Lyotard's discourse, in its inconsistencies and contradictions, articulates even as it seeks to conceal the crisis in these arrangements: This is the case insofar as experimentation in knowledge and the kind of free subject it presupposes are both necessary and impossible, according to Lyotard's own terms. The antinomy between performativity (the total reduction of knowledge production to the status of material production) and paralogy (the autonomy of knowledge production not only from material production but from social relations of production and control) reproduces the crisis in advanced knowledges (the contradiction between the possibility for rational collective control and the actual subordination to profitability) by articulating it in cultural and political terms: terror versus legitimation. In this way, one can remove oneself from terrorism not by abolishing the relations that support it but by committing oneself to the paralogic, experimental forms of legitimation characteristic of small language games and narratives.

Another prominent figure who has determined the parameters of the discussions of postmodernity is Jean Baudrillard. Baudrillard's work has moved from attempts to develop critical theory with the aid of structuralist semiotics, in order to conceptualize the political economy of the sign in advanced capitalist societies, to an understanding of contemporary society as governed by the production and dissemination of "simulacra." According to Baudrillard, simulacra are copies for which there is no original; simulacra produce reality or "hyperreality" as the effect of an abstracted and self-reproducing "code." Reality, in this case, becomes "that of which it is possible to give an equivalent reproduction" (1983, 146).

Baudrillard draws upon post-Saussurian linguistics to support his claims—if signs are constituted through their differential relations with other signs within a semiotic system, then it follows that the uses of signs that necessarily mediate any relation to reality are determined not by their relationship to that reality but by the various combinations that semiotic systems enable. At the same time, Baudrillard seeks to ground the dominance of simulacra in a historical process, which reads like a caricature of the Marxist theory of the transformation of one mode of production into another: "This would be the successive phases of the image: it is the reflection of a basic reality—it masks and perverts a basic reality—it masks the *absence of* a basic reality—it bears no relation to any reality whatever: it is its own pure simulacrum" (1983, 11). Baudrillard connects this historical process with capital accumulation and the application of autonomized knowledge to production:

> As soon as dead work wins out over living work—that is, as soon as the era of primitive accumulation is over—serial production yields to generation by means of models. And here it is a question of a reversal of origin and finality, for all the forms change once they are not so much mechanically reproduced but even conceived from the point-of-view of their very reproducibility, diffracted from a generating nucleus we call the model. . . . Here are models from which proceed all forms according to the modulation of their differences. . . . Finally, it is not serial reproducibility which is fundamental, but the modulation. Not quantitative equivalences, but distinctive oppositions. No longer the law of capital, but the structural law of value (100–101).

Baudrillard's analyses of the regime of simulacra in contemporary life are directed at the way in which social phenomena are constructed and represented in conformity with a model based upon an exhaustive binary opposition. So, for example, according to Baudrillard, critiques of capitalism as immoral or irrational simply reproduce the moralistic and rationalistic binaries that capitalism produces and requires for its own legitimation. Antisystemic actions—strikes, protests, critiques, terrorism—have already been organized within the system they attempt to oppose. They merely follow the media script, expert analyses, and institutional modeling and preparation that are ready to absorb them as evidence of the system's power, reality, and capacity to adjust to and contain the new or oppositional. Baudrillard describes this process using the category of digitality:

> This regulation on the model of the genetic code is not at all limited to laboratory effects or to the exalted visions of the theoreticians. Banal, everyday life is invested by these models. Digitality is with us. It is that which haunts all the messages, all the signs of our societies. The most concrete form you see it in is that of the test, of the question/answer, of the stimulus/response. All content is neutralized by a continual procedure of directed interrogation, of verdicts and ultimatums to decode, which no longer arise this time from the depths of the genetic code but have the same tactile indeterminacy—the cycle of sense being infinitely shortened into that of the question/answer, of bit or minute quantity of energy/information coming back to its beginning, the cycle only describing the perpetual reactualization of the same models. The equivalent of the total neutralization of the signified by the code is the instantaneousness of the verdict of fashion, or of any advertising or media message. Any place where the offer swallows up the demand, where the question assimilates the answer, or absorbs and regurgitates it in a decodable form, or invents and anticipates it in a predictable form. Everywhere the same "scenario," the scenario of "trial and error" (guinea pig in laboratory experiments), the scenario of the breadth of choice offered everywhere (the "personality test")—everywhere the test functions as a fundamental form of control, by means of the infinite divisibility of practices and responses (1983, 115–116).

There are several noteworthy features in this passage. First of all, there is the assumption that the dominance of digitality is determined by the subordination of production and social practices to advanced, self-reproducing knowledges, knowledges that have themselves been modeled on the "infinite divisibility" of practices and technologically organized production. Second, it assumes that the opposing sides of the production-consumption cycle have been conflated ("the instantaneousness of the verdict of fashion") or that the opposition itself has "imploded." Third, the production of subjects who will be inserted into this cycle by the same means is proposed ("the personality test"). Finally, it is the form of advanced knowledges—the way in which they are structured so that their questions already include the answers, their interrogations their responses, and so on—that is at stake, marking the irrelevance of content (which particular questions and answers). Unlike Lyotard's version of similar processes, meanwhile, Baudrillard's account seems to exclude the possibility that these knowledges might attain a degree of autonomy that would transform them into a site of free activity.

However, despite the presumably self-contained nature of this process, it becomes evident even in Baudrillard's account that the binary structuring of the code serves social purposes that are irreducible to the code itself. So, for example, he argues that the

> "advanced democratic" systems are stabilized on the formula of bipartite alternation. The monopoly in fact remains that of the homogeneous political class, from left to right, but it must not be exercised as such. The one-party totalitarian regime is an unstable form—it defuses the political scene, it no longer assures the feed-back of public opinion, the minimal flux in the integrated circuit which constitutes the transistorized political machine" (1983, 131).

Despite Baudrillard's claims to the contrary, then, the binary structure of, in this case, the political system serves the purpose of stabilizing the system (which, presumably, is therefore not automatically or necessarily stable). Furthermore, this binarism conceals the fact that the political monopoly is, in fact, held by a homogeneous political class.

On the one hand, then, Baudrillard is rehearsing a fairly commonplace analysis of the way in which the two-party system is a stabilizing force in mass democracies, as well as advancing something resembling a Marxist theory of ideology based upon a notion of false consciousness that Baudrillard consistently rejects. However, there is an important difference in his account: According to the standard models of pluralism, two-party systems are stabilizing because they allow for the expression of opposing positions and for negotiations and coalitions between various interests, thereby giving subjects an interest in the political system that, to some degree at least, serves their needs. Also, for the theory of ideology Baudrillard is implicitly invoking, it is ideologies with a specific ideational content (those that, in one way or another, justify capitalist social relations) that are responsible for the production of false consciousness. For Baudrillard, though, the two-party system is stabilizing not because it allows for some kind of representation but because of the question/answer, interrogation/response model itself, which compels all the participants to presuppose the terms on which legitimate feedback will be determined. At the same time, it does not matter which ideological content is used to conceal reality: In fact, Baudrillard would argue that the very structure of conceal/reveal simply follows from the model he has outlined, in which case the fact that the masses are aware that there is only a single homogeneous political class would simply facilitate the operation of the code. Nevertheless, Baudrillard's argument assumes that something like a "reference effect," which implies some desire for reality, is required, while at the same time finding it necessary to refer to some outside of the code that needs stabilization.

In addition, Baudrillard's analyses suggest that there is some coherence or logic to the types of binaries that are most useful to the system: The oppositions that he finds to be predominant are invariably the classic liberal oppositions such as nature/culture, moral/immoral, and just/unjust, on the one hand, and Marxist oppositions (which he generally assimilates to liberal ones) such as rationality/irrationality, domination/subordination, and productive/unproductive, on the other hand. In particular, the destruction (but also the simulated incorporation) of the private/public distinction is central to Baudrillard's notion of "obscenity," outlined in "The Ecstasy of Communication":

> In a subtle way, this loss of public space [to "gigantic spaces of circulation, ventilation and ephemeral connections" (1985, 130)] occurs contemporaneously with the loss of private space. The one is no longer a spectacle, the other no longer a secret. Their distinctive opposition, the clear difference of an exterior and an interior exactly described the domestic scene of objects, with its rules of play and limits, and the sovereignty of a symbolic space which was also that of the subject. Now this opposition is effaced in a sort of obscenity where the most intimate processes of our life become the virtual feeding ground of the media. . . . Inversely, the entire universe comes to unfold arbitrarily on your domestic screen (all the useless information that comes to you from the entire world, like a microscopic pornography of the universe, useless, excessive, just like the sexual close-up in a porno film): all this explodes the scene formerly preserved by the minimal separation of public and private, the scene that was played out in a restricted space, according to a secret ritual known only by the actors (1985, 130).

This passage reveals a nostalgia for both the classical bourgeois private space and private individual and the public sphere in which he or she entered as a rational and free subject. At the same time, Baudrillard's argument excludes the possibility of any outside to this private/public division or any possible transformation in the relations between private and public. These two positions are closely connected: The apparent imperviousness of the (post)modern world to any change depends upon the (liberal) standard of evaluation Baudrillard employs. This is why he cannot explain why these liberal binaries are appropriated by the "gigantic spaces of circulation;" for example, by analyzing the transformations in private property and the wage relation that have situated capitalism on new terms, creating new problems and possibilities but without resolving any of the contradictions articulated by the private/public relation. The nostalgic standpoint Baudrillard adopts also determines the response he proposes, which is to rescue privacy and the private space in a manner commensurate to contemporary conditions.

This is why the obscenity Baudrillard denounces ultimately lays the groundwork for a kind of free praxis that involves driving the implosion of the system to its limits. In "Toward a Principle of Evil" he argues for a type of practice he calls "fatal strategies," in which the subject realizes that any attempt to categorize and control objects fails to recognize that the system of objects is fundamentally indeterminate and characterized by a duplicity that undermines such attempts to privilege the subject. Instead, Baudrillard suggests going over to the side of the object, a strategy that is itself inscribed in the hyperreality his work describes:

> When I speak of the object and of its fatal strategies I am speaking of a person and of his or her inhuman strategies. For example, a human being can find a much deeper boredom while on vacation than in daily life—boredom intensified by the fact that it contains all the elements of happiness and recreation. The important point is that vacation is predestined to boredom, along with the premonition of being unable to escape it. How can one imagine that people would repudiate their everyday life in search of an alternative? On the contrary, they make it their destiny: by intensifying it in the appearances of the contrary; by submerging themselves to the point of ecstasy; and by fixating monotony in an even greater one. Super-banality is the equivalent of fatality. . . . No matter how boring, the important thing is to increase boredom; such an increase is salvation, it is ecstasy. It can be the ecstatic amplification of just about anything. It may be the increase of oppression or abjection that acts as the liberating ecstasy of abjection, just as the absolute commodity is the liberating form of commodity. This is the only solution to the problem of "voluntary servitude," and moreover, this is the only form of liberation: the amplification of negative conditions (1993, 357).

Like Lyotard, Baudrillard theorizes an all-encompassing system of signs and abstracted knowledges that organizes and posits reality according to self-generating categories and models and yet nevertheless provides within itself the possibility of reversing that absolute domination and yielding a mode of liberation that is somehow internal to the system. For Lyotard, as we saw, liberation lies in the inherently experimental and unregulated character of advanced knowledges that creates the conditions of possibility for language games that can be freed from the terroristic conditions of performativity. For Baudrillard, meanwhile, this possibility lies in "amplifying the negative," in exacerbating the obscenity of the simulacrum, in being more "hyper" than an already hyperreality. In both cases, this is made possible by the sublimation of material production into knowledge production, so that the opposition between antagonistic ways of organizing material production can be displaced onto the opposition between totalitarian modes of organizing knowledge (on the model of material practices in which all the elements are determined and controlled in advance) and the irreducibility of knowledge to this mode of organization and control.

Baudrillard's proposal that we amplify the negative presupposes a relation between that hyperreality and something else, which at least potentially escapes being subordinated to it. As I noted earlier, the structure of hyperreality, of the regime of simulacra, according to Baudrillard, depends both upon the abstraction of signs from any reality and upon a desire for such a reality. This desire may be a lingering or nostalgic one, but the workings of the system of simulacra demands that it be systematically reproduced, in an intensified and exaggerated form. Why this would be the case cannot be accounted for in Baudrillard's theory. It is itself constituted by precisely such a nostalgia, a nostalgia that accounts for why he views the possibility for escape in the amplification of the negative or the self-conscious exaggeration of both the desire itself and the knowledge of its unreality.

The question of the relation between hyperreality and the reality it posits can also be addressed by raising the issue of where the code acquires the resources for its own reproduction. Either it contains within itself the capacity for infinite recombination (which would contradict both its need for external materials and its actually fairly limited repertoire, as described by Baudrillard) or it requires the very simulations of its logic, for which it also provides the model. The code would then be two-sided: On the one side, it governs by simulacra; on the other, it requires the responses and resistances of the masses it organizes and obliterates. In this latter case, then, the total system described by Baudrillard takes the form of the access of subjects to the code, their appropriation of it, and their ability to put it to use—that is, it requires precisely the kind of resistance prescribed by Baudrillard. These are subjects who are able to recognize the reality of their understanding of the unreality of their simulated understandings, which, in the end, reproduces a moral center (supported not through seriousness but through parody and sensationalization) that is not all that different from the one problematized by postmodernity. Thus, the mode of resistance offered by Baudrillard actually provides the dominant order with the resources needed to reproduce its simulated models, and these resources are the autonomous activities of the simulated subjects themselves.

This resistance that is immanent to the system can be understood in relation to Baudrillard's claim that the system of simulacra has become absorbed into the very masses it has helped to produce. On the one hand, *"their* [the masses] *representation is no longer possible.* The masses are no longer a referent because they no longer belong to the order of representation" (quoted in Kellner 1989, 85). That is, the masses have been so thoroughly constructed by and integrated into the system that they no longer respond to it: "More and more, [information] creates an inert mass impermeable to the classical institutions of the social and to the very contents of information" (86). At the same time, this gives the masses a privileged insight into the "game": "They know that there is no liberation and that a system is abolished only by pushing it into hyperlogic, by forcing it into an excessive practice which is equivalent to a brutal amortization" (88). Now, contends, Baudrillard,

> the masses *aren't* the social, they are the reversion of any social and of any socialism. . . . This revolution by involution is not theirs; it is not critical explosive, it is implosive and blind. It proceeds by inertia and not from a new and joyous negativity. It is silent and involutive—exactly the reverse of all speech making and consciousness raising. It has no meaning. It has nothing to say to us (quoted in Kellner 1989, 88).

In another reversal of a Marxist thesis, Baudrillard argues that by creating the masses in its own image, the regime of the simulacrum has produced the force capable of undermining it, not, however, through a "critical-revolutionary" activity that would overthrow social structures but through a kind of defiant apathy that resists all calls to recognize the legitimacy of any principle or practice. Baudrillard, as Kellner points out, is indicating the possibility of a legitimacy crisis in contemporary capitalist societies. This is because Baudrillard's discourse is a kind of inverted nostalgia for the exercise of the collective power of the working class. In this case, it is a collective power produced not by the organization of the proletariat within the production processes of capitalism but by their organization within simulated signifying practices. Thus, the most authentic expression of this resistance is silence, the refusal to respond to organized modes of participation and democracy. For the same reason, though, the antirevolutionary and antiproletariat content of Baudrillard's discourse is all the more visible and virulent. Put in the form of an imperative, his claim is that the working class must be reduced to the constant staging and imaginary reversal of the contradiction between its potential collective power and its actual collective dispossession and dispersal as a series of private individuals; to put it another way, according to this logic, the collective power of the working class is exercised precisely as an effect of the sensationalizing of its dispossession. These conclusions, meanwhile, ultimately follow from the presumed autonomy of the production of knowledge, which is no longer seen as dependent upon the accumulated labor expropriated from the working class but rather as the conditions of production of the working class (as an effect of simulated models).

The reason why the system of simulacra must nevertheless incorporate the superseded dichotomies of an outmoded liberal, productivist order, as well as the consequences of this incorporation, can be understood if we return to Marx's theory of commodity fetishism, which remains the starting point of Baudrillard's meditations on contemporary culture. According to Baudrillard,

> Marx set forth and denounced the obscenity of the commodity, and this obscenity was linked to its equivalence, to the abject principle of free circulation, beyond all use value of the object. The obscenity of the commodity stems from the fact that it is abstract, formal and light in opposition to the weight, opacity and substance of the object. The commodity is readable: in opposition to the object, which never completely gives up its secret, the commodity always manifests its visible essence, which is its price. It is the formal place of transcription of all possible objects; through it, objects communicate. Hence, the commodity form is the first great medium of the modern world. But the message that the object delivers through it is already extremely simplified, and it is always the same; it is the medium that imposes itself in its pure circulation. This is what I call (potentially) ecstasy (1985, 131).

However, Marx's denunciation of the obscenity of the commodity, or his critique of commodity fetishism, is not addressed at the principle of equivalence or primarily at its abstraction of exchange from use value. Rather, it is based on the fact that social labor is represented by products that are privately owned:

> As a general rule, articles of utility become commodities, only because they are products of the labor of private individuals or groups of individuals who carry on their work independently of each other. The sum total of the labor of all those private individuals forms the aggregate labor of society. Since the producers do not come into social contact with each other until they exchange their products, the specific social character of each producer's labor does not show itself except in the act of exchange. In other words, the labor of the individual asserts itself as a part of the labor of society, only by means of the relations which the act of exchange establishes directly between the products, and, indirectly, through them, between the producers (Marx 1906, 84).

That is, the fetishism of commodities is a result of the contradictory process of capitalist development that makes all labor social in the sense of being united within an ultimately global process of production that subordinates any particular act of production and does so precisely by making particular labors simultaneously private and abstracted from any conscious social control. For this reason, the value of the specific product appropriated as a commodity appears to be immanent to the actuality of the product itself, a quasi-natural property of it. Fetishism, in Marx's account, is an effect of the abstraction of an interiority that results from a set of relations from those relations and its establishment in opposition to them. What is in question, then, is not abstraction and equivalence as such. For example, the "community of free individuals" that Marx hypothesizes in the chapter on commodity fetishism, which determines collectively the distribution of all available labor time, also presupposes the abstraction of "labor" from specific labors and the equivalence or homogeneity of different labors within the total social production process. The fetishism of commodities expresses a relation between a one-sided abstraction (human labor as such, rather than human labor at a particular level of social development and within a specific set of social relations) and an empiricist or sensationalist "concrete" (the immediately perceptible object, as opposed to the division of labor that is responsible for the product).

(Post)Modernity and Postmodernism as Ideology

The erasure of the distinction between materiality and discursivity, economics and culture characterizes most attempts to understand contemporary culture in terms of the replacement of modernity by postmodernity as the cultural dominant. However, this transformation can be theorized quite differently within a materialist framework that continues to make such distinctions. That is, modernity and postmodernity are categories that enable us to analyze particular modes of producing the types of subjects required for the prevailing relations of production. For example, most accounts stress the difference between the universalistic self-representation of modernity (with its reliance upon rationalism, a linear notion of progress, the autonomy of the various spheres of knowledge, etc.) and the self-conscious particularism of postmodernity (with its emphasis on the hybrid, multiple, and indeterminate character of reality, the fluidity of identity, and so on). However, if we are to avoid simply describing these cultural processes and preferring one to the other or some eclectic combination of the best aspects of both, it is necessary, I would argue, to understand both modernity and postmodernity materialistically, that is, as modes of producing and reproducing subjectivities in accord with transformations in the processes of production.

I will now develop the discussion on the problem of fetishism that I began in the previous section in order to advance a theory of (post)modernity that explains the intersection of economic and cultural relations, rather than simply conflating them. A theory of modernity based on Marx's theory of capitalism can, I believe, be formulated as follows. Modernity is the cultural articulation of the unity of the contradictory processes of collectivization (the organization of abstracted labors into social production processes) and privatization (the control and representation of this process by the owners of private property). The general cultural forms of modernity, like the fetishism of commodities, are attempts to articulate, institutionalize, explain, and resolve the contradictions that follow from this structure. For example, the contradictory structure of bourgeois rationality as means-end calculation and as totalizing, transcendental theory reflects the contradictory situation of the owner of private property who is interested both in profit, insofar as he or she is in competition with all other private property owners, and in the general conditions of bourgeois rule and therefore in a kind of solidarity with all other property owners, thus sharing a kind of common interest. At the same time, the existence of this form of rationality as a product of the collective labor commanded by the individual capitalist (which, of course, underlies any effective means-end calculation) is rendered invisible, as rationality appears to be a property inherent to the individual subject himself.

In this case, the cultural condition of postmodernity signifies the end of the domination of this general cultural form, predicated on the unity of the processes of collectivization and privatization. The final form taken by modernity was, then, "corporate liberalism," based upon the reorganization of the global liberal order through the domination of multinational corporations, the centralized organization (and segregation) of the production of advanced knowledges, and the articulation of producer-consumer networks through the reproduction and generalization of the nuclear family in the post–World War II period. I would argue that what finally made this form of modernity untenable was the demand of advanced capitalist structures that labor power no longer be left to the private initiative of individual workers but rather be publicly regulated and reproduced on a collective scale. This means that the public and collective social structures constitutive of modernity are compelled to intervene in the production of the private, which nevertheless cannot be abolished or fundamentally reconstructed because of the enduring capitalist requirement that products of labor and the capacity for laboring take the form of commodities. The significance of this is that as the private and the public become increasingly interdependent, they also become openly antagonistic and can no longer be seen as complementary forms of the dominant culture. However, if this represents the exhaustion of a particular historical project, it only does so by reproducing the social and cultural contradictions of capitalism in new forms.

It is then possible to resituate Baudrillard's descriptions if we understand what he calls "hyper-reality" as a "hyper-empiricism," or "sensationalism," which is the dominant ideological form in publicly organized capitalist society. I would define *sensationalism* as the fabrication of an imaginary immediacy of perception and meaning. I mean by this that under late capitalism, the empiricism and fetishism that condition private subjectivity are organized, centralized, and deployed as crisis-management devices. The sensationalist image or text is thoroughly political, since it is directed against some threat to the existing order that appears to be crystallizing "here and now." An excellent example is the pornographic text, as MacKinnon understands it. The pornographic image, as I argued in the previous chapter, concentrates the relation of sexuality as male domination/female subordination. It does so by eliminating all complications, all historical and social relations, all contesting possibilities. The containment of the threat to order or the restoration of order through the destruction or rehabilitation of some threat thus appears highlighted against a normalized background, all of the features of which can be taken for granted. Sensationalism, as an ideological form, then, is central to the production of subjects in contemporary capitalist societies: It organizes desires around the desire for order, stability, and control over the other—those actions and knowledges in contestation with the social and cultural props of private individuality. Sensationalism proposes the possibility of the immediate appropriation of reality (the proximity of desire and satisfaction) on the condition that one identifies with and hence desires that reality. Sensationalism presents social contradictions to the individual as a series of disordering differences constructed by liberal binaries (good/bad, responsible/irresponsible, reasonable/violent, etc.), which makes the narrative of the reestablishment of order a site of desire and pleasure. As I argued in Chapter 2 in relation to pornographic texts, sensationalistic representations are necessary because of the specific nature of the (ultimately global) challenge to the dominant subjectivities. That is, these threats, since they are the results of the collectivization of subjects, are actually internal to the construction of private individuality.

I would define postmodernism as an immanent critique of postmodernity that begins from the knowledge of the fabricated nature of this immediacy. This, I contend, is the source of the postmodernist critique of universalistic liberal categories. Postmodernism deconstructs the seeming naturalness of the liberal categories reproduced by the sensationalist text, and it is able to recognize them not only as artificial but also as outmoded. The limit of this is that the sensationalist text can still be enjoyed in a more self-reflexive manner. In fact, it can, in this way, be consumed even more pleasurably, since the knowledge of its artificiality and implicit self-referentiality transforms the sensationalist text into a layered one that can be appropriated in a variety of ways, on many levels, and in relation to the presumably autonomous sign systems against which the text explicitly or implicitly defines itself. Postmodernism, as a form of cultural politics, therefore does not really contest sensationalism; rather, it sensationalizes the immediate resistance to the dominant ideology (for example, by locating materiality in the body and thus regarding resistance as immanent to existing power relations). In other words, while tracing its genealogy back to critiques of private property, postmodernism, in the end, reproduces within critical discourses the reprivatizations imposed by the ruling class from the mid-1970s on. That is, it is complicit with the dominant ideology, since it conflates power relations with institutional stability (the same means by which the dominant culture sensationalizes opposition), and thus effective resistance with destabilization—by sensationalizing destabilizing resistances, postmodernism precludes recognition of the ways in which hegemony is reproduced precisely through the mechanisms of de- and restabilizations. The limits of postmodern theory, then, coincide with the limits of identifying the production of subjectivities with technocratic forms of knowledge and organization or with specialized discourses as such (since postmodern theory is thereby compelled to share the technocratic assumption that order and stability as such are equivalent to domination and therefore fails to see that the ruling class can maintain its domination through various combinations of order and disorder, stability and instability).[2]

Postmodernism, therefore, is a product of the various modes of resistance to postmodernity from the standpoint of the new petite bourgeoisie, which ideologically displaces exploitation onto domination, the system of material production onto knowledge production, economics onto culture, and class domination based on private control of the means of production onto the regulation of knowledge production by reified and sensationalized categories. Postmodernism is then determined by the various modalities of critique of the irrationality of private control from the standpoint of socialization. However, this standpoint is also abstracted from the possibilities of collective power—against which the postmodernist critique is also directed—which compels this critique to take the form of a rearticulation of the modes of private individuality available to the petite bourgeoisie and, through its ideological domination, the oppressed classes. It is this contradiction that takes the form of postmodernism. The liberal categories that produce the abstract subject and the social relations that produce the private individual are recognized as constructed—they are denaturalized and de-essentialized—and recognized as partial and limited (and dangerous, if taken literally). At the same time, the private individual is to be equipped with the capacity to reverse the sensationalized liberal categories that interpellate it ideologically (according to postmodernism, what the dominant culture claims is public in the sense of general and universal is really partial and a concealed effect of private power relations; what the dominant culture claims is private is really a result of publicly arranged institutions). However, this meets a need the dominant or mainstream culture cannot easily meet, and it does so on the terms of that culture itself: It provides resolutions to the ever more visible contradictions of a society and culture in crisis by highlighting crisis points, at which hegemonic operations in the form of the production of more complex modes of managing collective subjects and reproducing complex labor powers must be directed.

Materialism, Production, and Critique

What is at stake in the theories of postmodernity developed by and via Lyotard and Baudrillard (and, more broadly, by way of theories of "postindustrialism," such as that of Daniel Bell) is the usefulness of the category of material production in understanding contemporary capitalist society. There is no reason for either Lyotard or Baudrillard to reject Marx's theory of capitalism with regard to the nineteenth-century "classical" form of capitalism that he analyzed: In fact, both have claimed that they do not reject this analysis, and Lyotard at least has asserted that he still considers it relevant today. The rejection of Marxism or the claim that it has been superseded by theories of postmodernity depends upon the claim that the significance of material production is now secondary to the production of knowledges, which has acquired a degree of autonomy such that it now determines the forms taken by material production and production relations as a whole. If this claim is accepted, then it follows that struggles within knowledge and discourse production are paramount in our contemporary situation, whether these struggles take the form of the paralogies that the inherently experimental and complex nature of postmodern sciences make possible, according to Lyotard, or of the implosion of simulacra, as proposed by Baudrillard. This places very strict limitations on the ability of cultural critique to show how specific instances are effects of general conditions of possibility that can be grasped and transformed through collective practice.

However, the contradictory logic of both Lyotard's and Baudrillard's theories, which claim that postmodernity is constituted by a totalizing and totalitarian dynamic and at the same time contains multiple spaces for immanent resistance, points, I would argue, to the necessity for maintaining the distinctions between materiality and discursivity (or material production and knowledge production). This requires a reworking of the Marxist categories of the forces and relations of production that, Marx argues, come into contradiction in the course of social development. As I have suggested in the previous chapters, I believe that this contradiction, under late capitalism, takes the form of the contradiction between the maintenance of private property (and all of its social and cultural supports, such as the nuclear family and the private individual) and the production of collective labor power, which must now be publicly regulated. These categories enable a materialist critique based upon a theorization of the contradictions of the present order that, in turn, make it possible to produce a theoretical outside (as opposed to postmodernist immanence) that can oppose the potential to the actual.

This erasure of the distinction between the material and the discursive also takes place under the auspices of Marxism, in the work of Antonio Negri, his Italian collaborators, and American followers such as Michael Hardt. The "autonomists" contend that collective, socialized labor has become the new political subject, superseding the mass worker of Fordism. Drawing upon some of Marx's analyses and projections in the *Grundrisse* and his distinction in *Capital* between the formal and real subsumption of labor under capital, they contend that socialized labor now takes the form of the "general intellect," i.e., not merely performing "Taylorized" tasks within the economic division of labor but managing, controlling, and therefore theorizing, speculating, and communicating regarding the general forms, conventions, and models regarding the entire production process. The problem here is with the abstraction and hypostatization of a single tendency within the development of the productive forces and a very hasty liquidation of the distinctions between economics/politics/ideology/theory (i.e., base and superstructure). Contrary to the assumptions of the autonomists, labor is not the source of sociality or even of all wealth, as Marx points out in the *Critique of the Gotha Program*. Nor does the emergence of the conditions of possibility of the general intellect guarantee an increase in worker self-management or resistance; this process can easily coincide with new forms of petit-bourgeoisification and entrepreneurial subjectivities and sharper distinctions (between skilled and unskilled, educated and uneducated, employed and unemployed) within the working class.

By claiming that the distinction between economic class struggle and political class struggle is obsolete, the autonomists are compelled to ground political action in spontaneity: As the collective, socialized laborer comes to recognize and actualize itself as general intellect, thus unfolding its own immanent capacities, it will be able to slough off existing social relations and avoid decisive confrontations with the state and other forces organized around the defense of private property. Along with the privileging of spontaneity, then, we have the erroneous assumption that the capitalist class has become merely parasitic, in the sense of having no integral or directive role in the production process. This leads, in turn, to a privileging of domination over exploitation and an at least implicit portrayal of the state as already a remnant of itself.

These assumptions take us to the otherwise inexplicable convergence of the writings of the autonomists—deriving from the Marxist tradition—and the postmodern Nietzscheanism of Gilles Deleuze,[3] reflected, somewhat closer to mainstream cultural studies, in the work of Brian Massumi. If labor is taken not only as the value-producing activity organized within the process of production but as the production of sociality as such—i.e., domestic labor, community organizing, leisure, etc.—resistance can appear (or seem to appear) in the most heterogeneous places. It can appear in the valorization of the most advanced and complex forms of theorizing, on the highest level of social organization, or in the most micro of micropolitics, that is, in various "intensities" and "lines of flight," which deterritorialize and reterritorialize the plane of capitalist existence. And this latter approach will be the path of least resistance once the "asceticism" of the "old" revolutionary project is denounced, and, as Michael Hardt says, "the collective pursuit of pleasures is always in the forefront—revolution is a desiring-machine" (1996, 6). As Hardt correctly concludes in his introduction to *Radical Thought in Italy: A Potential Politics* (a volume of some autonomist and related writings), "this is why, although these authors follow many aspects of Marx's work, they seldom develop either the critique of the commodity or the critique of ideology as a major theme" (6–7).

This is why I speak, in this book, of the public regulation of the reproduction of labor power, rather than the socialized laborer. The distinction between labor and labor power (the basis of exploitation) needs to be carefully maintained as the ground of an outside against the immanence privileged by the autonomists (and what we could call the entire "Spinozan-Nietzschean line" in contemporary thought, which has also emerged among many Althusserians[4]). The capacities and needs developed under capitalism remain incommensurable as long as the wage relation remains in place (i.e., as long as capitalism exists)—there is no shortcut whereby one could reduce or overcome this incommensurability as a new basis for revolutionary politics. These incommensurabilities (labor/labor power, capacities/needs) are, in turn, articulated in the vast array of reconstructed and innovated juridical, military, political, and administrative machineries taking shape now internationally and where, in turn, new accountabilities will emerge. The fantasy of labor realizing and releasing itself from the boundaries of sovereignty obscures all of these issues and, more important, transforms politics into an affair driven by desires, contingencies, and affiliations.

All of these issues come out clearly in Paolo Virno's interesting and symptomatic essay "Virtuosity and Revolution: The Political Theory of Exodus." It is his view that with contemporary forms of production, the distinctions between politics, work, and theory have been abolished: Work has been "taking on many of the attributes of Action: unforeseeability, the ability to begin something new, linguistic 'performances,' and an ability to range among alternative possibilities" (1996, 190); theory has been absorbed within work as the general intellect organized in the production process, thereby losing its distinction and distance from praxis; and, in turn, work has become actionlike, i.e., public and "virtuosic."

Virno is clear that, by themselves, these transformations have no emancipatory consequences: Under capitalist conditions, virtuosity and intellect as work become *servile*—"its characteristic publicness is . . . inhibited and distorted. Ever anew called upon to act as a force of production, it is ever anew suppressed as public sphere, as possible root of political Action, as different constitutional principle" (1996, 194). In this case, the "key to political action . . . consists in developing the publicness of Intellect outside of work, and in opposition to it" (196). For such political action, Virno proposes a range of models, all of them encompassed in the notion of "Exodus": Since, today, "*a realm of common affairs* has to be defined by scratch . . . the political action of the Exodus consists . . . in an *engaged withdrawal*" (197). Radical "civil disobedience" (in relation to the law as such, not merely particular laws in the name of more fundamental laws), "intemperance," "acting minorities," "virtuosic cooperation," and "example and political reproducibility" are some of the principles, dispositions, and tactics Virno recovers and proposes to identify this new politics. What he calls the "soviets of the multitude" are said to "elaborate actions that are paradigmatic and capable of blossoming into new combinations of knowledge, ethical propensities, technologies and desires" (203).

Virno does recognize the danger that a politics predicated upon Exodus, by downgrading the "absolute enmity" implicit in the traditional Marxist assumption that class struggle in its revolutionary form issues in civil war, leads to the assumption that one is "swimming with the current" or is being driven "irresistibly forward" (1996, 203). A politics aimed at the establishment of liberated zones within capitalism under the assumption that the state will wither away without actually being "smashed" leads to the problematic one sees over and over again in postmodern cultural studies: "doing what comes naturally" as radical praxis. To counter this, Virno redefines the "unlimitedly reactive" "enmity" of the "Multitude" in terms of the "right to resistance" (206):

What deserve to be defended at all costs are the works of "friendship." Violence is not geared to visions of some hypothetical tomorrow, but functions to ensure respect and a continued existence for things that were mapped out yesterday. It does not innovate, but acts to prolong things that are already there: the autonomous expressions of "acting-in-concert" that arise out of general intellect, organisms of non-representative democracy, forms of mutual protection and assistance (welfare, in short) that have emerged outside of and against the realm of State Administration. In other words, what we have here is a *violence that is conservational* (206).

The decisiveness of the question of absolute enmity becomes clear if we ask a rather obvious question: What distinguishes autonomous expressions from any privatized space (say, Internet chat rooms) that withdraws from the common in the name of friendships, mutual aid, or, for that matter, networks, gated communities, or whatever? In short, nothing can lead more directly to the death of revolutionary politics than the assumption that the days of absolute enmity are over. Autonomous expressions necessarily lead to the esoteric and the singular as the paths of least resistance. Therefore (as in all Left-Nietzscheanisms), they take as their main enemy the programmatic and the decidable, transforming liberation into a private, simulacral affair, regardless of their denunciations of capitalism. I will return to this issue in the next two chapters, but I want to conclude this discussion by stressing that only theory and action that establish spaces that bring the common out into the open—before an outside (theory and judgment) so as to make visible the concentrated political-economic force of the ruling class—can count as a genuinely "new" politics.

꒰꒱

The privileging of autonomous expression explains why critique has such a problematic status for postmodern cultural studies, as can be seen in Andrew Ross's "New Age Technoculture." According to Ross, one of the leading representatives of postmodern cultural studies, New Age rationality "can be seen as a counter-cultural formation in an age of technocratic crisis" (1992, 533). As such, it has a kind of critical relationship to dominant technocratic ideologies and practices, formulating in more articulate terms the widespread distrust and questioning of the authority of organized modes of expertise (medical, technological, etc.) based on positivist notions of science. At the same time, the New Age movement, through its interest in transforming the existing institutions and science, must, to some extent, conform to those institutions: "As a result, the shape and language of holists' claims about alternative scientific knowledge are mediated through appeals to the rationalist language and empiricist procedures of the dominant paradigm" (532). The New Age movement is, therefore, according to Ross, constituted by the contradiction between its critical stance and its potential for co-optation. As he writes,

> [It] is here that we can see the tension within a social movement founded on an *alternative* scientific culture, distinct from dominant values, that is increasingly obliged to wage *oppositional* claims lucidly obedient to the language and terms set by the legitimate culture. Therein lies a story about the contradictions of New Age culture as it exists today, but it may also be a story about the evolutionary structure of all such social movements which display a slow evolution from marginal, utopian origins to mainstream encounters with professionalization and institutionalization (532).

Although Ross's interest in the contradictions of New Age culture indicates, as he acknowledges, some degree of critical distance from it, he also states that he is not "primarily interested in speaking against the New Age belief systems and their political implications" (1992, 537). He defines his position as "that of the speculative critic who thinks and feels that there are political lessons to be drawn from the shape and development of New Age culture" (537). This is because he is concerned to avoid both an interventionist polemical approach that does not "respect the lived experiences of cultures other than the intellectual" (537) and a relativism that completely relinquishes the position from which one can speak authoritatively as an intellectual (since that position will then simply be filled by other, more conservative voices). For Ross, cultural studies has done especially useful work in addressing these problems.

Thus, New Age culture, on the one hand, and cultural studies, on the other, are both contradictory and constituted by struggles that are internal and external. Both attempt to affirm the specific and experiential and yet, at the same time, still address their claims to dominant institutions, and they are therefore in danger of co-optation. Furthermore, in addition to situating of New Age culture within contemporary cultural crisis, Ross provides a detailed account of its relationship to historical shifts in the relation between alternative or marginal subcultures and dominant (especially expert) ones, including contemporary articulations of these categories. In addition, he relates "New Ageism" to the counterculture of the 1960s, with its own contradictions. Finally, he connects the contradictions and conservative elements in New Age culture and politics (its individualism, its ahistoricism, its abstraction of personal transformation from larger, structural changes, and so on) with the class position (upper middle class) of "the articulate majority of New Agers" (1992, 543). However, Ross resists an explanation of New Age culture on these terms. Despite the series of historical determinations that enter into his analysis of New Age culture, he still argues that

> New Age politics might be seen not as a wayward, pathological creature of the New Left's imagination, but as a political innocent in candid, questioning dialogue with the unclaimed mainstream territory of progressive, rather than atomistic, individualism. Indeed, if we were to examine some of the social and political threads that run through the aery fabric of New Age thinking, we would find much that resonates with necessary conditions for a left version of progressive individualism (545).

This progressive individualism, meanwhile, has its roots in a "powerful desire for self-respect, self-determination and utopian experimentalism" (Ross 1992, 547), and it "feeds off the popular desire for more democratic control of information and resources" (538). This popular desire accounts, according to Ross, for the coherence and effectivity of New Age culture.

This popular desire lies outside of any explanation. It is authentic, according to Ross, and "it cannot be dismissed as a 'petty-bourgeois' obsession" (1992, 538), nor can it be understood in terms of any other theoretical category. In this case, it is significant that Ross concludes "by suggesting that New Age culture can also be seen as a particular version of the arguments raised in the debates about postmodernism" (547). That is, it is a critical response to the project of modernity that has been "distorted by capitalist forms of instrumental reason and techno-rationality" (547). In this way, its concerns and problems are parallel to those of culture studies: Both discourses address the desire for community and personal and collective self-determination that more traditional left-wing discourses have neglected or devalued. The subject positions of both problematics are also equally unproblematized. Both the popular desire reflected in New Age rationality and the speculative criticism interested in learning political lessons reflected in work of cultural studies are taken as self-evident, remaining uninterrogated.

However, problems arise if we try to address the question of what is the most appropriate political response to technocratic reason and its present crisis. If existing relations of domination depended upon technocratic reason remaining unproblematized, then it would indeed be possible to argue for the subversive potential of New Age and related alternative cultures. However, if those relations require the perpetuation of this mode of reason but can easily tolerate (or perhaps even benefit from) its problematization, then we would reach a completely different conclusion. New Age ideology, precisely through its apparently critical aspects, serves to assist the cultural mainstream—as a kind of cultural subcontracting—in producing the kinds of subjects required for its operations. The same critique can be advanced of the cultural studies with which Ross aligns himself, insofar as it presents as opposites what are actually two sides of the cultural and ideological hegemony under present social conditions—in other words, a "bad" technocratic rationality that serves domination and a "good" desire for personal control and subjective wholeness. Placing one of these aspects against the other in a subversive relation provides a resolution of the cultural contradictions of capitalism by, like the dominant culture itself, staging an apparent struggle that never leaves the terrain of that dominant culture and simply confirms its terms. This is possible because technocracy is abstracted from the material conditions that produce it and from the class interests it supports. Rather than critique technocracy as an ideology that serves particular interests that could also be served by other means, Ross conflates it with the prevailing structures of domination. In this case, the "progressive individualism" he promotes is simply the reprivatization of the process of socialization, reduced to a kind of "care of the self" and presented as oppositional. This conflation is unavoidable for any analysis that starts from (in the sense of taking as a foundational categorical structure) the opposition between reified forms of knowledge and meaning production and the (ultimately circularly defined) needs of already constituted subjects, rather than with an inquiry into the historical conditions of the production of meanings and subjects. Needs, in other words, undoubtedly come into conflict with existing social relations; however, in their immediate and self-evident forms, these needs are also the needs of those social relations, which require constant modifications in the types of subjects that are produced.

Thus, technocracy as the master category against which New Age philosophy (or cultural studies) defines itself is a construct of the ideological formation of progressive or social individualism advanced by Ross's argument. Technocracy represents the abstraction of social relations from capitalist relations of production and the presumed transfer of power to self-reproducing "experts" who are able to distinguish arbitrarily between acceptable and unacceptable knowledges. Both New Age rationality and culture studies, meanwhile, cross intellectual and cultural boundaries without acknowledging their self-evidence or legitimacy, and they both return emphasis to the importance of subjectivity in ways that both mainstream and leftist scientific discourses (such as Marxism) supposedly exclude. However, they both accept the basic assumption of technocratic reason—that the production and reproduction of knowledges determines relations of domination. In either case, contradictions grounded in material production are represented in the cultural sphere as an opposition between regulated and unregulated forms of meaning production. This enables those with access to the more advanced forms of knowledge to oppose regulation in the name of a populist redistribution of knowledges but, in fact, in the interest of a freer exploitation of the advantages possessed by those with access to the more complex knowledges needed by contemporary modes of reproduction. The stress upon coherence and the unity of the self (a kind of updated, utopian humanism) characterizes New Age. Meanwhile, postmodern cultural studies is characterized by a kind of posthumanist politics of difference or nonidentity. However, as I argued in the previous chapter, it is precisely the interdependence of these discursive orientations that produces the ideological forms that contribute to the reproduction of advanced or complex forms of labor power under contemporary capitalism. In fact, it is precisely in the sphere of reproduction (of labor power) where a free bricolage is possible in ways that are excluded from the organization of material production: In this way, free bricolage serves to resolve the contradictions inherent in material production and reproduce subjects willing and able to take up their positions in material production.

Thus, despite Ross's references to economic and historical determinations, his investigation into New Age philosophy ultimately considers it to be a cultural matter, determined by inexplicable needs and desires. This means that although the critic can mark its differences from his or her own practices and commitments, he or she cannot critique it in the sense of inquiring into its conditions of possibility and political effects. The notion that desire is a mechanism of hegemony and articulated within the dominant ideology and that it is therefore what most needs to be explained is completely excluded in the dominant discourses of postmodern cultural studies. All that is called for in these discourses is an updating of cultural forms, to allow for greater freedom—for some—within the existing social arrangements. The role of the critic, then, is to sympathize with this desire and establish its legitimacy regardless of the various and at times questionable forms it might take.

These problems are not superseded in the work of Fredric Jameson, the most powerful and widely discussed attempt to theorize postmodernity within a Marxist framework. In his *Postmodernism, or the Cultural Logic of Late Capitalism*, Jameson is concerned both to account for the features of postmodernity described by theorists such as Baudrillard and Lyotard within a global historical materialist framework and to take up the challenge posed by these and other writers on postmodernism regarding the possibility of a revolutionary or oppositional politics and cultural criticism under contemporary conditions. (I recognize that Jameson does not, as I have done here, distinguish between postmodernity as a cultural condition and postmodernism as a series of interrelated responses and resistances to postmodernism. In fact, the two are conflated in his argument, a point that is reflected in his theorization of the postmodern.)

Jameson characterizes postmodernism in terms of transformations in the dominant modes of subjectivity available in culture and discourse. He contrasts the realist approach to nature and society, which he argues was available to subjects during the classical or free market period of capitalist development, and the hermeneutic or interpretive model of subject-object relations, which he claims was characteristic of modernism (the cultural dominant of the monopoly-imperialist period), with the fragmentation and superficiality characteristic of subjectivity in the present, multinational capitalist or postmodern period. What this transformation involves, according to Jameson, is the availability of a "depth model" constructing the relations between subject and object. In terms of realism, the depth model enables a knowledge of social reality that allows the subject to act effectively in relation to that reality; in relation to modernism, meanwhile, the depth model of the subject (above all in relation to categories such as alienation and the unconscious) enables one to address subjects in terms of the contradiction between their appearance (say, their conformity to existing social relations) and an essence (for example, some desire or need that goes unsatisfied under those relations) that contradicts that appearance, thereby opening up the possibility for transformation, such as through vanguard political organization or avant-garde artistic practices. This cultural transformation, for Jameson, raises the question of the possibility of achieving the kind of critical distance required for subjective and social transformation: If subjects are nothing more than shifting signifiers within global systems that articulate them as mere elements of that system, it is very difficult to see how one could posit some other standard against which contemporary social and cultural relations can be measured and critiqued.

Jameson wishes to distinguish his theorization from those dependent upon some version of the postindustrial society thesis that, I have argued, provide the underpinnings of the accounts of Baudrillard and Lyotard. He argues, on the contrary, that postmodernism is a result of a vast new expansion of capitalism in the post–World War II period, such that the last remnants of precapitalist societies and relations (for Jameson, symbolized by "Nature" and the "unconscious") have been obliterated. In other words, what characterizes this stage of capitalism is that there is no outside of capitalism and therefore no standpoint of critique. Meanwhile, culture, which, for Jameson, here means intellectual and aesthetic culture, has itself been so thoroughly commodified that it has lost its relative autonomy from the economic. However, in turn, the economic seems to have lost its autonomy from the cultural. Jameson argues that

> we must go on to affirm that the dissolution of an autonomous sphere of culture is rather to be imagined in terms of an explosion: a prodigious expansion of culture throughout the social realm, to the point at which everything in our social life—from economic value and state power to practices and the very structure of the psyche itself—can be said to have become "cultural" in some original and yet untheorized sense" (1991, 48).

Postmodern theorists such as Baudrillard and Lyotard might point out that this claim undermines the very categories of economic determination Jameson is working with, and in fact, that it is precisely the argument they themselves have been making in terms of the reversal and collapse of the relation of determination argued for by Marxism. Indeed, Jameson's dependence upon such claims also produces an antinomy in his attempt to discover a critical position in relation to postmodernism. Jameson, in other words, calls for a kind of "cognitive mapping" that is impossible according to his own argument. He argues that even the most "distorted and unreflexive" (1991, 49) attempts at representation, precisely as a result of the immediacy with which they reflect the reality of multinational capitalism, can be read as new forms of realism: This kind of reading would, then, presumably enable the development of the conceptual articulations required for the cognitive mapping Jameson proposes. However, how these partial and distorted reflections of reality can add up to a global cognitive mapping is unclear, for his cognitive mapping is really a kind of empiricism. More important, the theoretical transformation Jameson's account requires is impossible without conceptualizing some external vantage point from which the categories of postmodernism could be critiqued and their contradictions explained—and no such vantage point can be conceived as long as postmodernism is understood as the (noncontradictory) cultural logic of late capitalism, rather than the result of contradictions produced outside of this cultural logic. Despite his references to the *Communist Manifesto* as a model for the kind of dialectical rigor he would like to apply to postmodernism, Jameson ends up in this problematic situation because his argument assumes that it is, above all, categories such as nature, the unconscious (desire), and culture that provide Marxist theory with a standpoint of critique.

However, this is not the case: Marxism develops a critical standpoint by theorizing the contradiction between the forces and relations of production, which is to say by aligning itself with the most progressive possibilities implicit in the productive forces that are restricted, concealed, and prevented from realization due to the outmoded nature of the relations of production. Such an analysis is grounded in the category of material production that is material not in the sense of physical but in the sense of determining and extending the interchangeability of practices and subjects in the production process. It is this materiality, then, that determines the combinations, articulations, and transformations in the conditions, means, needs, and subjects that are associated in the labor process. The category of commodification is ultimately limited in analyzing transformations in material production because it tends to identify interchangeability with the structure of the commodity, whereas this is only one possible form taken by this process of the development of the production forces. Insofar as transformations in material production under what Jameson calls "multinational capitalism" take the form of collectivization, the conflation of this process with commodification determines a nostalgic resistance to the development of the productive forces, precisely from the standpoint of "Nature," "Desire," or "Culture." On the contrary, from a Marxist position, these processes represent the most advanced aspects of the productive forces in that they entail reductions in required labor time, the production of new needs, and, above all, the production of new types of subjects capable of managing new modes of material production and hence transformations in the apparatuses committed to the reproduction of labor power. The cultural logic of late capitalism would, in this case, be located not in postmodernism (which articulates this logic within bourgeois discourses that abstract the crisis from social contradictions) but in the contradiction between the need for this type of subject (and the needs and capacities of this type of subject) and the maintenance of private property and the subordination of all institutions to its reproduction, which requires that the working class be "just as much an appendage of capital as the ordinary instruments of labour" (Marx 1906, 628).

By subsuming the extension of capitalist relations under the category of commodification, Jameson abstracts capitalism from its contradictory developments. This, in turn, determines his "reflectionist" or "epiphenomenalist" approach to the relations between base and superstructure (which, if taken to its logical conclusion, leads to the collapse of this distinction). So, for example, the schizophrenic condition of subjects directly reflects the global and unrepresentable movements of capital. However, Jameson's own account of the condition of subjectivity in postmodern capitalism is problematized or qualified by his development of the category of the technological sublime. He distinguishes between the modernist approach to technology, in which the most advanced forms of technology served a representational function (in the sense of embodying in a graphic way social energies and possibilities that had yet to be realized) and the significance of contemporary technology, which "no longer possesses this capacity for representation" (1991, 36). According to Jameson, dominant technologies today, such as the computer and television, are "indeed machines of reproduction rather than production, and they make very different demands on our capacity for aesthetic representation than did the relatively mimetic idolatry of the older machinery of the futurist moment, of some older speed-and-energy sculpture" (37).

According to Jameson, this type of technology serves to produce a different kind of social imaginary, one consisting of vast, intricate, and integrated systems of control that cannot be grasped by the individual mind but that "our faulty representations of some immense communicational and computer network" (1991, 37) enable us to at least orient ourselves toward them. The kinds of aesthetic representation that he considers most characteristic of this technological sublime are those that articulate some type of "conspiracy theory," which he considers a "degraded attempt . . . to think the impossible totality of the contemporary world system" (38). Here, we have a paranoiac rather than a schizophrenic subject, one that is interested in developing (in however errant a manner) totalizing accounts of the global system and in comprehending and in some sense determining how it is to be constructed. However, it is hard to see how paranoia is better than schizophrenia. In fact, if we follow the logic of Jameson's account, the two are complementary; it is precisely the fragmentation of the subject that calls for some paranoiac representation that can resituate the subject on recognizable terrain. And the necessary collapse of any such paranoiac system reproduces the schizophrenic isolation and affectless-ness of the subject. This complementary structure (or, rather, antinomy) is, in fact, what is important, since it should make it impossible for Jameson to privilege (analytically) one "side" over the other. The same would, of course, hold true for whatever complements the other symptoms of postmodernism Jameson describes. For example, the lack of affect would also have to be seen to have a similar relation to the new intensities he describes, in which, as I outlined earlier, the contradiction between private dispossession and potential public power takes the form of a sensationalized amalgam of private and public in relation to which the subject is indifferent (affectless) but that the subject also appropriates for postprivate modes of populist reversals (producing new intensities, etc.).

Jameson's account, in other words, remains within an individualistic and psychologistic framework that ultimately reproduces the object of analysis by simply rehearsing its own simulated binaries. Jameson does not provide a way of distinguishing a genuine from a paranoid mapping, and his account in effect excludes doing so. He remains within the very logic he describes: An intensification of paranoia will, implicitly, bring one closer to an adequate map. The task of Marxist analysis, to account for the transformations in the relations between base and superstructure as effects of the development of the contradiction between the forces and relations of production, has been thoroughly abandoned here. Insofar as culture totally infiltrates the economic, it is impossible to occupy a position outside of culture by grounding culture in its external conditions of possibility. These external conditions of possibility are the ongoing class struggles that postmodernism, with Jameson's assistance, conceals. A better place than postmodern paranoia to initiate a genuinely political economic analysis, as I will suggest in the next two chapters, is with the constitution of the categories of universality and emancipation on the surface of late capitalism as polemical sites that make knowledge of social transformation a political and not merely a cognitive matter.

Notes

1. See his last book, *Postmodern Fables* (1997), especially the essay "A Postmodern Fable."

2. For another recent discussion of postmodernism from a position indebted to Marxism, see Eagleton 1996. My difference from Eagleton stems from the fact that he really doesn't clarify the social and historical terrain that is presupposed, exploited, and shaped by postmodernism. Despite his disagreements with it, he tends to take postmodernism at its own word and presuppose a common ground of concern about issues of freedom and domination. That is, his approach is ultimately dialogic. Furthermore, if the categories Eagleton supports—such as rationality, solidarity, humanity, and so on—are to be defended effectively, this will not happen through a more nuanced description of their real, historically sedimented

meanings or experiential manifestations, nor through debunking various distortions, simplifications, and misrepresentations. Eagleton wants to reach the "reasonable" reader; the assumption, ultimately, is that postmodern fallacies will dissolve upon closer examination and confrontation with reality. Emancipatory concepts, though, can only be secured, deepened, and clarified under the polemical conditions wherein the forces of production compel theory to take up those concepts against determinate political-economic and ideological violence.

3. Hence, Geoff Waite cannot so easily excise Nietzsche(anism) from Negri's list of materialist democrats (see the introduction in this volume).

4. See Montag and Stolze, eds., 1997.

4

CULTURAL STUDIES AND
THE PUBLIC SPHERE

Politics and Theory

The main effect of postmodernism with regard to the public sphere has been to replace the "universal" with the "specific" intellectual. Postmodernism has articulated social movements based on identity with poststructuralist discourses aimed at dismantling the presuppositions of the liberal public sphere: the free and rational subject who enters a neutralized public arena predicated upon disinterested discussion. Postmodernism exposes the disavowed violence fundamental to that model of publicity and traces it back to the predication of the subject him- or herself.

However, the figure of the universal intellectual as the enunciator of a critique from the outside depends, it would seem, upon the same set of assumptions. In an on-line "symposium" on *Public Intellectuals and the Future of Graduate Education,* Cary Wolfe argues,

> At first, the critique of representation seemed liberating for the left intellectual, for if it could be shown that any hegemonic discourse was contingent and not "grounded" in the usual sense, then it was easy to imagine that a different (i.e., more just) hegemony might be established. The problem, of course, is that once you have appealed to a social constructionist argument, and thereby kicked the theoretical foundations out from under those who pretend their power is grounded in the very order of things, you have also put your own (putatively more progressive) claims in jeopardy as well, insofar as those claims need a foundationalist claim to be effective (3).

Clearly, then, postmodern cultural studies must raise and address the question of public, political responsibility attendant upon intellectual work. What, exactly, is the relation between the delegitimation of subjectivity that follows from the critique of the constitutive structures of the subject and the boundaries and terms constitutive of legitimate public discourse and political action? Postmodern cultural studies takes the easy way out here: The activity of articulation that accounts for the formation of political agents within a decentered hegemony is also that which gives intellectual work its purchase on the social. In both cases, the popular is resisting the totalizations of modernity.

The liquidation of the critical concept of ideology has precluded any inquiry into the possibility that responsible political and intellectual work might be determined in a very different way than the social construction of subjectivities allows. In particular, the violence that constitutes subjectivities inscribed by the justification of inequality is a different mode of violence than that which threatens the space of legitimate political action and radical, interested theoretical inquiry. The violence constitutive of subjectivities is ultimately prepolitical, and the violence against the articulation of theory and action is antipolitical: The location of politics on the plane of subjectivity offers no resistance to antipolitical violence.

Wolfe's conclusion regarding the implication of leftist politics in antirepresentationalist critiques is predictable: "We need to be more savvy media manipulators, sound-bite rhetoricians, and, sometimes, snake oil salesmen and demagogues for causes we deem worthy—and this *includes* mobilizing incoherent or historically obsolete terms like 'the public sphere'" (6). Wolfe is perhaps being deliberately provocative here. He is arguing against Michael Bérubé's more sober proposal that cultural studies intellectuals tie their work more explicitly to policy, contending that this often involves an evasion of the need to come to terms with the state of contemporary critical theory. Even if we grant this, though, the argument would underline the extent to which these discussions of the public intellectual have become an entirely insider affair, almost caricaturing Peter Sloterdijk's "cynical subject"("we know better, but if we want to be effective, we must . . . "). In other words, Wolfe's critique is not so much of Bérubé's proposal but of the fact that he actually seems to believe it, that is, he has not attained the necessary distance between what we say among ourselves and what we say out there.

As I will make clear, I am not proposing a Habermasian understanding of the public sphere, predicated upon the counterfactual "ideal speech situation." In my view, Habermas's core claim, at least in terms of its political implications, is that any speech act necessarily implies equality between the interlocutors, in the sense that one cannot address another (which is to presuppose his or her "response-ability") and simultaneously hold the contrary assumption that the other is incapable of responding and of addressing oneself in turn. The main problem with this is not its counterfactuality (this is precisely what makes it a ground for critiquing actual speech acts); it is not that the claim is merely logical or, insofar as it has the empirical basis Habermas wants to claim for it, that it must always depend upon ultimately contestable "evidence"; nor is it even the historical implications of the assumptions regarding equality that Habermas takes for granted. Most important is the fact that even—especially—if Habermas is right, the very attempt to secure the ideal speech situation has no legitimacy because as a prepolitical move to set the procedural terms for public discourse, it must seek to neutralize the ideological struggle that is the inaugural political act. What needs to be introduced into the speech situation is, in fact, a form of discursive inequality necessary for the establishment of pedagogical relations. This would locate the speech situation on the boundary of the extension and operationalization of rights, where their constitution becomes visibly polemical. (Where, for example, does the question of rights become, at the same time, a question of the possibility of knowledge and theory?)

The issue is not, in other words, that Habermas must presuppose a univocal, fixed meaning, as Judith Butler claims: The equivocity of the ideological statement is an articulation of a very univocal intent. Nor is the issue that consensus totalizes a plurality of language games, as Lyotard charges: The differend is always ready to become a litigation. Rather, the issue is that Habermas's claim is not nearly universal enough. Just as political action must distance itself from the postmodern multiplication of subjectivities and a sensationalized public sphere, theory must distance itself from ideology and common sense in order to see where legitimate action appears against the force of political-economic violence. Universality lies not in the speech situation but in political action as "seen" by theory and in theory as distinguishing itself from the theoretical presuppositions actualized by and necessarily cut short by political action.

Any discussion of the public intellectual, especially in connection with the various crises framing such discussions (of the humanities, of the Left or leftist intellectuals, of the university, of the public sphere) needs to be grounded in the assumption that only as a result of sustained theoretical struggle—the contention of foundational claims made exoteric—will any genuine critique emerge from the site of theory. Also, it will only be possible to do anything more than conceal the roots of the aforementioned crisis if such critiques make visible the polemics constitutive of the public sphere and if they do so by siding with the polemic of theory against common sense. This, of course, requires implicating common sense in the operations of global capitalism through ideology critique. Only in this way, by defending the public "rights" of theory and the theoretical grounds of politics, will it be possible to explain anything, that is, to offer critiques of ideology and expose the structures of violence appearing (anti)politically.

The Political Function of the Intellectual

In an essay entitled "Cultural Studies and Its Theoretical Legacies" (which appears in the volume *Cultural Studies*), Stuart Hall poses the problem of theory and politics for postmodern cultural studies in an exemplary way:

> There is no doubt in my mind that we were trying to find an institutional practice in cultural studies that might produce an organic intellectual. We didn't know previously what that would mean, in the context of Britain in the 1970s, and we weren't sure we would recognize him or her if we managed to produce it. The problem about the concept of an organic intellectual is that it appears to align intellectuals with an emerging historical movement and we couldn't tell then, and can hardly tell now, where that emerging historical movement was to be found, we were organic intellectuals without any organic point of reference; organic intellectuals with a nostalgia or will or hope (to use Gramsci's phrase from another context) that at some point we would be prepared in intellectual work for that kind of relationship, if such a conjuncture ever appeared. More truthfully, we were prepared to model or simulate such a relationship in its absence: "pessimism of the intellectual, optimism of the will" (1992, 281).

The structure of the simulated organic intellectual is identical to the structure of (non)identity I examined in Chapter 2. On the one hand, there is the desire to define intellectual work in terms of its direct affiliation to some actually existing historical agent. On the other hand, there is a recognition that no such affiliation exists and that one's actually existing work must therefore depart from an altogether different set of historical coordinates. Hall should be read as attempting, however weakly, to resist postmodern cultural studies' "solution" to this dilemma. This solution (evident in the vast majority of the contributions to *Cultural Studies,* including Hall's piece) has been to eliminate the contradiction between simulated and organic (the organic being merely an effect of simulations) and situate intellectuals in the general cultural process of producing representational machines. Hall wants to hold on to a more traditional notion of the political intellectual, facing two fronts. First, he says, the organic intellectual must "be at the very forefront of intellectual theoretical work because, as Gramsci says, it is the job of the organic intellectual to know more than traditional intellectuals do: really know, not just pretend to know, not just to have the faculty of knowledge, but to know deeply and profoundly" (281). At the same time, he speaks of an equally crucial second front: "that the organic intellectual cannot absolve himself or herself from the responsibility for transmitting those ideas, that knowledge, through the intellectual function, to those who do not belong, professionally, in the intellectual class" (281).

But it is impossible for Hall to move beyond such banal generalities as long as he is presiding over the bandwagon of cultural studies. This is particularly true as long as he is unwilling to actually challenge and critique the prevailing tendencies in this field that undermine the kind of critical distance, theoretical rigor, and political accountability he seems to be calling for here. And Hall certainly cannot trace those tendencies back to the culturalist organicism that expelled Marxism from cultural studies. At any rate, he simply drops the question. What might be politically necessary now for cultural studies is never addressed.

John Frow, in *Cultural Studies and Cultural Value*, discusses Hall's same statement in some detail. For him, "the sheer virtuality of that link [between the organic intellectual and his or her constituency] shoots through with irony the notion that attachments to another class or bloc is the right and proper way for intellectuals to work" (1995, 129). This comes as part of Frow's critique of the mystified transparency of intellectual work, which can manifest itself either in the construction of the popular as degraded other or in a self-effacement of the elitist position of the intellectual in the name of letting the popular speak for itself. Frow sees much of cultural studies as an example of this latter option, often in unreflective reaction to the former. His proposal is that intellectual work should not be a matter of "preparation or anticipation but of work conducted in its own time, work with its own impetus and its own historical goals; we might propose, that is to say, that work in cultural studies could be taken seriously in relation to the specific interests of the class of intellectuals rather than in relation to a non-existent historical bloc" (129). In short, the politics of cultural intellectuals, as cultural intellectuals, "should be openly and without embarrassment presented as their politics, not someone else's" (169).

Frow's contention ties together a series of arguments within postmodern philosophy (Lyotard's theory of heterogeneous phrase regimes, for example) and the sociology of what is variously called the "new class," the "new petite bourgeoisie," the "knowledge class," and so forth. He does address issues connected to the logic of late capitalism—including "the integration of knowledge into commodity production" (1995, 91); the "developing autonomy of management functions" (113); and "the protracted development of a public sector in which a range of ethico-disciplinary functions—those of education, of public health, and a variety of welfare services—are removed from the family or the kinship network and assumed as state responsibility" (117). But he does not address them in terms of a new global regime of global capitalism and consequently a new terrain of class struggle in which the new petite bourgeoisie would be implicated and its interests thereby sharpened, made somewhat more determinate than Frow allows.

This is why his conclusion returns to the same position he had earlier critiqued: The specific capacities of cultural intellectuals, "who are specifically trained in the ability to switch codes, to move readily between different practices of valuation" (Frow 1995, 154), are, in effect, best suited to mediate between different, heterogeneous value regimes. So, despite his warning, Frow does "universalize the competencies [intellectuals] possess as norms which can be used to totalize the cultural field" (169). It is symptomatic that, with such a close fit between class and ideology, Frow never seriously considers whether the theory of an unbounded, pluralized field of discourses and identities might not be the ideology *of* this class, its imaginary representation of its relation to real conditions. But breaking with this ideology cannot be understood in local terms, that is, by finding some "positive" or progressive aspect of the petite bourgeoisie to counter the "bad" side. Rather, it is necessary to theorize the conditions of class struggle across all the fields of late-capitalist society. And this, in turn, will require a universalization not of the interests of the petite bourgeoisie but of the conditions of possibility of theory, which is under attack by a whole range of forces, from the Left as well as the Right. I will return to this point toward the end of this chapter.

Another attempt to deal with this issue, which highlights the problems of trying to generate a new, "specific" intellectual, is made by Nancy Fraser. Fraser argues that "academic radicals" occupy a mediating position. Accordingly, she says,

> we, too, are in the business of building bridges. In relation to our academic disciplines, we function as the oppositional wing of an expert public. In relation to extra-academic social movements, on the other hand, we function as the expert wings of an oppositional public. In addition, many of us relate to still other publics. As teachers, we try to foster an emergent pedagogical counterculture. As faculty advisors, we try to provide guidelines and legitimacy to radical student groups on our campuses. Finally, as critical public intellectuals, we try to inject our perspectives into whatever cultural or political public spheres we have access to. The point is we function in several distinct institutionalized publics. Necessarily, then, we speak in several voices. Insofar as we find ourselves talking both to experts and to activists, we are situated between movements and professions. One way to think about this "between" is as a point where oppositional discourses and expert discourses intersect. One thing, then, that critical intellectuals do—apart from speaking to movements, on the one hand, and to experts, on the other hand—is to find ways to knit their disparate discourses together. In other words, we are engaged in creating bridge discourses and in opening new hybrid publics and arenas of struggle (1989, 11).

But these disparate publics are differentiated aspects of a unified process of reproducing class domination. There is no space in Fraser's conception for a position outside of the negotiations between publics, from which one could theorize their conditions of possibility. In a more extended discussion of Fraser's understanding of counterpublics later in this chapter, I will examine the logic that brings her from seemingly self-contained public arenas (expert, activist) to an ethics of difference and hybridity, not a global logic. For now, I want to stress the point that her portrayal here excludes the possibility of transforming the essence of these various publics: one is the political opposition within an expert discourse, one does not posit that discourse as necessarily political; one is the intellectual wing of an activist discourse, rather than positing it as necessarily theoretical and enabling that discourse to theorize its practices at a higher level of abstraction as a precondition of political action.

As I suggested in the previous chapter, the function of creating bridge discourses gives a privileged position to the petit bourgeois postexpert, of the subject initiated into expert discourses but equipped with self-reflexivity regarding them, that is, with the ability to recognize their constructed, partial, and limited character. However, this tends to protect rather than transform knowledges by revaluing them and thereby situating them in an accommodating or laissez-faire relation to one another. In Fraser's attempt to develop a mode of intellectual and political activity adequate to the postmodern condition, we can see the political consequences of postmodernist assumptions on critical intellectual work. The presupposition of the autonomy of discourse, which means the independence of self-reproducing, heterogeneous sites of discourse and subject production, supports a politics interested in negotiating differences at the expense of comprehending the global production of the system of differences.

The example of Fraser, who on one level is actually quite critical of the postmodernism of figures such as Lyotard and Derrida (and certainly more so of Baudrillard), demonstrates the more general character of this problematic. This problematic is not limited to those who can be labeled postmodernist in unambiguous ways or those who would accept that label. This point can be seen more clearly in the concluding chapter of Patrick Brantlinger's *Crusoe's Footprints: Cultural Studies in Britain and America*, where he argues against the predominance of postmodern theory in cultural studies. Brantlinger sees Baudrillard's version of postmodernism as a result of the contradiction into which contemporary theories of mass culture have become mired: "At one pole, the mass media and mass culture are conceived as 'monologic' and anti-democratic, 'interpellating' the masses in the strong sense intended by Althusser: the 'subject' becomes the product (or even the mere identity-effect) of the ideological 'apparatus'," while at the other pole, "mass culture is . . . conceived not as a monolith enforcing what Baudrillard calls 'hyperconformity,' but (at most) as a set of limits within which all sorts of 'resistances' are not only possible but ironically inevitable" (1990, 179). Postmodernism, then, ar-

ticulates this contradiction, as I suggested in the previous chapter, by uniting the all-encompassing system (performativity for Lyotard, the code for
Baudrillard) with the simultaneous production of seemingly autonomous
sites of freedom and resistance.

Brantlinger goes on to claim that although postmodernism ultimately
ends up celebrating late-capitalist society, Habermas's theory of communicative action "is different from deconstruction in that it seeks to salvage
the possibilities of truth, ethics, politics, and history from the mounting
post-structuralist ruins" (1990, 181–182). Whereas postmodernism, for
Brantlinger, focuses correctly upon the ways in which the project of
modernity has been distorted and subordinated to the growth of technocratic power, its critical insights get stranded in that it does not recognize
the potential for progress and Enlightenment that has also been part of
these developments. For Habermas, this potential is located in the immanent tendency within communication for the engaged subjects to strive
for "mutual understandings" (as opposed to speech directed at strategically conceived ends).

So, according to Habermas, the crisis of contemporary capitalist societies is a result of the colonization of the "lifeworld" (sites governed by
other than functionalist criteria) by the organized economic and bureaucratic systems during the historical process of modernization and rationalization. This leads him to conclude that the most promising sites for political struggle are "in domains of cultural reproduction, social integration
and socialization" (1987b, 392). This is because those domains are where
"system imperatives *clash with* independent communication structures"
(391), as subjects seek to prevent the erosion of the lifeworld by system
imperatives. Such political struggles, though, can be aimed only at preserving the autonomy of the lifeworld, not at transforming the system imperatives themselves. Thus, these struggles are essentially local and defensive, interested more in processes of communication than in the
abolition of class rule.

Habermas's understanding of undistorted communication is situated
within the same problematic as the postmodernism of Lyotard in a much
more fundamental sense than would be indicated by the apparent opposition between them. Both locate emancipatory knowledges and politics in
the liberation of language from technocratic imperatives. And the political
consequences are the same as well. In both cases, local transformations
(the deconstruction and reconstruction of distorted modes of communication) that create more democratic or rational sites of intersubjectivity are
all that is seen as possible, "with the goal," as Brantlinger says, "of *at
least* local emancipations from the structure of economic, political and
cultural domination" (1990, 191–192, emphasis added). The addition of
"at least" to the kinds of changes sought suggests a broader, potentially

global role for critique, such as showing "how lines of force in society can be transformed into authentic modes of participatory decision making" (197). However, the transition from one mode of transformation to another—what should be the fundamental task of cultural studies—is left unconceptualized and is implicitly understood as a kind of additive or cumulative spread of local democratic sites until society as a whole is transformed. What this overlooks, of course, is the way in which, as long as global economic and political structures remain unchanged and unchallenged, local emancipations can only be redistributions—redistributions that actually support existing social relations by merely shifting the greater burdens onto others who are less capable of achieving their own local emancipation. This implicit alliance between the defenders of modernity and their postmodern critics (at least on the fundamental question) also suggests that we need to look for the roots and consequences of this alliance in the contradictions of the formation of the cultural studies public intellectual.

Power, Sovereignty, and Knowledge

To a great extent, the Habermasian turn in cultural studies defines itself against the project of Michel Foucault, who, among postmodern thinkers, has done the most to address issues of power and political struggle. Foucault's understanding of politics and power is directed against the assumption, common to both liberal and Marxist theories of politics, that power is exercised by some relatively coherent agency (for liberalism, the state as the representative of the people seen as a series of autonomous individuals; for Marxism, the ruling class) over another agency (anyone who undermines civil peace; the exploited class or the class of former exploiters and their allies in the case of the proletarian dictatorship) for a determinate purpose (the protection of rights, ultimately of property owners; the maintenance of exploitation—or its abolition). In both liberalism and Marxism, the possession of general social power by such an agency is designated by the term *sovereignty*. The evaluation of sovereign power, meanwhile, is carried out according to the degree of legitimacy it possesses (that is, whether the aims it advances are just and whether it indeed advances those aims). Foucault, in one of his best-known descriptions of his work, explains that his

> general project over the past few years has been, in essence, to reverse the mode of analysis followed by the entire discourse of right from the time of the Middle Ages. . . . I then wanted to show . . . the extent to which, and the forms in which, right (not simply the laws but the whole complex of apparatuses, institutions and regulations responsible for their application) transmits

and puts in motion relations that are not relations of sovereignty but of domination (1980, 95–96).

Foucault's approach is, then, best understood as an attempt to undermine the categories of sovereignty and legitimacy, and it is necessary to inquire into the causes and effects of this effort.

This shift or inversion of functional theories of power involves the following. First, there must be a move away from the analysis of power in terms of how it is used to advance some kind of right or interest (which, in principle, precedes the exercise or application of power) toward an inquiry into the "how" of power—"not the uniform edifice of sovereignty, but the multiple forms of subjugation that have a place and organ within the social organism" (Foucault 1980, 96). Second, with the abandonment of the categories of sovereignty and legitimacy, related distinctions such as those between oppressive and emancipatory forms of power (i.e., those required for determinations of the legitimacy of uses of violence) can no longer be maintained. In fact, these distinctions themselves must be seen as effects of the articulations of power relations.

As Nancy Fraser and others note,[1] this, of course, raises the issue of the grounds of any critique of particular manifestations of power. I will return to this problem soon, but first, it is essential to examine how Foucault's discourse is in fact compelled to incorporate these distinctions without actually justifying or analyzing them. In order to "substitute the problem of domination and subjugation for that of sovereignty and obedience" (1980, 96), Foucault argues that

> there were a number of methodological precautions that seemed requisite to its pursuit. In the very first place, it seemed important to accept that the analysis in question should not concern itself with the regulated and legitimate forms of power in their central locations, with the general mechanisms through which they operate, and the continual effect of these. On the contrary, it should be concerned with power at its extremities, in its ultimate destinations, with those points where it becomes capillary, that is, in its more regional and local forms and institutions. Its paramount concern, in fact, should be with the point where power surmounts the rules of right which organize and delimit it and extends itself beyond them, invests itself in institutions, becomes embodied in techniques, and equips itself with instruments and eventually even violent means of material intervention: . . . in other words, one should try to locate power at the extreme point of its exercise, where it is always less legal in character (96–97).

Foucault seems to be claiming simply to put forth a productive methodological proposal that still accepts the distinction between centralized, legitimate, and legal forms of power and the more extreme, unmediated, brutal, and therefore ultimately illegitimate modes of application of power. In this case, he would be asserting an interest in the dimension of force as opposed to (but also in relation to) that of consent; he would merely be interested in studying this problem beyond the domains in which it has conventionally been located (the central state, the "bodies of armed men" that Friedrich Engels refers to as constituting, in the last instance, the state, etc.). However, this more conventional notion of power could hardly be reconciled with the third methodological precaution listed by Foucault, which

> relates to the fact that power is not to be taken to be a phenomenon of one individual's consolidated and homogeneous domination over others, or that of one group or class over others. What, by contrast, should always be kept in mind is that power, if we do not take too distant a view of it, is not that which makes the difference between those who exclusively possess and retain it, and those who do not have it and submit to it. Power must be analyzed as something which circulates, or rather as something which only functions in the form of a chain. It is never localised here or there, never in anybody's hands, never appropriated as a commodity or piece of wealth. Power is employed and exercised through a net-like organisation. And not only do individuals circulate between its threads; they are always in the position of simultaneously undergoing and exercising this power. They are not only its inert or consenting target; they are always also the elements of its articulation. In other words, individuals are the vehicles of power, not its point of application (98).

In this passage, the methodological and ideological break with the problematic of sovereignty is complete. Power is understood here as an immanent set of relations, which requires no external reference for its comprehension. At the same time, the notion of extremities advanced in the passage I just examined loses any sense in this connection: extreme in relation to what? And this is the case with regard to both the spatial meaning of the term (extreme in relation to a center) and the term's normative sense (as beyond the norm). In the former case, the possibility of any center (from which power primarily proceeds) ultimately impacting upon the extremes has been dissolved in the perpetual circulation of power. In the latter case, the grounds for distinguishing between more and less legitimate exercises of power no longer exist. Why, that is, should subjects be considered vehicles or elements exercising power any less in more immediately physical forms than in other forms? We can begin to grasp the significance of these contradictions by looking at the way in which Foucault proposes uniting the local and global levels of analysis:

It seems to me—and this then would be the fourth methodological precaution—that the important thing is not to attempt some kind of deduction of power starting from its centre and aimed at the discovery of the extent to which it reproduces itself down to and including the most molecular elements of society. One must rather conduct an *ascending* analysis of power, starting, that is, from its infinitesimal mechanisms, which each have their own techniques and tactics, and then see how these mechanisms of power have been—and continue to be—invested, colonized, utilized, involuted, transformed, displaced, extended, etc., by ever more general mechanisms and by forms of global domination (1980, 99).

This passage again attempts to articulate the contradictory positions implicated in Foucault's discourse by merely reversing rather than abolishing the relation between global and local modes of domination and, by implication, between the how and the why of power. Foucault argues that investigations can proceed from the local to the global by examining how "these mechanisms of power, at a given moment, in a precise conjuncture and by means of a certain number of transformations, have begun to become economically advantageous and politically useful" (1980, 101). Advantageous to whom? And useful for what? If the distinction between more and less useful implementations or forms of power is meaningful, Foucault is once again depending upon a functional notion of power, and he is simply advancing a more complex way of inquiring into the effectiveness of various modes of power. However, if the general theory of power advanced by Foucault (power as circulation, not as a top-down application) is to guide the investigation, then the global determinations could only be the accumulation of articulations between local sites of power. In addition, these sites would need to be explained in a way consistent with this theory of power, not by implicitly positing those who, presumably outside of the circuit of power, would find this or that technique advantageous or useful.

Foucault's discussion itself moves from these precautions to their historical situation, in relation to a "new type of power, which can no longer be formulated in terms of sovereignty. . . . This non-sovereign power, which lies outside the form of sovereignty, is disciplinary power" (1980, 105). Foucault associates the emergence of disciplinary modes of power with the development of industrial capitalism in the eighteenth and nineteenth centuries. However, I would argue that this is a projection into historical investigations of tendencies that perhaps can be seen in embryonic form in this earlier period of modes of domination specific to a more advanced kind of capitalism. This can be demonstrated by examining Foucault's response to a question he himself raises: "Why has the theory of sovereignty persisted in this fashion as an ideology and an organising principle of these major legal codes (of Europe)?" (105). His answer is extremely instructive. The theory of sovereignty, he says, is an ideology that has served the purpose of advancing (by concealing) the development of disciplinary modes of social control. There are two aspects to this answer. First, there is the claim that the theory of sovereignty was useful in overcoming the obstacles posed by feudal society to the implementation of the disciplinary regime; put another way, the theory of sovereignty was a kind of superstructure of the base of disciplinary power. Second, and more important,

> [the] juridical systems [based on the theory of sovereignty] have enabled
> sovereignty to be democratised through the constitution of a public right ar-
> ticulated upon collective sovereignty, while at the same time this democrati-
> sation of sovereignty was fundamentally determined by and grounded in
> mechanisms of disciplinary coercion. . . . The powers of modern society are
> exercised through, on the basis of, and by virtue of, this very heterogeneity
> between a public right of sovereignty and a polymorphous disciplinary
> mechanism (105–106).

The contradiction and conflict between these heterogeneous domains and the increasing domination of the area of right by that of discipline, he continues, "can explain the global functioning of what I would call a *society of normalisation*" (107).

In this case, the heterogeneous notions of power incorporated into Foucault's discourse would reflect the heterogeneous modes of power articulated in the social order itself and historical transformations in the relative significance of these modes. One could argue, then, that those forms of power that appear—from the standpoint of sovereignty—to be located at the extremities and to be extreme in a normative sense are in fact (as revealed by a genealogical analysis of disciplinary power) the dominant, normal (in the sense of general and normalizing) mode in which power circulates through society. In other words, these are forms of power that ultimately exceed and are inexplicable in terms of the category of right; nevertheless, they are only visible and open to analysis at the limits of the concept of rights. This interpretation would account for the fact that Foucault's analyses of disciplinary power are not primarily interested in the most obviously egregious exercises of power (torture, concentration camps, etc.); rather, they focus on those sites and functions that appear the most normal and beneficial from the standpoint of sovereignty, although the actual practices of these sites and functions can seem most scandalous from the standpoint of consent (in particular, scientific and medical knowledges, "rehabilitation" systems, etc.). The point here is that the very concept of disciplinary power is formulated in both direct theo-

retical and ethical opposition to and dependence upon sovereignty, without it ever being possible to make this clear or explain it.

In other words, the global perspective offered by the category of sovereignty is still necessary if both senses of extreme are to retain any meaning or usefulness. Critiques of disciplinary power would only be intelligible as ideology critiques of the category of sovereignty. This critique,
though, still presupposes the category of right underlying sovereignty as
its basis; otherwise, terms such as *coercion* lose their meaning. Thus, Foucault implicitly maintains notions associated with sovereignty (for instance, human rights) as a basis for critiquing the society of normalization, but this analysis is really aimed at liberating disciplinary power from
the obfuscations of sovereignty and rethinking the possibility of freedom
on this new terrain.

So, the category of sovereignty is still absolutely necessary for Foucault,
even if as a phantom against which positions taken on the field of disciplinary power can situate themselves. If one is not able to theorize some
differentiation or contradiction constitutive of the field of disciplinary
power, which would provide a basis of critique intrinsic to the concept itself, then one can only critique those modes of disciplinary power that
continue to produce the "mystification" of sovereignty. In this case, the
"tightly knit grid of material coercions" (1980, 105)—exercised "over human bodies and their operations" (104), located in "continuous and permanent systems of surveillance" (105), involving a "calculation . . . in
terms of the minimum expenditure for the maximum return" (105)—can
be attributed to those modes of power still implicated in sovereignty.
Meanwhile, the categories tying theoretical understandings to emancipatory power can be evacuated of content, cannibalized so that "net-like"
power (which can always be reversed and recirculated) can be implicitly
portrayed as so many liberated zones where the appearance (and brutal
reality) of sovereignty no longer holds. Foucault needs to be able to say
that what passes as right is really (mere, illegitimate) power, and he needs
to be able to say this to avoid overtly valorizing disciplinary power as
such, while covertly doing so.

Foucault, then, needs sovereignty (as putative illusion, vanishing normative basis, and real scapegoat) in order to avoid the appearance of a
wholesale abandonment of any claims to emancipation and an unqualified embrace of neoliberal, postmodern individualism. His aims, that is,
are no different from other libertarian attacks on the state or the New Age
rejection of experts, which also need the representation of the state as a
dying yet still dangerous dinosaur. Arguably, in his later work on governmentality and the history of sexuality, he dropped these hedges and qualifications with a more direct endorsement of ethical self-fashioning. Nevertheless, the work developed along the lines I am discussing now has
had by far the greater impact upon Left discourses and practices and cul-

tural studies in particular. To clarify exactly what Foucault provides to the cultural studies intellectual formation, it is necessary to examine the kind of resistance he has proposed.

Foucault argues that the conditions of possibility of the type of analysis he offers lie in an event of the historical period dating, according to his account, from the early 1960s, which he terms an "insurrection of subjugated knowledges" (1980, 81). By "subjugated," he states that he means two things. First, he uses the term to refer to "those historical contents that have been buried and disguised in a *functionalist coherence* or formal *systematisation*" (81)—those that have been systematically excluded by dominant, institutionalized, and disciplinarily sanctioned modes of discourse and yet in some way mark those discourses and problematize their apparent coherence. Second, he uses the term to refer to popular knowledge, meaning knowledges that have some regional or local existence and articulation but are degraded or posited as illegitimate according to the terms and norms of the dominant knowledges. Foucault admits that it is a

> strange kind of paradox to assign to this same category of subjugated knowledges what are on the one hand the products of meticulous, erudite, exact historical knowledge, and on the other hand local and specific knowledges which have no common meaning and which are in some fashion allowed to fall into disuse whenever they are not effectively and explicitly maintained in themselves (82).

However, what actually unites these disparate forms of knowledge, according to Foucault, is that they are constituted by a "historical knowledge of struggles" (83) that the dominant knowledges suppress.

The genealogy proposed by Foucault, then, is an attempt to aid this insurrection by producing a "painstaking rediscovery of struggles together with the rude memories of their conflicts" (1980, 83). The work of intellectuals situated within the institutions of knowledge production and interested in emancipatory social change can, in this way, be aligned to the struggles of oppressed groups whose local forms of knowledge have never been recognized by those institutions. This kind of work could support a "non-disciplinary form of power" (108), one that is produced in the "struggle against disciplines and disciplinary power" (108) and that, furthermore, would not be grounded in the category of sovereignty (a contest of rights). Above all, this struggle would be carried out against "the tyranny of globalising discourses with their hierarchy and all their privileges of a theoretical *avante-garde*" (83).

However, following up on the critique I have advanced, what is not said here is that the local knowledges Foucault wishes to ally himself with cannot be anything other than the effect of the disciplinary knowledges against which he announces the struggle. The local knowledges are appealed to in order to make this struggle appear as if it is waged in the name of anything other than the liberation of a mode of knowledge production that is now to be deregulated. The subjugated knowledges are nothing more than new, postdisciplinary forms of knowledge, free from the restraints of the formalism and the embarrassment of the too-evident complicity of the dominant disciplinary knowledges. This accounts for the attractiveness of Foucault's analysis for so many leftist intellectuals, as well as the convergence of that analysis with cultural studies. Foucault's discrediting of the categories of sovereignty and legitimacy recapitulates the grand narrative and political logic of postmodernism: the simulated struggle between increasingly pervasive and undifferentiated global violence and ever more local, subtle, elusive, and yet paradoxically readily available sites of resistance. But nothing is more urgent today than theorizing the relations between legitimacy, sovereignty, and violence—a legitimacy that doesn't culminate in sovereignty while nevertheless depending upon it; a political assessment of violence dependent neither upon humanist common sense (such as moderate/extreme) nor upon the postmodern assumption that violence produces its own resistance and is itself nothing more than the resistance to that resistance; and a sovereignty that enables a political form to present itself before its outside without presupposing either a global state of nature or a nonstate of culture.

Counterpublics

Nancy Fraser's theory of counterpublics, which was largely responsible for introducing the issue of the public intellectual into cultural studies, is an attempt to reconcile Habermas and Foucault. It is exemplary for its understanding of cultural studies precisely through its welding together of a Left-liberal notion of publicity, feminist understandings of identity and difference, and postmodern conceptions of politics and culture. Fraser has criticized Foucault for his rejection of any normative ground for critique while nevertheless maintaining a "crypto-normativism," an implicit, libertarian ground for critique. However, she reduces her criticism to a thesis of the "two Foucaults." On the one hand, she says, there is the "transgressive" Foucault, who is interested in transcending and replacing humanism, and on the other, there is the Foucault whose work "constitutes humanism's own immanent counterdiscourse or critical conscience" (1989, 64). The first (transgressive) Foucault, according to Fraser, "lacks political seriousness" and is "wanting in the theoretical, lexical, and critical resources necessary to sustain a viable political vision" (64). However, Fraser contends, "we owe a profound debt of gratitude" (65) to the "immanentist" counterdiscourse to humanism produced by the second Foucault, which points to the hypocrises and unintended oppressive effects of humanist discourses.

However, Fraser's own theory disproves her claim that the transgressive Foucault can be kept at a distance while his theory provides resources for a reconstruction of emancipatory theory. Foucault's main assumption, that resistance is immanent and simply the other side of power, is reproduced in Fraser's own theory. First, though, it is necessary to look at the other, more visible side of Fraser's theory: her critique of Habermas's theory of the public sphere and its transformation under late capitalism.

In "Rethinking the Public Sphere: A Contribution to the Critique of Actually Existing Democracy," Fraser acknowledges that some notion of the public sphere, in the sense of an arena designated to the participation of social agents in opinion formation and decisionmaking processes, is essential. However, she contends, Habermas's understanding of the public sphere, drawn from his ultimately idealized version of classical bourgeois publicity, is inadequate for the task of formulating such a notion. She argues that, rather than a sphere that was, at least in principle, inclusionary and committed to no other criteria than the force of the better argument, the bourgeois sphere was constituted by its exclusions and its contestatory relation to other, unsanctioned, and subordinate public spheres. This set of relations, in turn, means that the bourgeois public sphere's claims to be inclusive and rational must not be taken as an unrealized yet valid ideal; rather, the claims themselves must be understood as means of exercising these exclusions, therefore indicating the need for a fundamentally opposed conception of the public sphere.

More specifically, Fraser calls into question the following four assumptions, which she considers central to what she calls the "bourgeois masculinist" conception of the public sphere:

1. the assumption that it is possible for interlocutors in a public sphere to bracket status differentials and to deliberate as if they were social equals; the assumption, therefore, that societal equality is not a necessary condition for political democracy;

2. the assumption that the proliferation of a multiplicity of competing publics is necessarily a step away from, rather than toward, greater democracy and that a single, comprehensive public sphere is always preferable to a nexus of multiple publics;

3. the assumption that discourse in public spheres should be restricted to deliberation about the common good and that the appearance of private interests and private issues is always undesirable;

4. the assumption that a functioning democratic sphere requires a sharp separation between civil society and the state (1990, 62–63).

Two main presuppositions underlie Fraser's questioning. First, there is the recognition of the need to inquire into the relations between the positions taken up by members of a public sphere within that public sphere and the positions they occupy outside of it. In other words, if the presumed equality within the public sphere actually conceals power differentials supposedly external to it, then it is necessary to investigate how these inequalities structure the public sphere, determining which issues will be allowed in (considered genuinely public), how discursive chances will be organized within the public in accord with external determinants, and so on. Second, there is the assumption that the more general public spheres (whether socially comprehensive or not—I will return to this point) are not strictly autonomous relative to social practices but are, in fact, articulations constructed on the basis of the relations between a multiplicity of heterogeneous and specific public spheres. That is, the common interest that is putatively the concern of the public sphere is not constructed in abstract opposition to special interests but arises out of the various local or specific struggles over what are designated as special interests. These two issues can be seen to be connected if we keep in mind that the relations of power between these more specific publics determine the structure of the more general publics.

However, these concerns make unavoidable the problem of determining what constitutes the power exercised by a given public sphere. This problem is reflected in Fraser's attempt to answer the question of whether "the institutional confinement of public life to a single, overarching public sphere is a positive and desirable state of affairs, whereas the proliferation of a multiplicity of publics represents a departure from, rather than advance towards, democracy" (1990, 66). By raising this question in a quasi-Kantian way (in the form of an "ought," abstracted from an "is"), Fraser is able to argue that, in stratified societies, "arrangements that accommodate contestation among a plurality of competing publics better promote the ideal of participatory parity than does a single, comprehensive, overarching public" (66). Given Fraser's own contention that public equality cannot be separated from social equality, it is unclear just how the former can be significantly advanced while obstacles to the latter remain intact. In fact, Fraser does recognize an "is" that stands in counterfactual relation to this "ought": a comprehensive, dominant public sphere that excludes the interests of subaltern groups. She therefore argues that "counterpublics emerge in response to exclusions within dominant publics" (67) or, in other words, in a contestatory relation to them. However, by positing a "plurality of competing publics" as an ideal, Fraser is able to situate the changes brought about by counterpublics as internal to the public sphere itself, separate from changes in relations based on social inequality: Counterpublics "help expand discursive space" (what Fraser refers to as "politicization" elsewhere, as in her essay "Struggle over Needs: Outline of a Socialist-Feminist Critical Theory of Late Capitalist Culture"). She concludes that "in principle, assumptions that were previously exempt from contestation will now have to be argued out. In general, the proliferation of subaltern counterpublics means a widening of discursive contestation, and that is a good thing in stratified societies" (1990, 67).

Fraser's argument, then, is following the same assumptions she critiqued in Habermas's conception of the public sphere. It assumes that the public sphere is an arena in which transformations are possible independent of changes in the broader, social sphere. Again, this assumption relies upon another—that changes are ultimately changes in discourse and not in power, much less property relations. So, Fraser understands subaltern counterpublics as "parallel discursive arenas where members of subordinated social groups invent and circulate counterdiscourses, which in turn permit them to formulate oppositional interpretations of their identities, interests, and needs" (1990, 67). Furthermore, "they function as spaces of withdrawal and regroupment" and also "as bases and training grounds for agitational activities directed towards wider publics" (68). However, questions about what constitutes their power relative to the dominant public sphere and what enables them to impose redefinitions of the political upon that sphere are not addressed at all; even more, they cannot be addressed on the terms established by Fraser's discourse. But they must be addressed if Fraser is to justify her claim that more publics is better or even to distinguish genuinely subaltern, bottom-up publics from those that are ultimately extensions of a dominant public sphere that finds it necessary to pluralize itself.

The implications of the absence of such questions and of any means with which even to pose them are apparent if we look at Fraser's consideration of "the relative merits of multiple publics versus a singular public for an egalitarian, multicultural society" (1990, 68). Here, again, Fraser comes to the conclusion that "public life in egalitarian, multi-cultural societies cannot consist exclusively in a single, comprehensive public sphere. That would be tantamount to filtering diverse rhetorical and stylistic norms through a single, overarching lens" (69). By once again formulating this question in terms of a principle, ideal, or norm, Fraser's discourse is able to bypass the mechanisms by which a stratified society might be transformed into an egalitarian one. Even more, the discourse does nothing to discourage the notion that this transformation might just as conceivably take place through the very process of the proliferation of subaltern counterpublics she describes here as in any other way.

Indeed, if the notion of power is reduced to the power exercised by competing discourses, it is completely consistent to assume that the accumulation of discursive transformations or reversals in relative power of discourses will add up to socialist transformation. In this connection, it should also be noted how the defining characteristic of counterpublics has now become rhetorical and stylistic norms, which must be protected from being reduced to a single, overarching lens: In other words, resistance is no longer resistance to exclusionary conceptions of the common interests but to discipline. Fraser further argues that in order to question the relation between singular and pluralized publics, "we need to take a closer look at the relationship between public discourses and social identities." She continues:

> *Pace* the bourgeois conception, public spheres are not only arenas for the formation of discursive opinion; in addition, they are arenas for the formation and enactment of social identities. This means that participation is not simply a matter of being able to state propositional contents that are neutral with respect to form of expression. Rather, as I argued in the previous section, participation means being able to speak "in one's own voice," thereby simultaneously constructing and expressing one's cultural identity through idiom and style (68–69).

The formation of public opinion (what Fraser refers to as the function of weak publics), not to mention the translation of opinion into effective change (the function of strong publics), requires an inquiry into political-economic relations—the way in which property relations constitute private interests and thereby structure political and public practices to benefit the most powerful interests. Since, as I have argued, Fraser has no way of addressing this issue, it is easy to understand how this second function of the public sphere, the formation of identities, becomes, at least implicitly, the primary one. Put another way, there is a shift in Fraser's discourse from an understanding of the public sphere as the site where common interests are determined to an understanding of the public sphere as the site where diverse identities are negotiated and preserved from a totalizing, monologic public sphere. Social transformation is therefore reunderstood as the granting and protecting of new identities, which are, in turn, reduced to voices, styles, and idioms.

Despite her critique of both Habermas and Foucault, then, her discourse fails to move beyond either the abstract ideal of the public sphere propagated by Habermas or the conflict between disciplinary and nondisciplinary (local) forms of knowledge posited by Foucault. Rather, she uses one to complement the other. Thus, although Fraser recognizes the coercive power exercised by the dominant, mainstream public sphere, she defines counterpublic activity as the protection of identities that are ultimately bearers of insurrectional knowledges and yet capable of their own ideal speech situation. In this case, the main function of counterpublics is not to theorize the political resources produced by the contradictions of the mainstream (and thereby establish a space for ideology critique from the outside) but rather to maintain an outside that is, in the end, part of the inside, since it is defined in terms of the imperative to pluralize a monologic public arena.

This project coincides with that undertaken by Richard Rorty, who has made one of the most prominent attempts to reconstruct bourgeois liberalism on a postmodern terrain. In "Postmodernist Bourgeois Liberalism," a chapter in his volume *Objectivity, Relativism, and Truth,* Rorty argues that

> there is no "ground" for such loyalties and conviction [i.e., that tie one to a particular community] save the fact that beliefs and desires and emotions which buttress them overlap those of lots of members of the group with which we identify for purposes of oral or political deliberations, and the further fact that these are *distinctive features* of that group, features which it uses to construct its self-image through contrasts with other groups. This means that the naturalized Hegelian analogue of "intrinsic human dignity" is the comparative dignity of a group with which a person identifies herself (1991, 200).

In addition, Rorty argues that the "morality/prudence distinction" (200), which roughly corresponds to the distinction between common or public and self or private interest,

> now appears as a distinction between two parts of the self—parts separated by blurry and constantly shifting boundaries. One part consists of those beliefs and desires and emotions which overlap with those of most other members of some community with which, for purposes of deliberation, she identifies herself, and which contrast with those of most members of other communities with which hers contrasts itself (200).

According to Rorty, "most moral dilemmas are thus reflections of the fact that most of us identify with a number of different communities and are equally reluctant to marginalize ourselves in relation to any one of them. This diversity of identifications increases with education, just as the number of communities with which a person may identify increases with civilization" (200–201).

The moral dilemmas Rorty refers to here are identical to the problem of the comprehensive public sphere as it is posed in Fraser's argument: "The question is: would participants in such debates [those affecting everyone] share enough in the way of values, expressive norms, and, therefore, protocols of persuasion to lend their talk the quality of deliberations aimed at reaching agreements through giving reasons?" (1990, 69). Fraser suggests that the possibilities of this being true "expand once we acknowledge the complexity of cultural identities" (69). In both cases, what is valued is arriving at discursive agreements, which presuppose overlapping identities; the possibility of articulating these overlapping identities, meanwhile, depends upon recognizing their complexity and plurality and offering people the chance to embrace more identities. Rorty calls the progress in this direction "civilization," whereas Fraser calls it "egalitarian multiculturalism" or "socialism," but these differences are, in the end, nuances determined by the specific publics in which these different figures participate, as well as the identities they adopt.

The intrainstitutional side of what Fraser calls counterpublics is the "border-crossing" pedagogue argued for by Henry Giroux. Giroux develops this concept in his linking of critical pedagogy with cultural studies in his essay "Resisting Difference: Cultural Studies and the Discourse of Critical Pedagogy." Here, he specifically tries to connect the struggle for a democratic public sphere to radical pedagogy, and he argues that the discourses of cultural studies and postmodernism are useful for this project. Cultural studies, according to Giroux,

> is important to critical educators because it provides the grounds for making a number of issues central to a radical theory of schooling. First, it offers the basis for creating new forms of knowledge by making language constitutive of the conditions for producing meaning as part of the knowledge/power relationship. . . . Second, by defining culture as a contested terrain, a site of struggle and transformation, cultural studies offers educators the opportunity of going beyond cultural analyses that romanticize everyday life or take up culture as merely the reflex of the logic of domination. . . . Third, cultural studies offers the opportunity to rethink the relationship between the issue of difference as it is constituted within subjectivities and between social groups. . . . Finally, cultural studies provides the basis for understanding pedagogy as a form of cultural production rather than as the transmission of a particular skill, body of knowledge, or set of values. In this context, critical pedagogy is understood as a cultural practice engaged in the production of knowledge, identities and desires (1992, 201–202).

I will begin my analysis of Giroux's argument by looking at the first two of these issues. Insofar as language is constitutive of the conditions for producing meaning as part of the knowledge/power relationship, power is, in effect, subordinated to knowledge and language. In this case, the critique of the supposed transparency of language and knowledge ("in some kind of correspondence with a self-enclosed objective reality" [Giroux 1992, 201–202]) or a modern, liberal notion of language (enabling a postmodern understanding of language and knowledge as always implicated in and constitutive of power relations) is itself a liberating act. Thus, Giroux is being consistent when he argues that the consequence of starting from the knowledge/power nexus is to attempt to "reshape knowledge according to the strategy of transgression; to define the traditional disciplines as much by their exclusions as by their inclusions; and to reject the distinctions between high and low culture" (202). If we assume that language and knowledge determine power relations and that the transformation of traditional or conventional boundaries, exclusions, and categories within the dominant knowledges therefore necessarily entails the transformation of power relations, such an argument is unproblematic. In this case, the second claim made by Giroux would also hold. That is, the claim that defining culture as contested terrain is really a "going beyond" of what are, in effect, the culturalist and structuralist alternatives I examined in Chapter 1 in my discussion of Stuart Hall. Regardless of Giroux's references to inequalities, to posit culture as a site of contestation in opposition to understanding culture as a reflex of the logic of domination (i.e., as superstructure) leads to the conclusion that this contestation, the positions available within it, and its outcome(s) are strictly indeterminate. This is to place political struggles within inherently heteroglossic discourses, where transformations in discourses and "social and cultural forms" (202) are equivalent to social transformation as such.

This brings us to the third of Giroux's claims and what he calls "the politics of voice and difference." Making an argument identical to the postmodern feminist ones I discussed in Chapter 2, Giroux argues that although "theories of difference have made important contributions to a discourse of progressive politics and pedagogy, they have also exhibited tendencies that have been theoretically flawed and politically regressive" (1992, 205). The positive side of theories of difference has involved the recognition, "primarily from feminist women of color" (205), that differences can be relational and creative, rather than inherent and hierarchical. On the negative side, meanwhile, "the discourse of difference has contributed to paralyzing forms of essentialism, ahistoricism, and a politics of separation" (205). Thus, the theories of difference, which Giroux associates with identity politics, are both an enabling challenge to a hegemonic Eurocentric liberalism and a potentially damaging essentialism, which privileges the interests of one subordinate group over another. For Giroux, this suggests that the discourse of difference and voice should be "elaborated within rather than against a politics of solidarity. By refusing to create a hierarchy of struggles, it becomes possible for critical educators to take up notions of political community in which particularity, voice, and difference provide the foundation for democracy" (209).

In this context, democracy is founded not upon any institutional or material structures or transformations but upon the ultimately discursive categories of particularity, difference, and voice. And if we are to take Giroux's injunction against creating a hierarchy of struggles literally, this also means that democracy must be founded on a refusal to set, theorize, and debate priorities regarding various ways of using energy, resources, capacities, and the like. The politics of (non)identity proposed by Giroux is supported by what he calls a "border pedagogy." If there can be no hierarchy of struggles and if struggles are situated within language, then the only position available to radical pedagogues is

> [to] become border crossers through their ability to not only make different narratives available to themselves and other students but also by legitimating difference as a condition for understanding the limits of one's own voice. By viewing schooling as a form of cultural politics, radical educators can bring the concepts of culture, voice and difference together to create a borderland where multiple subjectivities and identities exist as part of a pedagogical practice that provides the potential to expand the politics of democratic solidarity and community (1992, 206).

Pedagogy, then, involves enabling students to both discover or forge their voices and cross the borders between different voices, creating new cultural forms and identities and thereby expanding the realm of existing democratic politics.

Democracy, in this case, is defined not in terms of a mode of collective power or control but in terms of the capacity, first, to revalue experiences within a discursive terrain that has devalued them and, second, to become fluent in that transformed discursive terrain itself or to be able to participate in the exchanges that constitute the processes of valuation itself. This is a postmodern notion of pedagogy and democracy in the sense that it presupposes the intrinsic heterogeneity of subjectivities and discourses, both as fact and value. But it is a postmodern notion modified by the introduction of the modern categories of emancipation and solidarity, which prevent the discourse of difference from precluding alliances and cooperation and which, in turn, become contingent upon specific alliances and border crossings. The maintenance of modern alongside postmodern understandings is necessary if Giroux is to maintain some notion of democracy and public life. What really happens, though, is that these modern categories are thoroughly undermined by this help from postmodernism. The politics of border crossing necessarily subordinates the multiplicity of voices to the arena in which they are articulated in various ways. In other words, the pedagogy proposed by Giroux produces a new identity—that of the border crosser who identifies not with any group, collectivity, or principle but with the means of articulating and evaluating identities and the relations between them. This identity is ultimately incompatible with the more specific ones it is presumably based on, since it is defined in contrast to the un-self-reflexivity of experientially based identities, rather than in relation to a given set of experiences or constituency.

In that case, far from being the ground of border-crossing politics and pedagogy, voice, identity, and so forth are actually pretexts for the production of an independent realm in which revaluation takes place. Thus, what is at stake in postmodernist politics is the seizure of the (modern) means of authorization, of the means of producing social authority (i.e., subjectivities) that have been released as a result of the hegemonic crisis of post-1960s capitalism and that are presumed to hold the key to a redistribution of power and hence more democracy. As long as the independence of these means from the direct control of the main contending classes (that is, the relative autonomy of the petite bourgeoisie) is assured, then a high degree of pluralism will be legitimate, as with any relatively secure regime of private property. The privileging of heterogeneity represents the minimum level of agreement necessary for this system of class practices because it guarantees the independence of the discursive terrain of revaluation from the oppressed class and therefore its corporate possession by the border-crossing petite bourgeoisie.

Within the framework of this agreement, various forms of postmodernism, with marginally different political commitments, are possible. A Left postmodernism supports this notion of pluralism and democracy by refusing to establish or theorize a hierarchy of struggles (which requires an inquiry into the material conditions of social transformation), thereby ensuring that politics will not go beyond the arena of the exchanges of discourses and identities and that it will continue to require the diplomatic practices of postmodern pedagogues. The identities organized by a Left postmodernism, then, would best be characterized as neoidentities, since they are posited as identities that are in principle exchangeable within the system of circulation established by the counterpublics themselves. And it is the border crossers, who can participate in many counterpublics, who will have access to the means of exchange. That is, just as the availability in principle of private property to any individual in fact secures its possession by the capitalist class, so the liberation of the means of authorization in fact guarantees its possession by the class whose position within the social division of labor provides it with privileged access to those means.

The Practice of Border-Crossing Counterpublicity

An excellent example of the counterpublicist border-crossing subject position is the one Cary Nelson has prominently proposed for the public cultural studies intellectual. Nelson's position is worth examining because it is simultaneously a response to the "crisis" in cultural studies that has been the other of mainstream cultural studies from the beginning: its availability to commodification and opportunism. The willingness of cultural studies intellectuals to go public serves, for Nelson, to "draw a much needed boundary . . . around the cultural studies alliance," based on "who will and those who will not join that struggle"—the "struggle against the global inequities following the Reagan-Bush era, the struggle against the Allan Bloom–Lynne Cheney consensus about American education and American culture" (1997, 72–73). The "constitutive antagonism" for cultural studies is the struggle against the Right, particularly the cultural Right.

The identity of cultural studies can articulate this antagonistic site as follows:

> Now that recent theory as a whole has been accused of being politicized . . . cultural studies can willingly occupy the site of theory as politics. Now that efforts to open up the canon and expand the cultural reach of academia's field of vision have been scandalized for abandoning the transcendent and eternal standards of Western high culture . . . cultural studies can cheerfully occupy the site of standard-free omnivorousness. Everyone else may choose to respond to the Right's assault by filling and backsliding and denying they are now or have ever been political in their aims or interests. Cultural studies can step in and be the very thing the Right loves to hate (Nelson 1997, 73–74).

This proposal exemplifies the "strategic essentialism" proposed by Gayatri Spivak, in which one seizes an essentialized identity imposed by the oppressor and rearticulates it in order to present demands and open a new political space. This same strategic essentialism is also, of course, signaled in the title of Nelson's work: *Manifesto of a Tenured Radical,* which, as befits such a project, is "both serious and ironic." Its seriousness lies in its "progressive cultural commitments within academia" (2), commitments that have become radical because "the country has moved to the political right." This also accounts for the irony, for in themselves, as Nelson acknowledges, these commitments are not particularly radical: He is merely interested in making "a series of statements about what higher education must do to heal itself" (2).

As an "articulation," Nelson's strategic essentialism draws together a series of heterogeneous discourses and identities. One of these is the essentially Habermasian discourse implicit in helping higher education heal itself. Nelson often occupies this position throughout his book, speaking for the university in the name of its professed and utopian values—rationality, equality, critical discourse, modernization, and so on. Thus, for example, he argues that "higher education remains the only proven means of social mobility, the only antidote to poverty, and the only large scale corrective for the ravages of capitalism. It is in short the only workable solution to some of America's worst social problems" (1997, 8). Elsewhere, he defends the "social mission" of universities to help America "move more blacks into the middle class" (100). On another level, he argues for contesting the cultural Right's claims that cultural studies has abandoned the norms of American nationalism and Western universalism with the claim that recovering excluded works and traditions will, in fact, deepen our sense of commonality and allow us to more properly assess what really belongs to our heritage. Furthermore, much like Michael Bérubé, Nelson spends a lot of time refuting and correcting lies and assertions made by the Right, distinguishing what has been conflated, historicizing what has been presented in conspiratorial terms, and so forth.

Nelson's construction of the cultural studies public intellectual, though, presupposes that this Habermasian mode is insufficient: "While it is necessary to point out the inaccuracies and distortions in work like Roger Kimball's *Tenured Radicals* and [Dinesh] D'Souza's *Illiberal Education* . . . that kind of reasoned counterargument will not suffice . . . public dialogue is only useful if it has the potential to reach other people" (1997, 109). This claim is ambiguous, even if reasoned counterargument is insufficient if the point is to change the minds of the Kimballs and D'Souzas of the world; is the dialogue with the Kimballs and D'Souzas worthwhile if one might reach other minds that way? In the latter case, we are still within a Habermasian framework aimed at mutual understanding, even if the partner in the dialogue is not the one sitting right there. Nelson is clearer in challenging this framework when he argues that

> [the] struggle for power and influence in American culture proceeds, like all hegemonic conflicts, by way of articulating diverse cultural forces, images and discourses into new configurations that constitute possible ways of understanding our culture as a whole. Merely taking issue with local claims can only have limited use. We must also take on the larger cultural vision that is at stake when dealing with local issues (111).

Reasoned counterargument, then, would be a component of this larger task but not a privileged one.

For whom, exactly, are the reasoned counterarguments intended? Whom does one want to convince that deconstruction is not cultural studies, that canon expansion is not always political, that cultural studies and deconstruction have a tenuous and contingent relationship with political correctness and multiculturalism, etc.? "These are distinctions we need to

draw for our students and colleagues, but we are unlikely to do so suc-
cessfully for the media or the public" (Nelson 1997, 73). The public intellectual's relation to the media and the public is what leads Nelson to the
strategic essentialism I examined earlier: "These are different intellectual
traditions, but their points of partial correspondence are sufficient to convince people they are part of the same general cultural pattern. Our audiences, in other words, will smell a rat. Since we can do little to resist that
moment of recognition, it might be better to welcome it. Cultural studies,
in other words, might set out to *be that rat*" (73).

So, the Habermasian ideal speech situation is the model for dialogue
within the academy (and perhaps those sections of the general public that
are like academic interlocutors) but in relation to *outsiders* to cultural
studies, that is, in those spaces where institutional norms of free inquiry
and open discussion are taken as operative. The rat, or the articulation of
the identity of cultural studies through the suturing of the constitutive antagonism with the cultural Right, is the model of engagement for the general public and media *and* for the *internal* constitution of the boundaries
of cultural studies. A third, more Foucauldian conception of subjectifica-
tion must now be taken into account. I am referring to Nelson's calls
throughout his book for a self-reflexive postdisciplinarity, giving voice to
the insurrection of subjugated knowledges. For example, he speaks of an
inquiry into the historical constitution of disciplinarity ("we need to inquire how and why certain concepts—like 'literature' or 'freedom'—have
their inner contradictions precipitated out and become elevated to a transcendental status within the social formation" [1997, 27–28]) and of
"putting the left at the center" (133), a "project of rearticulation which is
a violation of the logic of directionality," "set[ting] off chain reactions
here and elsewhere" (133). This Foucauldian position is asserted primarily in relation to the *institution,* as an *insider* subverting that institution's
universal claims by accessing its constitutive exclusions.

Finally, there is the counterpublicist logic concerning the internal regulation of identities within cultural studies itself, for *the insiders as insiders.*
This identity is of the type we saw articulated by figures such as Fraser and
Giroux: For Nelson, it takes the form of a "multiculturalism without guarantees," concerned with "what sort of voices they will have within what is
necessarily a very selective frame" (1997, 32). Nelson is talking about inclusion within anthologies, but the logic is easily extended: His descriptions of multicultural anthologies (a mix of utopianism and realism, bases
for strategic alliances and the "forces that will resist and undermine those
same alliances"), where "competing constituencies will construct their in-
tertextual implications in diverse and contradictory ways" (37–38), is easily transferred to his sixteen-point definition of cultural studies. This definition can be reduced to self-reflexive, politicized, postdisciplinary theory,

which is, for Nelson, "an enterprise in which people can explore their race, ethnicity or gender and articulate its relations with the larger culture" (67).

This is the logic behind the strategic essentialism on which the cultural studies public intellectual is based. The assumption here is that the general public is, like the cultural studies community, a multiplicity of dialogic voices and identities. Insofar as cultural studies knows this, it can present itself as the truth of the larger culture. The local democratizations brought about by cultural studies can therefore move outward, osmotically, into the public as the semblance of universality taken on by local cultural democratic, counterpublic spaces becomes a more genuine universality in the articulation of hegemony. According to Nelson, the "current attack on universities is part of a struggle for power and influence in American culture" (1997, 109); hence, various alliances should be possible with other targets in this same struggle. But, then, how is it possible to relate the victory over some local antagonist to the larger political-economic transformations that might produce that victory as a downsizing of unwanted ideological themes? Which vision should be propagated? Since the cultural Right has been selected as antagonist precisely because it is constitutive (i.e., it produces a coherent identity for cultural studies), there is no escape from the assumption that simulating this antagonism *as* the proliferation of resistant cultural studies voices is the academic Left's contribution to social change.

In this case, Nelson's project cannot maintain any distance from its other, as Nelson constructs it: "Of all the intellectual movements that have swept the humanities in America over the last twenty years, none will be taken up so shallowly, so opportunistically, so unreflectively and so ahistorically as cultural studies. It is becoming the perfect paradigm for a people with no sense of history—born yesterday and born on the make" (1997, 54). The depoliticization of cultural studies, though, is constitutive of cultural studies, not an accident that befalls it. It is a result of its exclusion of its real other, Marxism. What Marxism cannot tolerate, as Nelson notes, is a "contextualization so radical and relative that no universal generalizations about human history could be made" (23). Radical contextualization is a synonym for opportunism, and every component of the identity for cultural studies Nelson seeks to articulate is thoroughly contextualized and opportunistic. This applies to the Habermasian posture with those concerned with the university's mission. It applies to the subversion of disciplines whose power/knowledge formation is already shifting toward a postdisciplinary radical contextualization. And it applies to the fantasy of gaining hegemony by marginalizing the cultural Right—easily the weakest link in the current remaking of global capitalist hegemony—the purpose of which, as Nelson implicitly acknowledges, is primarily to hold "our" identity as progressive intellectuals together.

It is symptomatic that the only outsider position Nelson seems willing to adopt is that of the rat to the cultural Right's constructions—that of a "political animal attuned to assuring the survival of his or her interests" (1997, 73). He never considers the possibility of positioning himself outside of the Habermasianism of "students and colleagues" (i.e., those who, by virtue of their social and institutional interests, are necessarily Habermasian). He overlooks the Foucauldianism of immanent critiques of disciplinarity—when the university is itself more and more interested in "pragmatic" knowledges. And he also bypasses the counterpublicity of radically contextualized cultural studies insiders attuned to their own interests. Each imagined interlocutor is addressed on his or her own terms: the ideals of the university as they are implicated in its downsizing; the "insurrection of suppressed knowledges" in terms of the institutional opportunism of cultural studies; and the counterpublics of multiplied subjectivities in terms of the depoliticization of the boundaries of knowledge constitution. The only logic that transcends all these local skirmishes is the inside/outside representational machine producing Nelson's text, whereby the self-differentiating identity of cultural studies becomes the logic of democracy itself. Thus, the totality of the present situation is never addressed: What is excluded is the possibility that, despite their local quarrels, the Habermasians, the Foucauldians, the cultural studies subjectivities, and even the cultural Right might not be all that different. All of them are interested in embodying local liberations and cultural transformation. So, the graduate student organizing an activism upon which much of the moral authority of Nelson's argument rests is bracketed out from the rest of his discussion. Cultural studies doesn't seem to have much to say about this organizing, nor do these practices imply a critique of cultural studies; the function of this pure appreciation is ultimately to mark as extreme and impossible any theorization that doesn't contribute to the presentation of cultural studies before its outside as a democratic force. (The same is also true for the volume edited by Nelson entitled *Will Teach for Food: Academic Labor in Crisis*, in which each text has its separate strategic analysis and its experiential affirmation but no attempt is made to theorize the politics of intellectual activism.)

Another recent book that aims at producing a cultural studies public intellectual corporate identity within identical parameters is *Class Issues*, edited by Amitava Kumar. Here, the counterpublicist, border-crossing paradigm is maintained, and so is the innovation we saw in Nelson's book—the use of the urgencies of concrete political struggles (now, especially, those within the institution) to liquidate theoretical polemics. An instructive way to begin examining the construction of this formation is by noting that the most antitheory (i.e., anti-intellectual) contributions to the collection come from self-identified Marxists. Carol Stabile's diatribe against "academic ultraleftism" (1997, 215) is a good place to begin. Academic ultraleftism is, for Stabile, "characterized by its fashionable theoretical posturing, dense theoretical jargon, and a refusal to participate in building or organizing anything but a career" (215). The greatest crime of academic ultraleftism, she contends, is its abstractness, both theoretically and in its relation to its context. In fact, the two go together:

> Having taken note of the institutional context, declared its independence from that context, academic ultraleftism cultivates a sense of marginality—if not autonomy—from the institution, thereby seeking to deny the material conditions of production. . . . Because academic ultraleftists seldom have contact with organized political struggles, they can maintain a level of ideological purity and dogmatic certainty whose very existence is based on its unaccountability (215).

This abstraction—of intellectual work from its institutional conditions, of theoretical discourse from public dialogue and concrete practice—has devastating effects, according to Stabile: It is reactionary in that it "reinforces the already existing anti-organizational tendencies of the institution" and "reproduces pedagogical and academic authority"; it mystifies the "contemporary economic context of the U.S. economy," to which it is merely an epiphenomenal reflex; and it is "extremely alienating" (215).

One would like to know who these extremely dangerous academic ultraleftists are, where their power lies, and how they have been able to do so much damage—not to mention what they might have to say for themselves. Unfortunately, Stabile is not very helpful here, content as she is with a caricature. But perhaps we can reconstruct the academic ultraleftist position through an analysis of the gaps and contradictions of her own discourse. Let's, for example, look at the "alienating" character of academic ultraleftism. Here is what I think Stabile must mean here. She describes an extraordinary class she recently taught "in which knowledge flowed out of and into the classroom [and] students began to think critically about the official histories and information they had received. They argued passionately, worked through conflicts, moved each other, and were deeply moved" (1997, 217). However, all this movement was ultimately blocked: "At the same time, however, students felt as though they had nowhere to move, no movement to build" (217). Their spontaneity was bottled up because of "the limits prescribed by the institutional setting itself" (217). The classroom, after all, is not a political organization. It doesn't "move."

Stabile is supposedly the one who takes into account the context that academic ultraleftists rudely and arrogantly ignore, yet those contextual limits have not, apparently, been accounted for in her pedagogy—they

just come from the outside and block its movement. It is precisely this extremely alienating moment, when interested theoretical inquiry is
blocked, that is the most productive site of pedagogy—it is not, in other
words, the moment when one has to go elsewhere. This is where abstraction begins, and the point is not to get moving again or find some outlet
"beyond the immediate context of the institution and learning lessons that
cannot be taught in a university classroom" (1997, 217). Abstraction, to
put it another way, begins when context ceases to be an alibi, when one
ceases to invoke life lessons as the supplement to one's own theoretical
backwardness. Abstraction takes as enabling the institutional and political-economic conditions that it seeks to grasp by positing the classroom as
a site of advanced theoretical struggle (as advanced as one can make it).
The point of pedagogy, in other words, is not to reduce alienation but to
theorize its symptoms.

   The job of the self-identified Marxists, Stabile among them, seems to be
to give a specifically humanist, activist legitimation to the cultural studies
public intellectual. This would also account for the essays of Neil Larsen
and Alan Wald, both of whom make every effort to downgrade the significance of the theoretically constituted classroom. Larsen is against the
idea that "the spontaneity of culture can or should be transcended in the
name of an abstract, theoretical 'politics'" (1997, 84), which he considers
a "subjectivist reification of theory" (84); he goes on to argue that "theory
must both consciously orient the pedagogical process as a whole and also
grow spontaneously out of the process itself at each successive phase of
development" (85). In this case, theory must become methodology, recognizing a concrete, immanent object. For Larsen, this necessity points to an
important contradiction: The extent to which theory can't be grasped by
students (and hence has to be turned into a methodology emerging spontaneously from student and text) also indicates an "extreme crisis" that
"severely curtails the capacity of the system to legitimate itself theoretically" (86). Dumbed down students who can't tell a contra from a Communist won't be very helpful ideologues. The seemingly momentous implications of this ("radical theorists and pedagogues, take note") are
unclear. Are the students therefore open to a radical leftist interpellation—
and, perhaps, is a shortcut to this possible, if "high theory" can be bypassed? This, in the end, seems to be Larsen's point: The introduction of
theory assumed that questions of reading needed to be addressed in terms
of their conditions of possibility. The problem with this, for Larsen, is that
"conceived along radically subjectivist lines, theory inevitably becomes its
own object" (81). But pedagogy has no justification except insofar as it
uncovers the theoretical question lying beneath apparently more real and
concrete ones. What Larsen has discovered, it seems, is that the very need
to start at ground level with the students has a dialectical upside, for one
no longer needs the detour through theoretical polemics.

Alan Wald, meanwhile, wants a domesticated Marxism in a dialogic relationship to multicultural politics. "Historical materialism today," he argues "is dead without the vital infusion of feminism, antiracist theory, ecology, gay and lesbian theory, advanced cultural theory, and many other fertile perspectives" (1997, 146). In this way, a unified "socialist" position can make it to the outside—moving "aggressively into the public sphere" (146). Socialism becomes one identity among many others, as long as "sectarianism" is abandoned and "socialist intellectuals . . . build forums of debate and discussion with an institutionalized policy of including a range of voices from the non-sectarian left" (145). For Wald, like Stabile, the point of pedagogy is to maintain "a connection to the egalitarian social movements that first opened up the doors of the university in the 1960s for the democratization of cultural study and pedagogy that we now enjoy" (143). Again, movement is everything. The seeds of cultural democratization flow into the university, fertilize, and flow back out again; as long as mutual recognition of plural, nonsectarian identities is institutionalized, everything should be fine. But the egalitarian social movements have developed theories of their own, each time systematically institutionalizing in their basic theoretical presuppositions the struggle between postmodernist and Marxist theses, usually to the marked advantage of the former. These theses must be addressed as consequential, not in terms of whether or not postmodernists "seek to join socialist activists" (145). Theoretical assumptions have consequences beyond what one joins.

The other essays in *Class Issues: Pedagogy, Cultural Studies and the Public Sphere* do the real work of constructing the post-Marxist, border-crossing public intellectual. Kumar's introduction sets the tone. First of all, since the attack on progressive education is part of an attack on education as such—"the loss of schools and universities as a viable public sphere" (Kumar, ed., 1997, 2)—a Habermasian entrance into the public sphere in the name of education is possible, "engaging in a public defense of education and the values threatened by a dangerous culture of corporate downsizing" (3). Here, one can take on the role of correcting errors, countering falsehoods, and "inform[ing] the reading public of the devastation wrought by the economic and political priorities of the ruling elite" (3). (The use of "elite," rather than "class," should here be taken as a rehearsal of such a nonalienating mode of public address.) At the same time, the institutional consolidation of such forays into the public sphere has a Foucauldian underpinning. "This volume," Kumar tells us, "signals an unwillingness to surrender to that kind of disciplinary terrorism, holding sway over left intellectuals in the past, that has dictated a silence on issues of one's own self-formation as well as a lingering inattentiveness to the operations of power in and through the production of values, identities and social relations" (3–4).

This, in turn, leads into the counterpublicist stance: "We are learning to invent our publics and ourselves: as teachers, as students, as activists, as global workers. Or not" (Kumar, ed., 1997, 3). Among ourselves, Kumar suggests, we should focus on "process"—not which knowledges are acquired but how one's self has been formed. "Disciplinary terrorism" is Kumar's translation of Stabile's "academic ultraleftism": We should reveal our "scars" (3) to each other while giving the public information. But isn't informing the public an example of such terrorism, of the assumption that "knowledge is acquired to be applied" (4)? Why shouldn't we inform each other and address the public in terms of its self-formation? This might foreground theoretical polemics (rather than survival) internally and the polemic between theory and common sense externally, thereby making ideology critique the foundational mode of engagement, which would never quite be convenient in Kumar's approach.

Mike Hill and Jeffrey Williams take similarly cynical and economistic approaches to the questions of cultural studies and pedagogy, respectively. According to Hill, cultural studies (CS), due to the academic job slump, has become implicated in its object:

> If CS's politics has arrived, it has done so after the fact, and with precisely the ambivalences and disruptive banalities CS thought for a moment it could merely study. The split condition of the popular subject, where identity teeters between ideology and the material desires it doesn't yet know it has, is no longer the masses' business to experience, and the job of Enlightened CSers to write up (1997, 159).

While cultural studies was worried about how to be organically connected to the people, labor came to cultural studies. What is good about this for Hill is not that class struggle and intellectual work might bear more forcefully upon one another; rather, he is fascinated by the inherent aporia opened up between theory and experience and how this aporia will be experienced instead of theorized—"we" are now just as "hybrid" (159) as "they" are. None of this calls for a return to basic theoretical and political questioning or concepts. In fact, such a possibility is openly denied:

> CS has at the moment been denied the "mastery" of "philosophical privilege," and it is a denial that marks both its arrival and its ineffectiveness. That materiality has provided for both the death and, one hopes, an accidental politics for CS is an irony immanent in CS from its inception. Still it is an irony that brings about some alternative, if "ordinary" possibilities (159).

Hill doesn't say just what possibilities those would be—it is enough that cultural studies has gone if not public then simulacral, a parody of its own depoliticizing antinomies. But, again, the point is that such theoretical questions are dead, ironized out of existence (any politics will be accidental, so what is to be said or done?). Something more elemental is suggested by Hill's text, some "coming to terms" (159), but it's hard to see what it would mean to try to figure any of this out.

For Williams, meanwhile, the entire concern with pedagogy and the public sphere is merely symptomatic of a crisis in the profession: "It speaks to a professionalist concern and legitimation, to reinvoke a public purpose and thereby to relegitimate its threatened professional status—intensified by contemporary fiscal and ideological pressure for accountability" (1997, 303). For him, as for Stabile, a pedagogy that prioritizes theory "has a profoundly conservative function and reaffirms rather than reconfigures the current distribution of academic knowledge production" (305). It goes without saying, though, that Williams's dissection of the self-interest of academic professionals does not lead to any theorization of a universal or disinterested conception of the intellectual. Like Frow, he wants academics to own their self-interest, which for Williams means to "struggle for the ground of the pedagogical contract as employment, radicalize our labor practices, resist administrative mandates for downsizing, speed up and the like, and reform the inequitable distribution of labor that presently constitutes the university" (307).

There is nothing wrong with any of this, of course, but what should be asked is why this agenda currently needs to be asserted at the expense of theory and the "radicalizing of pedagogy" (Williams 1997, 307). By what mechanism does this internal, institutional (at least proposed) politicization rely upon and strengthen the reduction of theory to a pragmatic, self-reflexive means of negotiating local issues? As urged by Jeffrey Di Leo and Christian Moraru, the volume's representatives of Williams's "posttheory generation," this would bring a "new eclecticism," a "pragmatic approach to theory, which enables them to assess various theoretical models on the basis of the sociocultural and political insights that these models bring about" (1997, 240). But as long as some empirical, local piece of reality (such as the job crisis) is used as a "limit case" to subordinate theory to its exchange value in negotiations on the construction of a corporate self-image, it will be unthinkable to push the boundaries of theoretical polemics and thereby constitute the classroom as a theoretical space organized around contending concepts as the primary responsibility of the intellectual and pedagogue. Therefore, too, intellectuals will not strive to be "outside of the outside of the other" (as I argued in Chapter 1), and occasions for broader, public interventions in the media and elsewhere will not aim at splitting and implicating the public in relation to the sedimented theoretical understandings that can only be made available from the outside.

Ronald Strickland does, at times, seem to argue along the lines I have just suggested, so I want to conclude this discussion by examining his chapter in *Class Issues: Pedagogy, Cultural Studies and the Public Sphere.* As is clear to any reader, I consider it urgent to theorize political accountability under contemporary conditions, and this does depend, as Strickland claims, upon a reunderstanding of publicness and pedagogy in the wake of theoretical critiques of the subject. Some of Strickland's proposals are productive for that end: for example, his attempt to organize the classroom along sharply drawn contestatory theoretical lines and his violations of collegiality by situating these contestations within a broader institutional space and, finally, in relation to questions regarding institutional structures and criteria. In other words, engaging in institutional struggles doesn't mean setting theoretical struggles aside or reducing them to the means of counterpublicist negotiations; instead, it entails an extension of those struggles. However, Strickland doesn't really, as he claims, move beyond the notion of "public accountability of higher education that we have inherited from the modernist and civic humanist traditions" (1997, 163)—rather, he extends these traditions to areas that have traditionally been off-limits. For instance, his insistence that students study "data on student enrollments, tuition costs, fees, faculty teaching loads, and so forth" (167) is really transporting a traditional notion of the informed citizen into the classroom. It is not clear what is empowering about this. Nor is it clear just what is empowering about his proposal for "engaging 'vocationalist' publics within the academy," who are to be held accountable "to the democratic and intellectual ideals of the university and society at large," while holding "academic humanists accountable to existing sociopolitical conditions" (170). These are simulated modes of accountability, assuming, along Habermasian lines, that change follows from more open, informed, and inclusive public deliberation. In other words, the entire argument collapses into localist and market-oriented, rather than world-historical, modes of accountability.

There are more important theoretical questions here. Evoking Fraser, Strickland raises the possibility of seeing the classroom and even the "entire academy as a potential counterpublic sphere" (1997). He seems to reject this possibility, since "universities and even humanities departments are overwhelmingly dedicated to serving the interests of postnational capitalism" (166). This is equivocal—does Strickland reject Fraser's theory? Or does he consider it simply unrealistic? In the university as a whole or even in the single classroom? Is his call for "a general deprivatization of knowledge and pedagogy" (166) therefore a compensatory project and perhaps an attempt to create the conditions for counterpublicity? Or is it a principled rejection of Fraser's position? This is an important issue because what is at stake is whether the pedagogue is accountable to theoretical clarification or to a broader dissemination and the proliferation of identities. This point is not clarified by Strickland's postmodern view of knowledge as "contingent, subject to dialectical contestation, and continually involved in the process of production and reproduction . . . not hypostatized and homogenized disciplinary canonical tradition filtered through the teacher as master and text as master-resource" (166). This view doesn't suggest anything beyond a vague dialogism.

This dialogic emphasis is reinforced by Strickland's conclusion that "it is time to hold ourselves, our colleagues, and our students accountable to constituencies beyond the universal human individual conceived as the subject of the liberal humanist academy" (1997, 175). The problem here is that one can only be accountable to the pedagogical relation to constituencies, to the theoretical clarification of their historical status as constituencies. The same problem holds for Strickland's uncritical celebration of "virtual spaces," in which the "power relations between student and teacher can be significantly altered, knowledge generated in the classroom . . . linked to other knowledges, other voices, thereby creating a participatory 'public sphere'" (166).

This last claim, grounding a more genuine (counter-) public sphere in the dismantling of pedagogical authority, the hybrid constitution of knowledge, and developments in communications technologies brings me to my fundamental objection to the essay. Although Strickland wants to "break down the walls of the classroom," I think that, in many ways, such walls need to be made stronger, thicker, and higher. The outside should be brought into the classroom but on terms set by the theoretical constitution of the classroom: The point of foregrounding the central concepts and problematics of the course is precisely to ensure that when other knowledges and voices enter, they do so as objects of theoretical inquiry and sites of theoretical polemics. Insofar as the classroom, meanwhile, engages its outside (via students, the instructor's relation to the institution, etc.), it is not for the sake of crossing borders but to make the tension between the rigorous classroom space and other spaces visible, to sharpen and theorize this tension and to make it a site of public pedagogy.

⚬

What Foucault came to call "governmentality," in essence a more generalized and self-reflexive mode of discipline in which the subject becomes responsible for the techniques of self-control, I would call "marketized sovereignty." From its legitimation by reference to a founding, revolutionary social compact, sovereignty is contracted out, whether it be the state as such selling its services to transnational corporations, the state subcontracting various functions (as with privatized prisons), or groups of citizens opting out of one mode of sovereignty and forming another or contracting with several modes at once (e.g., gated communities in the United States). In this case, one can account for various political spaces without finding it necessary to follow Foucault's liquidation of political concepts such as the "commons" and "legitimacy": Thus, it becomes possible to explain the manner in which "tiered" forms of citizenship emerge and are maintained in relationship to the development of the productive forces and the ongoing reconstruction of class relations.

Specific modes of knowledge and technique begin to appear fundamentally violent and illegitimate in relation to a different mode of sovereignty. Consequently, the primary responsibility of the specific intellectual, the self-reflexive inquiry into the modes of power/knowledge that have formed one, i.e., "unlearning privilege," is nothing but a transfer of allegiance to new modes of marketized sovereignty emerging around knowledge production. The counterpublics, meanwhile, and their border-crossing diplomats are simply negotiating points, playing one form of marketized sovereignty off against another. Such conditions complicate politics, of course—no one gets to choose which mode of marketized sovereignty they come into direct confrontation with—but this doesn't liquidate the universalizing political principles. The very fragmentation of the "common" is at stake in the multiplication of sovereign forms, since the legitimacy of any sovereignty is in the space it provides for theory, accountability, and power to be articulated before an outside. To put it differently, how wide a scope does a given mode of sovereignty provide for each to be "outside of the outside of the other," on a global scale? In this way, we can also account for the hierarchy arranging different modes of sovereignty, in terms of where the antagonism between privatized modes of sovereignty and transnational modes of accountability are most concentrated.

In this connection, I will conclude with an argument for the disinterestedness of the intellectual, but not in the sense of an unsituated position or speaking for an empirical subject or general interest (what Jean-Jacques Rousseau called the "will of all"). Rather, I would argue for what I will call "evident disinterest," disinterest that is on the "surface." This mode of disinterest surfaces the limits to the relation between action, accountability, and theory presupposed by any sovereignty, and it does so in defense of the outside that sovereignty neutralizes. The implication of a series of such spaces in the political-economic totality accounts for the disinterest of any discourse—a disinterest that is interested in the limits and conditions of any interest. Central to the postmodern critique of humanism, especially in its Foucauldian variant, is the dismantling of the link between sovereignty and disinterest—a link that presupposes that disinterest involves speaking from the standpoint of the real or ideal sovereign. In other words, the modern bourgeois state posits the will of the people as its ground; in critiquing the state from the standpoint of a pristine popular will, the critic of the state simply strengthens the ground of state action by providing its reality with a supportive ideality.

Evident disinterest, though, presupposes no such ground of the state nor any mode of sovereignty (including of the subject): Sovereignty is simply the protection of a space of action and accountability, meaning that the question is about which modes of power the state protects and which it destroys. The marketization of sovereignty draws upon the logic of protection and neutralization as well as that of collective power and consent (otherwise, it wouldn't be marketable), but it does so through a process of selection (what Zygmunt Bauman calls "spatial segregation" [1998, 3]), in which the capitalist logic of privatizing gain and socializing costs is aggravated. Hence, the "common" returns as aggregate cost. This reduces disinterest to local crisis management, and it leads to the association of progressiveness with the subject of crisis management. A position outside of the system of marketized sovereignties is thus necessarily disinterested (otherwise, it is merely playing one sovereignty off against another) and disinterested in a different relation to sovereignty.

A more insistent focus on the universalizing categories (such as reason) must characterize the text of evident disinterest, e.g., a defense of reason as such, and, simultaneously, a more grounded one—reason as a site where reasoned inquiries into global contradictions confront the antipolitical violence that neutralizes the conditions of possibility of such reasoning in collective action. In other words, an inaugural ideology critique founds any engagement and grounds the universality of disinterest. Thus, the starting point of any responsible engagement encompasses the critique of the norms of communicative reason with the Habermasians (where the assumption of reasoned grounds is founded on the irrationality of introducing communication into strategic and functionalist discourses); the critique of (anti)disciplinary knowing contra the Foucauldians (the "universal" is other than a cover for emerging modes of control and subversion); and the critique of pluralizing counterpublics with the border crossers (asking where the actual point of concentrated opposition that they must posit—as "democratizers"—and endlessly evade and dissimulate lies).

Only what I would call a "political-economic" universality, as I will explain in the next chapter, is adequate here. To anticipate, class struggle cuts across all the horizontally differentiated fields of communication and identity by locating the systematicity of local sites in the necessary violence of the "vertical." By the same token, theoretical struggle precedes the deconstruction of universalizing concepts in that it posits the contradiction between the original, animating principle of generalized commodity production and the equally original expansive political forms that abolish capitalism as constitutive of any local site. The point of critique, then, is to foreground not sovereignty's distance from founding political principles but rather the relation of that distance to social contradictions and/as fundamentally opposed spaces and modes of theory and action. The other always has a manifesto and a program; the other also has, therefore, certain presuppositions regarding the spaces of economics, politics, culture, and theory: Evident disinterest is interested in the articulation of those spaces and hence resists the violence dispersing them and rendering them opaque. Aid in this resistance is the purpose of struggles over sovereignty. It is therefore in opening spaces where theory and action can confront one another, where lines need to be drawn, discourses taken literally, foundations defended. These articulations of theoretico-political spaces, if evident on the surface of the text, make visible the distance between any mode of marketized sovereignty and the ground of political legitimacy. And the test of such disinterest is whether it opens a space for knowledge that would compel retheorizing that ground and situating the ideological struggle on a new terrain.

Notes

1. See Visker 1995 for a helpful analysis of the question of the contradictory epistemological ground of Foucault's critique of power/knowledge.

5

GLOBALIZATION, UNIVERSALITY, AND CULTURAL STUDIES

Foundational Polemics

The globalization debates and their ramifications within cultural studies have recapitulated the trajectory I have traced throughout this book: Globalization is overwhelmingly understood as a logic of homogenization, the primary violence of which is the assimilation and extirpation of difference. Resistance is hence located in difference. The main distinction that has emerged, for example, between the advocates of a postcolonial project allied with poststructuralism (among them Homi Bhabha and Gayatri Spivak) and critics of such a project (including Benita Parry, Arif Dirlik, and Aijaz Ahmed) is whether difference is "always already" located in the center (the norm is constituted by the exception) or in an empirical margin. The seemingly radical move of conflating the violence of exploitation with the violence of exclusion (i.e., joining "top-bottom" relations with "inside-outside" relations) in fact has the effect that disrupting prevailing inside-outside relations can be presented as an attack on relations of domination. The exemplary critical position is thus that of the constitutive outside of the same-becoming-other. As opposed to this, I am arguing for a political-economic universality wherein one is the outside of the outside of the other. Rather than an ethical space, such an outside is a space of pedagogical accountability. First of all, one is interested in the polemic of the other (not the body or experience); second, one aims at implicating that polemic in the articulation of economics, politics, and theory.

Since I am arguing for foundations and universality, it will be helpful to develop my argument through another recent attempt to recover and resituate these categories. David Harvey, in his *Justice, Nature and the Geography of Difference*, begins with the contention that "the task of critical analysis is . . . to find a more plausible and adequate basis for the foundational beliefs that make interpretation and political action meaningful, creative, and possible" (1996, 2). Harvey argues that the best way to arrive at such a basis is provided by what he calls, following Raymond Williams, "militant particularisms": "Ideas forged out of the affirmative experience of solidarities in one place get generalized and universalized as a working model of a new form of society that will benefit all of humanity" (30). As Harvey recognizes, there is nothing necessarily progressive about militant particularisms or their "global ambitions." First, if "political and social identities formed under an oppressive industrial order operating in a certain place [cannot] survive the collapse or radical transformation of that order," then the "perpetuation of those political identities and loyalties requires perpetuation of the oppressive conditions that gave rise to them" (40). Second, the very search for militant particularism presupposes, as Harvey also acknowledges, "that capitalism has fortuitously taken a path these last 20 years toward the elimination of many of the militant particularisms that have traditionally grounded socialist politics" (40). Nevertheless, Harvey sees no option but to "search for new combinations of both old and new forms of militant particularisms to ground a rather different version of socialist politics" (41).

I consider this a mistaken way to recover and resituate the revolutionary communist project today, for the simple reason that once you start searching for militant particularisms in order to elaborate them and align yourself with their global ambitions, you are already assuming your own freedom and contingency; by thus making a virtue of intellectual and political dispossession, you simultaneously ensure that whatever militant particularism you find will be a simulated one. When I, by contrast, speak of "foundational polemics," I start from the way in which Lenin (in an argument that, of course, became crucial to Althusser) understands the fundamental struggle between idealism and materialism in philosophy. This struggle is fundamental because neither materialism nor idealism can prove its own presuppositions, nor can one refute the other: In fact, any attempt to do that would be akin to allowing the presupposition of the opponent to constitute one's own discourse. All idealism and materialism can do is seek to dislodge the other from one or another position occupied within the realms of knowledge and politics.

Any foundational polemic (some world-historical ones being faith/reason, rhetoric/philosophy, and Marxism/liberalism) must, I would suggest, do at least the following: (1) establish borders separating it from its outside; (2) establish internal boundaries, categories delineating a hierarchy and division of faculties, values, tasks, etc.; and (3) constitute itself before its outside, that is, put the legitimacy of its marking of boundaries and defense of borders in question. To put it another way, it must present itself in any articulation before a space of judgment that transcends any specific articulation but is unthinkable without the possibility of articulation as such.

In addition to founding and being legitimate by reference to some (its) polemic, political action is the recovery and actualization of that polemic, first, in relation to the polemic's distance from its present manifestations and, second, in opposition to or engagement with other polemics.

It is possible to judge acts issuing from the actualization or crystallization of a particular foundational polemic because any polemic presupposes an outside (whether it be indifferent strangers or hostile enemies) that accounts both for the relative freedom of occupants of that outside (their movements can't be totally predicted) and therefore for possible contacts and confrontations. To give one example of the implications of this argument, in these terms the proper way for a materialist to critique an idealist is not to address the "flawed" foundations of idealism; rather, the point is to make visible the failure to follow that idealism to its logical conclusions, perhaps by reserving a certain esotericism in the name of making idealism more presentable. To conclude this point, it also follows that one can be outside of the other in the sense, say, that one accepts or takes literally the charge coming from idealism that materialism is amoral and Machiavellian, as a polemical, interrogatory ground (this would involve a kind of transferential relation to the other). I want to distinguish this move, though, from taking a position outside of the outside of the other: Here, one is interested in having the attacking polemic miss its target because that target no longer exists (it has moved on) or, to put it differently, because the polemic one is issuing is situated on a new historical boundary. The point of this is to implicate the attacking polemic in its preemptive reproducibility (i.e., its reduction of the outside to a derivative of the inside). This move of implication addresses antipolitical violence against the space of accountability, and critiquing that violence is an effort to reopen the space of articulation of economics, politics, and theory.

The notion of foundational polemics as constitutive of and concealed by one's entry into the world in a determinate set of economic and political relations that are a priori addressed theoretically is opposed to a more or less stable identity or experience as constitutive of subjectivity. The concept of foundational polemics also answers the caricature widely circulated by postmodern cultural studies that Marxism must see the oppressed as dupes (as opposed to the presumably positive alternative of seeing the oppressed as creative, deconstructive, self-(un)making hybrids). In fact, if the point of ideological struggle is to surface foundational polemics, the interest is in opening spaces where accountable relations of (relative) enmity and unconditional theoretical struggle are possible. This thesis is thus an attempt to contest the concealment, within postmodern cultural studies, of relations of exploitation behind reversible inside/outside processes: The inside/outside desiring machine of postmodernism eliminates the possibility of surface/depth or appearance/essence relations, which, in turn, are necessary in order to make systemic relations of oppression visible. The defense of the outside, not as constitutive outside that is produced by the instability of the inside itself but as a space of theory that is the result of critique, makes it possible to see systemic relations as they appear politically or, to use Trotsky's term, to see politics as "concentrated economics."[1] This outside of the outside is what I will call political-economic universality, which I consider necessary to challenge global capitalism.

The Globalization of Cultural Studies

Analyses of globalization can go in one of two directions. First, they can be theorizations of the expansion and consolidation of capitalist relations of production on the terrain established by, successively, the post–World War II reconstruction, the international recession of the 1970s, and the post-Cold War "New World Order." Second, they can identify globalization with "culturalization," undermining Marxist accounts by claiming that the defining feature of globalization is precisely the increasing causal (or postcausal) importance of culture, identities, communication, symbolic exchange, and so on. Two early examples of the first type of analysis are Robert Ross and Kent Trachte's *Global Capitalism: The New Leviathan* and M. Patricia Marchak's *The Integrated Circus: The New Right and the Restructuring of Global Markets*, both of which seek to explain how capitalism, since the 1960s, has been resituated on new boundaries. Both make the argument that the restructuring of capital has produced conditions under which, instead of national capitalist classes confronting national working classes within a relatively unified national economy (within which the working class can wield considerable power), an increasingly global capitalist class confronts an ever more fragmented working class with few if any powers of resistance. This accounts for the decentering of the institutions and norms of the welfare state and state responsibility for economic conditions, what we could call a substantial reprivatization of the reproduction of labor power.

More recently, analysts such as William Robinson, in his *Promoting Polyarchy: Globalization, US Intervention and Hegemony*, and Saskia Sassen, in her *Losing Control?: Sovereignty in an Age of Globalization*, have extended this analysis in productive directions. Robinson focuses on the U.S. global strategy of exporting liberal democracy (what another book calls "low intensity democracy"[2]) in which the formal "balances" of liberal democratic institutions are put in place in the wake of the autocracies sponsored during the Cold War in such a way as to remove from the agenda substantive questions of production and real inequalities. Sassen addresses issues of new forms of global "citizenship" granted to transnational corporations. Meanwhile, Frederick Buell's *National Culture and the New Global System,* Malcolm Waters's *Globalization,* and the work of Roland Robertson and Mike Featherstone have advanced "culturalist" analyses in which indeterminacy and hybridity are privileged.

It should also be noted that analyses coming from the neoconservative Right, such as John Gray's *False Dawn: The Delusions of Global Capitalism,* and the neoliberal center, such as Thomas Friedman's *The Lexus and the Olive Tree,* have also explained globalization as an outcome of the inexorable logic of capitalism. What a genuine critique of capitalist globalization must address, then, is not simply the causal logic producing the integration of political-economic, social, and cultural forces but also the question of whether there is an outside to globalization, that is, whether it can be theorized not simply as inevitable—in which case, there can be nothing but local accommodations and maneuvers—but also in terms of the theoretical and political categories that make it possible to posit capitalist globalization as a contradictory unity that can be transcended. As Alan Scott argues, "interpreting globalization as historically inevitable and unstoppable" "contributes to its political puissance" and thereby conceals the "extent to which globalization is a *political project*" (1997, 2). In what follows, I will concentrate not on the globalization debate per se but on its manifestations within an internationalized cultural studies, keeping in mind the question of focusing on "glocalization" as itself a political project, aligned with neoliberal globalization, and developing some of the arguments and analyses required to defend a political-economic universality outside of globalization.

◆○

The internationalization of cultural studies in recent years has, as I suggested earlier, conformed to the overall trajectory of cultural studies—the focus is invariably upon some new subaltern, "excessive" subjectivity (such as "diasporic," "nomadic," "hybrid," etc.) that subverts in some local space the logic of a totalizing modernity. The most important reference point here is Gayatri Spivak's understanding of subalternity. Spivak's focus is on intellectual and institutional privilege that reads the subaltern either from a distanced, vanguard position, which imposes extraneous narrative logics on the subaltern, or from the complementary position of assuming a self-representing subaltern, which already knows what it wants and hence frees one from complicity in its conditions. For Spivak, the point is to subvert from within the Eurocentric knowledges that silence the subaltern and to thereby open a space where a critical discourse ethically aligning intellectuals and subalterns becomes possible.

The single most consistent target of Spivak's critique is the possibility of a political-economic universality: "No historically [or philosophically] adequate claims can be produced in any space for the guiding words of political, military, economic, ideological emancipation and oppression. You take positions in terms not of the discovery of historical or philosophical grounds, but in terms of reversing, displacing, and seizing the apparatus of value-coding" (1993, 63). In this way, one makes visible the irreducible, contingent, founding violence of all claims to rationality and truth that, in a Foucauldian manner, produces its subjects and objects. It is thus precisely the universal "one cannot not want to inhabit" that is the site of one's inaugural and persistent critique. But the universal one cannot not want to inhabit is open to critique because it presupposes, actualizes, and sets in crisis certain historical and philosophical grounds. There can be foundational polemics surrounding differing notions of, say, equality because equality articulates the conditions of possibility of theorizing political appearances as a concentration of economic relations (the relation between cause and accountability). In the name of what, exactly, does one "reverse, displace, and seize the apparatus of value-coding"? Clearly, one does not do this in the name of a value but rather in the name of opportunistically gaining greater proximity to the apparatus.

Rather than historical and philosophical grounds, it is the inaccessible subaltern that legitimates one's practices. So, Lisa Lowe and David Lloyd locate resistance to capitalist global modernity in "alternative" cultural practices that emerge in the wake of colonial and neocolonial capitalism's appropriation of traditional elements for the maintenance of domination. These cultural elements are therefore transformed into sites of resistance: "Culture becomes important where a cultural formation comes into contradiction with an economic or political logic that tries to refunction it for exploitation or domination" (1997, 24). To make this argument, it is first necessary to project the logic of capitalism beyond the primary opposition of capital and labor ("a totality governed by the globalization of capitalism or the superordination of the proletarian subject" [15]) and toward the logic of homogenization and differentiation. The modes of production narrative, i.e., the explanation of social transformation in terms of the contradiction between the forces and relations of production, must also be delegitimated as complicit with liberal and nationalist modernity.

In this case, those practices that cannot be accounted for in theoretical terms are thereby the most important sources of resistance. Ultimately, the assumptions here are Foucauldian, for a homogenizing, modern discipline produces the resistance of local subjects. Such resistance is therefore necessarily heterogeneous; it involves the linking of forms "below the level of the nation and across national sites" (Lowe and Lloyd 1997, 26). The new forms of subjectivity are produced by the "encounter between 'indigenous' forms of work and cultural practices and modern capitalist economic modes imposed upon them" (26). Only affirmation is possible here, not inquiry into the contradictions constitutive of such resistant practices:

Locating one's discourse outside of the outside of the other would necessarily be the most violent act possible. Culture, never actually defined by Lowe and Lloyd, is precisely this excess over capitalist modernization, in the name of which one seizes the apparatus of value-coding.

Kuan-Hsing Chen, in his introduction to *Trajectories: Inter-Asia Cultural Studies*, explicitly puts up resistance to some elements of the postmodern articulation of cultural studies. He defends the maintenance of a Marxist position in cultural studies, but he does so with endless qualifications that make it hard to see what, exactly, is left. Marxism, Chen says, "has not yet been sentenced to death" but only because "its critical elements have been saturated into different geographical sites, and can always be called upon to deal with difficult uncertainty" (1998, 7). Marxism, in other words, has become a supplement to the new identity politics, which is easy to understand because, for Chen, Marxism was in fact the first identity politics. In a strangely teleological narrative that echoes those of Stuart Hall, he writes of a "desire" that became "omnipresent" but is now implicated in a "whole series of 'unstoppable' 'epistemological breaks'": "Capitalist class, First World, male, whites, heterosexuals, etc., could not escape the fate of being decentered" (7). Likewise, the Marxist critique of capitalism could not escape becoming Foucauldian power/knowledge. Chen's Marxism is Stuart Hall's "Marxism without guarantees" (47), a "Marxism mediating through Nietzsche" (7) and resituated by the endless proliferation of new subjectivities.

At the same time, Chen wants to distance himself from this "universal abandon" and maintain the critical edge of cultural studies by redirecting its focus to decolonization within an international framework. He argues for superseding identity politics with a new "critical syncretism," the "bottom line" of which "is becoming others, to actively interiorize elements of others into the subjectivity of the self so as to move beyond the boundaries and divisive positions historically constructed by colonial power relations, patriarchy, capitalism, racism, chauvinism, heterosexism, nationalist xenophobia, etc." (1998, 25). But the tradition of Marxism Chen invokes has always aimed at setting limits to the "unstoppable . . . etc.," to prioritize some boundaries and hierarchies over others. Chen wants to distance his critical syncretism from Homi Bhabha's "hybridity," but the only difference seems to be in Chen's quintessentially cultural studies appeal to concreteness, coalitionism, alternative communities, cultural activism, etc. Again, the problem is not with any particular democratic or progressive struggle, like the many Chen and his contributors discuss. The problem is that theory becomes the immediate reflection of alliances, coalitions, and local activism and is therefore in no way able to critique them in fundamental ways. With a reinvented "Marxism," cultural studies becomes a traveling umbrella concept articulating the negotiations between various intellectual activists.

Chen's claim that his volume does not reject the original tradition of British cultural studies but instead "provincializes" (1998, xv) it is therefore true, if we add that it does so by globalizing the logic of that tradition. As with the tradition, what is absolutely precluded is the possibility of an outside that is not merely a utopian imaginary, to be deconstructed by a new utopian imaginary, etc., but a theoretical and political position from which one can actually try to stop the "unstoppable." In other words, one can ask any new identity several questions: Why multiply further, rather than explain and challenge others to explain, the cause articulated through your symptomatic practices? Why do you not inquire into the historical status of the principles by which you claim legitimacy—not strategically but as a foundational polemic, the border of which must be justified, the ground of which must be cleared? Rather than empathizing with the other, why do you not perform the historical service of being outside of the outside of the other?

Another project that rhetorically heightens its resistance to global capitalism precisely in order to devise new ways of valorizing the local is Rob Wilson and Wimal Dissanayake's *Global/Local: Cultural Production and the Transnational Imaginary*. Near the opening of their introduction, the authors announce:

> Regions and region-states increasingly override national borders and older territorial forms and create special economic zones of uneven development and transcultural hybridity. The global/local synergy within what we will track as the *transnational imaginary* enlivens and molests the texture of everyday life and spaces of subjectivity and reshapes those contemporary structures of feeling some cultural critics all too commonly banalize as "postmodern" or hypertextually consecrate as "postcolonial" resistance. Too much of cultural studies, in this era of uneven globalization and the two-tier information highway, can sound like a way of making the world safe and user-friendly for global capital and the culture of the commodity form (1996, 2).

So, the transnational imaginary stands opposed to the complicit postmodern and postcolonial. How? The main distinction, in terms of the postcolonial at least, seems to be that the postcolonial implies a failure to confront capital. It supports "in-between spaces of negotiated language, borderland being, and bicultural ambivalence" (2), whereas the transnational imaginary speaks of the "ongoing process of disruption and manipulation by global discourses and technologies" (2). In other words, there seems to be somewhat more weight given to questions of domination in the transnational imaginary. Nevertheless, Wilson and Dissanayake contend that "it is no longer adequate to map the globe into binary zones of center and periphery" (2), meaning that "enduring asymmetries of domination, injustice, racism, class dynamics and uneven spatial development" (8) are themselves localized. In fact, instead of theorizing new, global terms of struggle, Wilson, Dissanayake, and their contributors would rather focus on the "rehabilitation, affirmation, and renewal in disjunctive phases and local assertions" (3). The resistance to the "consecration" of the local, of which postcolonial theory is guilty, is thus resisted in the name of an even more intensely localized micropolitics.

The logic of resistance is now summed up in the "counter logic of the *both/and*" (Wilson and Dissanayake 1996, 6). As we saw in Lowe and Lloyd's argument, this involves focusing on local sites where resistance is produced as a result of globalization and thus undermines "any prefabricated metanarrative of teleological development," positing the global/local space "as one that disturbs prior analytical categories" (6). The local site doesn't resist "in-itself," nor is it assimilated to some larger transformation; rather, it unsettles the global/local binary itself, marking the local as "the rendering and deforming local of Western universality as standard, center, and dominant knowledge" (6). It is not clear what, exactly, separates this from the postcolonial logic Wilson and Dissanayake claim to reject: "The local posits interstitial spaces of alternative imagining: modes of living and memory undoing the dominant space-time of the nation-state and the transnational super-state" (7).

The local, to put it another way, becomes a site of resistance as globalization is taken to be the culmination of modernity and the point at which it therefore turns into postmodernity, confronting its limits and opening for the deconstruction of its metanarratives. By seeking to extirpate and/or assimilate every last bastion of the premodern, global modernity, on this account, transforms these residual sites into sites of resistance—resistance that is not so much in the site itself and that needs to be read in the slippages of the text of global modernity. Regardless of their resistance to the postmodern and the postcolonial, the "rendering and deforming of Western universality" can't mean anything else.

Something different would seem to be suggested by the notion that "local struggles . . . can be registered as a relational, multidimensionally conflicted social space of global contradiction" (6–7) and that local struggles are to "figure as allegories of larger, more systemic alteration" (7). In this case, the local is symptomatic, and one needs to explain the global contradiction—which, obviously, can't be the contradiction between global and local itself. Furthermore, if local struggles are to figure as allegories of "systemic alteration," it would follow that those local struggles must know this and must include the construction of global modes of theorizing in their political practice. That is, political struggles against capitalism would be located not in (or developing from) the excessive, residual site but in the global contradiction. And what could that be other than the contradiction between the relations and forces of production? But Wilson and Dissanayake can't follow up on such questions because that would implicate them in a teleology, in Western universality, the modern meta-narrative, or "the delusion of any total space-time alternative" (4). For them, grasping the global involves "representing an intensified vision of the local situation" (5), but this is a simulacral rather than theoretical logic: Intensification doesn't lead to truth or anything other than representational transformation.

The way in which postmodern categories frame questions of globalization so as to make it impossible to examine the material structures of oppression and emancipation is even more forcefully evident in Arif Dirlik's contribution to Wilson and Dissanayake's collection. Dirlik is, of course, very well known for his forceful critiques of the leading postcolonial theorists, in particular their evasion of the logic and consequences of global capitalism and their own place within it.[3] And that is, indeed, Dirlik's concern here, but in his piece, we find the same logic whereby the intensification of globalization simultaneously intensifies the stakes of the local. Dirlik argues for a "critical localism," and he is, of course, very careful to distinguish the claims he makes on behalf of the local from nostalgic, ethnocentric attempts to retrieve an authentic cultural identity. Among other things, he insists that the local must be "a site of negotiation to abolish inequality and oppression inherited from the past" (1996, 38), thus acknowledging the need for liberation struggles to endorse at least one side of modernity. Even more, he argues that local resistance "must be translocal both in consciousness and action if it is to be meaningful at all" (41). It must rely upon knowledge of the "conjunctures that produced it," he asserts, and moreover, it is actually nothing more than the "product of the conjuncture of structures located in the same temporality but with different spatiality" (39). In the end, Dirlik seems to reduce the local to "building bricks for the future" (41).

None of this, in other words, implies placing any value upon the local as such, that is, as anything more than a space produced by global forces and wherein, as for Trotsky's theory of uneven and combined development, those forces can be concentrated and hence made visible as part of an internationalist project of clarifying and seeking to aggravate global contradictions. But there is something else involved here, as can be seen in Dirlik's association of the new concern with the local and postmodernism's rejection of teleology.

Dirlik finds not only explanatory relevance in the connection between the two ("the concern for the local gathered force simultaneously with the rejection of teleology" [1996, 27]) but also a great deal of legitimacy in the concern for the local as part of a protest against a homogenizing modernity: The "postmodern consciousness that serve[s] as enabling conditions for a contemporary localism . . . is itself an articulation not of powerlessness, but of newfound power among social groups who demand recognition of their social existence against a modernity that had denied them historical and, therefore, political presence" (27–28). And this legitimization of the local as a politically productive site is reinforced by Dirlik's speculation—directly opposed to any "building block" model of local resistance—that "the very fragmentation of the globe by capital may be turned to an advantage by resistance movements: the demand for the authentically local against its exploitation as a means to assimilation may 'overload' global capitalism, driving it to fragmentation" (41). Dirlik takes the notion of overloading from Immanuel Wallerstein, but within the conceptual framework of a local that is always already mediated by the global modern, this notion fits better with a Baudrillardian simulacral politics of "fatal strategies" than with more traditional activist approaches.

With such contradictions, Dirlik's concluding affirmation of a politics of dialogue, coalition building and Henry Giroux's "border pedagogy" are, ultimately, evasions of the question of how to theorize resistance to glocalization without an affirmation of the local and cultural. Now, at this point, perhaps some readers will ask whether all resistance is not, on some level, local. Doesn't one resist a specific assault on someone's rights or some collective set of living conditions or some crucial condition of democracy? Doesn't a revolution always overthrow a single state? Leaving aside for now the way in which postmodern articulations of the global and local serve to avoid questions of the state and sovereignty, I would concede this point in its obvious, banal sense. The question is whether the logic of resistance, the materials of resistance, and the legitimacy of resistant practices can be found in the local, cultural site. This is what postmodern cultural studies, even more forcefully in its international phase, insists upon, and this is what I do deny. Resistance, in global capitalism, is, in the first instance, only resistance in any meaningful sense insofar as it theorizes (and provides occasions for other theorizations of) the articulation of the interlocking economic, political, and ideological forms constitutive of the globe.

The most productive way of theorizing the local in these terms is by prioritizing politics, as I suggested in the introduction and first chapter in particular, as a space of accountability to the conditions of openness that make politics possible in the first place; such an accountability situates any political action and space in relation to an outside—i.e., the theoretical struggles that are implicated in politics, before which politics "appears," and that come to meet or address political actions. Such a politics must secure its conditions of possibility in the name of the level and modes of world-responsibility that contemporary social conditions require. These conditions of possibility point in several directions: toward the economic, in the first case interference with and ultimately suppression of the logic of capital and private property; toward the reciprocally constitutive political and theoretical principles themselves, engaging political action as instances of theory and practicing theory as clarification of the articulation of the political and the economic; and toward the outside, seeking not a neutral judge but a surfaced polemic aimed at making visible the relevant economic/political/ideological articulation. So, there is, of course, a "direct" antagonist, but it exists *as* this articulation, in opposition to which political action pursues a different articulation via ideology critique. In other words, an antilocalist politics starts with the reciprocal clarification of principles, concepts, and globally situated antipolitical violence (manifested always ideologically)—not in some remainder where traditional, modern and postmodern, and local and global collide and deconstruct each other.

Aihwa Ong, in *Flexible Citizenship: The Cultural Logics of Transnationality*, effectively ties together all the conceptual mechanisms of the new, internationalized cultural studies: a localized, qualified Marxism, Foucault's governmentality, transnational cultural flows, the diasporic/nomadic/border-crossing subject, and counterpublics, now situated internationally. She argues that a new mode of "flexible citizenship" has arisen in response to capitalist shifts toward "flexible production" and new, "variegated" types of sovereignty, which locate subjects in diverse ways in relation to capital and state power. An important preliminary move in Ong's synthesis is a neutralization of the political presuppositions of many of the categories of postmodern cultural studies and their normalization as empirically verifiable hypotheses.

So, for example, theories of cultural globalization (Ong focuses here on Arjun Appadurai) and the "conjuncture of postcolonial theory and diaspora studies" (1999, 13) in the United States in particular "have much to recommend them, especially for furnishing useful concepts and opening up a whole new critical area for anthropological research and theorizing" (14). What Ong rejects is the uncritical celebration of cultural globalization and diaspora: Appadurai "gives the misleading impression that everyone can take equal advantage of mobility and modern communications and that transnationality has been liberatory, in both a spatial and political sense, for all peoples" (11). In addition, she writes, the "unified moralism attached to subaltern subjects now also clings to diasporan ones, who are invariably assumed to be members of oppressed classes and therefore constitutionally opposed to capitalism and state power" (13). To such normative constructions, "which seem primarily concerned with projecting the cosmopolitan intentions of the scholar" (14), Ong consistently opposes "lived realities" (12), "particular local-global articulations" (13), "how the disciplining structures . . . condition, shape, divert and transform such subjects and their practices and produce . . . moral-political dilemmas" (14), etc.

In other words, rather than assuming that diaspora, cultural globalization, and other phenomena represent new forms of liberation, one should study their actual dynamics and effects. Ong makes this case in the name of bringing political economy back into cultural studies: "When an approach to cultural globalization seeks merely to sketch out universalizing trends rather than deal with actually existing structures of power and situated cultural processes, the analysis cries out for a sense of political economy and situated ethnography" (1999, 11). She also makes this case in the name of resisting the way in which celebratory accounts of these new forms conceal increasing "global inequalities" (11). However, by tying political economy to situated ethnography, Ong neutralizes Marxism and reduces it to a set of analytical methods compatible with other methods, rejecting its "essentializing and homogenizing narrative about capitalist culture" (16). This ultimately subordinates political economy to culture, with the purpose of helping to render more specific, detailed, and nuanced analyses—showing how "capitalism . . . has become even more deeply embedded in the ways different cultural logics give meaning to our dreams, actions, goals, and sense of how we are to conduct ourselves in the world" (16), with the focus ultimately on "human imagination and agency" (22).

For Ong, this combination of political economy and cultural analysis ultimately privileges the indeterminacy of culture. Her interest in the "reciprocal construction of practice, gender, ethnicity, race, class and nation in processes of capital accumulation" (1999, 5) appears to give causal primacy to "capital accumulation," insofar as "cultural logics" make "economic rationality" "thinkable, predictable and desirable" (5) (i.e., insofar as they justify and protect it). Nevertheless, she goes on to argue that "people's everyday actions" should be analyzed "as a form of cultural politics embedded in specific power contexts" (5). A Foucauldian micropolitics relies upon and ultimately erases any consequential political economic analysis: Precisely to the extent that capitalism is increasingly embedded in cultural logics, its effects are localized and dispersed, allowing for no coherent political logic to emerge. This accounts for Ong's preference for "transnationality" over "globalization":

A model that analytically defines the global as political economic and the local as cultural does not quite capture the *horizontal* and *relational* nature of the contemporary economic, social, and cultural processes that stream across spaces. Nor does it express their *embeddedness* in differently configured regimes of power. For this reason, I prefer to use the term *transnationality*. *Trans* denotes both moving through space or across lines, as well as chang-

ing the nature of something. Besides suggesting new relations between na-
tion-states and capital, transnationality also alludes to the *trans*versal, the
*trans*actional, the *trans*lational, and the *trans*gressive aspects of contemporary behavior and imagination that are incited, enabled, and regulated by the
changing logic of states and capitalism (4).

Thus, the "trans" denotes a regime of indeterminacy, complexity, exchange, communication, and so on, all horizontal and inside/outside relations that, in the end, reduce capitalism to an analytical starting point and
reference but in no sense a determining instance. In fact, to see political
economy primarily as embedded in culture is to make invisible the externality structuring that embeddedness, meaning the way in which the economic (as class exploitation incessantly resituated by the contradiction
between the forces and relations of production) is articulated with the political (as a space of openness contending with antipolitical violence), theory (as the space of polemics versus ideology), and culture (as grounding
versus inside/outside representational machinery) from the outside in the
sense that it is the economic logic that produces and sharpens these antagonisms along with an interest in their resolution. Only in this way—by
grasping these antagonisms in the universality of the contradiction situating them—can practices be both outside and against political-economic
forces and not merely within them (5).

This is why Marx ("the strategies of capitalist exploitation and juridical-
legal power" [Ong 1999, 19]) must also be external and opposed to Foucault ("modes of governmentality associated with state power and with
culture" [19]). The reconciliation of Marx and Foucault enables Ong to
analyze flexible citizenship, shaped within a variety of relations constituting capital, nation-state, modes of discipline, and displaced subjects. But
no matter how much one insists that the "rise of flexible concepts and
practices in modernity . . . all point directly and indirectly to the workings
of global capitalism" (19), the logic of discipline and governmentality will
always acquire both explanatory and political primacy over the logic of
wage labor because Marxism is "built" to maintain its externality to bourgeois discourses, this externality being constitutive of the class-structured
field of theory. Postmodern discourses, by contrast, are built to undermine
and cannibalize universality from within. In other words, there can be no
reconciliation between a conception of the universal as a site where antipolitical, ideological violence is grasped and challenged and a conception of the universal as a "vanishing mediator" that enables the construction of new modes of control.

Ong's neutralization of categories such as diaspora and border crosser
as strictly analytical categories, separate from the celebration of mobile
subjectivities, therefore can't be maintained: This celebration simply gets

embedded in the construction of the subject and object of the analysis. So, Ong's goal is to "redirect our study of Chinese subjects beyond an academic construction of Chineseness that is invariably or solely defined in relation to the motherland, China" and to focus on the "ever growing pluralization of Chinese identities [and thereby] subvert the ethnic absolutism born of nationalism and the processes of cultural othering that have intensified with transnationality" (1999, 24). We are back to the very valorization of diasporic identities that was rejected earlier, only now it appears as a situated, postdisciplinary "anthropological" position rather than a "universal intellectual" one. The "practices and values of diasporan Chinese are characteristic of larger questions," whereas a border-crossing anthropology "oscillating between Western belonging and non-belonging and between the local and global . . . can provide a unique angle on cultural realities" (24). In other words, Marxism, the logic of capital, and the critique of inequality are all neutralized by a celebration of the diasporic subject even more firmly embedded in the constitution of knowledge. Rather than writing as a political intellectual, with a disembedded (i.e., principled and universal) project, Ong says that she writes "as a diasporan subject moving in tangent to the claims of the home country, always posited to discern the governmentality of the state, culture, and capital and the struggle against submitting fully to any" (23). The specific positionality of the anthropologist is identical to that of the flexible citizen: exploiting the tensions and ambiguities within each constitution of power so as to continually play one site off against the other.

Consequently, Ong's argument does not support her claims that "shifts in the relationship between governmentality and sovereignty have produced zones of differentiated sovereignty," some of which are "seedbeds for counterpublics that seek to articulate visions outside the structures of state and capital" (1999, 26). These counterpublics, as Ong herself acknowledges, are the site of the nongovernmental organizations (NGOs), which "have become vehicles for the middle classes to struggle for greater democracy and to define a substantive citizenship that is based on socioeconomic and cultural rights and is midway between formal citizenship and universalist human rights prescriptions" (237). But the counterpublics, a late-twentieth-century transnational version of Habermas's early modern bourgeois public sphere, must be completely embedded in global capitalism—and there is no way they can become disembedded if their entire activity is based upon pressuring one articulation of state and capital against another and playing new forms of sovereignty off against "biopower." Reliance on Foucault here ultimately means reducing sovereignty (the site where struggles over the protection and maintenance of a space of political action take place) to the mask, alibi, and support of struggles reduced to cultural articulations.

So, Ong concludes by calling for "a kind of nomadic thinking that allows us to stay outside a given modernity and to retain a radical skepticism toward the cultural logics involved in making and remaking our worlds" (1999, 244). The perspectivalism implicit here (outside of one modernity but obviously within another), along with Ong's "Foucauldian sensibility about power" (242) (the source of all the complexity of her analysis), makes it impossible for her to be skeptical of the new middle-class transnational counterpublics: To the extent that they are located in the continual negotiations between incommensurable processes, they are beyond critique. Postmodern cultural studies, in its international version, has succeeded in going back before Marxism to the "democratic middle class" as the limit of change. But postmodern cultural studies is incapable of getting beyond the middle class because its assumption that there is nothing but contexts articulating contexts is the pillar of middle-class ideology; theoretical concepts become (ultimately self-) regulatory techniques. This is a good place to point out that Ong's critique of cultural studies for being insufficiently rigorous and concrete in its analyses of contexts is one of the standard critiques produced by cultural studies itself, brought into play whenever contradictions and suppressed polemics come to the surface. In proposing another postdisciplinary reconciliation, Ong also avoids the question of critique, which must account for some mode of disembeddedness (some outside that is not merely a product of the capacity to shift from one disciplinary site to another). Only in this way might the middle class cease to be the horizon of social change.

This is not to invalidate the descriptive value of Ong's analysis: "Mobile" articulations of international human rights and liberal democracy do account for one important tendency in global capitalism. In fact, despite some superficial differences (easily explained contextually), Ong's analysis is completely compatible with those offered by Thomas Friedman in his book (*The Lexus and the Olive Tree*) and in his columns for the *New York Times*, which also trace the emergence of a new international civil society. It is precisely because of the descriptive accuracy of such analyses that firm conceptual lines need to be drawn, in particular between progress understood as installing in piecemeal fashion a new international regime—every advance in "human rights" is simultaneously an advance in capitalism, U.S. power, and postmodern glocalization (Friedman at least is perfectly clear on this point)—and progress as a heightening, clarification, and publicization of irreconcilable contradictions.

Cosmopolitics

As Ong's book suggests, the resolution of the glocalization question in international cultural studies seems to be headed toward a reconceptualization of "cosmopolitics," which, on one level, brings the state back into the discussion as a point of convergence between economic and cultural forces and, on another level, reproduces the same "glocal" problematic by reducing the state to a point of convergence of cultural forces. I will look at one example of this trend, Pheng Cheah's "Given Culture: Rethinking Cosmopolitical Freedom in Transnationalism," which appeared in the recent volume *Cosmopolitics: Thinking and Feeling Beyond the Nation*. I will also take a detour through the Derridean underpinnings of this trend.

Cheah tries to present an alternative to positions that privilege culture, especially culture operating below and above the level of the nation-state, as a new site of resistant agency. He defends the centrality of the nation-state to political thought and action (perhaps it would be better to say he defends the centrality of the ongoing articulations of nation and state), especially in Third World countries resisting neocolonialism. Against transnationalisms that presuppose the obsolescence of the nation-state, Cheah argues that "in the absence of a world-state capable of ensuring an equitable international political and economic order, *the unevenness of political and economic globalization* makes the nation state necessary as a political agent for defending the peoples of the South from the shortfalls of neo-capitalist restructuring" (1998, 300). His support for the state is, of course, not unqualified. He opposes a "nationalist communitarianism" (290) and recognizes that the postcolonial nation-state is the stake of a constant tug-of-war between "elites and the people," comprador subordination to global capital, and "popular national mobilization" (316).

Cheah's argument has much broader aims, though, than simply pointing out that the often celebrated transnational networks of NGOs, human rights activism, and so on are "neither mass based nor firmly politically institutionalized" (1998, 312) or that political legitimacy relies not merely upon symbolic means but also upon "political-organizational and economic factors, such as law enforcement, the provision of welfare and other services by the state, and the establishment of a framework for the distribution and regulation of economic resources and capabilities to satisfy human needs" (299). He is interested in developing a theory of culture (and national culture in particular) that breaks with the understanding of culture as transcendence, an understanding in which Cheah implicates Kantian and Marxian cosmopolitanisms as well as postcolonial theories of hybridity. The understanding of culture as freedom from the given, Cheah contends, has led to or lent support to the various Enlightenment and post-Enlightenment cosmopolitanisms that resist finitude and subordinate the nation to a telos of progress. As he puts it,

philosophical modernity resolves this problem [the contradiction between natural causality and moral autonomy] by reconciling the nature/culture opposition in a natural-teleological account of culture as nature's final end for humanity. The success of culture as a utopian project depends on an anthropocentric conception of nature as a totality in harmony or accord with human normative interests: because nature is amenable to human purposes, nature itself leads humanity beyond nature (307).

This critique of the theory of culture underlying modern nationalisms (including anticolonial ones) means that Cheah is tying his political defense of the material necessity of the nation-state to a poststructuralist theory of culture. This will depend heavily upon Derridean undecidability, even if Cheah is more explicit about this in another essay (which I will address briefly here). Accepting finitude and abandoning claims to transcendence and reconciliation leads, Cheah claims, to

> the *aporia of given culture*. The aporia is as follows. Culture is supposed to be the realm of human freedom from the given. However, because human beings are finite, natural creatures, the becoming objective of culture as the realm of human purposiveness and freedom depends on forces that are radically other and beyond human control. Culture is given out of these forces. Thus, at the same time that culture embodies human freedom from the given, it is also merely given because its power over nature is premised on this gift of the radically other (1998, 308).

There is some tension between the epistemological and political consequences of the "aporia of given culture." Epistemologically, the aporia would mean that one could no longer explain culture as the formation of a coherent, self-producing subject. If culture no longer reconciles necessity and freedom, then attention would need to be paid to the conditions of possibility of constructing a space of freedom through engagement with—recognizing the irreducibility of—necessity, rather than through its conquest. But Cheah also goes on to say that "the aporia of given culture implies a vulnerability that we have not learned to accept" (1998, 308). Vulnerability to what? And what would it mean to "accept" it? This claim suggests that the notion of the "gift" is central to Cheah's thinking here: From whom is this gift received? Without going through the entire Derridean discourse on the gift as a presocial, preeconomic moment of undecidability, we can focus the question in this way: Is the relation between the radically other and our vulnerability to be taken as ontological or historical? In other words, is the vulnerability an originary condition, suppressed by the violence of modernity, or is it a product of the contradictions of capitalist global culture (for example, the fragility of the ecological system or the uncontrolled spread of military technology)? The issue here is whether Enlightenment and universality are modes of violence to be resisted or sites of political struggle.

There is, for instance, a "radical alterity" inscribed in international human rights law. The Nuremberg laws instituted in the wake of the defeat of fascism by liberal democracy have established two principles that ultimately imply such a radical alterity in the constitution of contemporary citizenship.[4] First, there is the accountability of leaders of states for crimes against humanity and, by extension, other human rights abuses. Second, there is the accountability of the actual perpetrator of human rights crimes to international judgment, i.e., the removal of the alibi of adherence to state authority. Thus, the citizen no longer appears as reflected in his or her fellow citizens within the framework of formal equality enforced by the state and checked by the exercise of popular will enabled by that equality. Instead, the citizen is reflected in the absence of the rights of others: As soon as he or she speaks or acts and as a condition of speaking and acting, the citizen confronts the state as both bearer and object of an abstract international judgment. The state, meanwhile, is no longer defined by its responsibility for the defense of borders and protection of the rights and well-being of citizens. It is, at the same time, charged with actualizing this international judgment by establishing and participating in forums that provide it with material manifestations.

In this case, the liberal democratic problematic in which the citizen looks to the state for the defense of his or her rights is transformed into a problematic in which complicity and powerlessness are dialectically conjoined. I use the term *complicity* because if states and citizens alike are accountable to the external conditions of self-governance, then the human rights granted by international law are always implicated in the violations denounced by that law. In other words, the guarantees of democracy now provided by international law are coupled with a liability for the means by which that democracy is maintained through a series of exclusions and repressions (e.g., of immigrants); at the same time, responsibility for resisting human rights violations elsewhere also rises when the elimination of those violations is posited as a condition of the world order in which democracy is possible. This enables us to account, for example, for some of the contradictions in the NATO war against Serbia—a war explicitly justified in the name of democracy and human rights, which, because it had to be carried out democratically (with popular support or at least a lack of popular resistance), rendered the citizens of those countries literally complicit with the destruction wrought.

I also use the term *powerlessness* because this juridical structure in effect restores the international state system, in its most hierarchical form, as the limit of politics. This occurs because the structure actually presupposes the suppression of democratic political power; the enforcement of human rights law is dictated (hence raised above democratic contestation) and linked only to questions of means, reducing politics to criminology. This is why international human rights can easily be seen as the other side of capitalist globalization. As the NATO actions make clear, the universality of human rights in practice grants all rights to the enforcer of those rights, an enforcer who, like Hobbes's Leviathan, is, in the last instance, unaccountable and who emerges as the defender of those property rights that are by definition untouchable as the foundation of the law itself. Furthermore, the positing of the United States as the last-ditch defender of human rights also makes this nation the defender of world democracy by definition; as a/the democracy, which can only carry out a democratic war, it must simultaneously make every effort to render such wars marginal to social and political life (i.e., to remove citizens from decisionmaking and consequences). In turn, of course, this requires that the war be not only extraordinarily destructive for the other side but also "democratically" focused on the civilians' support for their government. Thus, the extension of democracy implicit in human rights law and politics simultaneously renders citizens increasingly complicit in the global policies of their governments and increasingly removed from practical, collective control of those policies.

At the same time, the Third World critiques of the imperialist nations of the North that this structure produces are implicated in the structure as well. To the extent that such critiques are themselves legitimated by an international human rights cosmopolitics, they are predicated upon the failure of resistance on the part of those political agencies in the name of an obligation to which those critiques are issued—that is, a failure to acquire the power needed to position the citizens of those states as defenders of the self-determination that international equality would require. Thus, each critique of the North, of the G-7, and so on depends upon and, at least on one level, reproduces the failure of internationalist solidarity that made the international human rights "juridical form" possible in the first place. All of this means that the "human rights worldview" is ideological, for it structures any action or text that can appear publicly. But this, of course, doesn't mean that it hasn't in actuality destroyed the modern democratic subject as the basis of politics.

Put another way, the subject of the human rights worldview must provide a reckoning of his or her active or passive support for antipolitical violence, antipolitical violence that is, furthermore, constitutive of the very legal and political discourses (human rights as ground, culmination, and limit of democracy) designed to contest it. This antinomic a priori cannot be resolved; it can only be negated through the exposure of its inner, "esoteric" core. The antinomy between sovereignty as simplest element and normative basis of international society and as condition of possibility of international values of peace, cooperation, and rights (and hence subordinate to those values) and the consequent antinomy of complicity and powerlessness produce a space that implicates and cannibalizes the position of external judgment they also presuppose. So, for example, human rights can only be politically effective if and when its advocates claim to be above politics; it can provide a space for proof and evidence and hence judgment only if it disavows the theory and knowledge that opens such a space in the first place.

The core of these antinomies is the unity of necessity and violence in the wage relation. This is the relation that requires daily ratification and thereby undermines the distinction between coercion and consent, that produces the conditions of its own reproduction and hence makes knowledge and apologia inseparable, and that requires a constant intellectual and material attack on the conditions of collective power required for submitting all hierarchical relations to public inspection. A certain polemical line—interested in pursuing questions of coercion and consent, knowledge and justification, and power and authority to their "logical conclusions"—is thus cut off at the roots. The human rights worldview produces and conceals the antinomy of complicity and powerlessness while rendering necessary, as historically concrete "radical alterity," the pursuit of that polemical line as it is cut off categorically (in actually existing relations between power, knowledge, and principles). That is, radical alterity is ideology critique as the foundational mode of political action.

Such an understanding would make it possible to engage international human rights as, first of all, placing all actions before an outside. Returning to the implications of Nuremberg (the initial historical move, I would contend, toward undermining the neutrality and neutralizations of universality) requires situating, for example, strictly "medical" categories under a theoretical-political lens. And it does so in a foundational way, not simply in terms of abuses: The very possibility of the autonomy of medicine is in question. Here, I would suggest that a more minimalistic account of human rights (rather than one that seeks to accumulate more and more rights—social, economic, cultural environmental, etc.) is going to be the more radical one. International human rights covers actions carried out by those in possession of political-economic power in the name of sovereignty, which undermine the international conditions of peace and justice. This is precisely what places internal actions before an outside. So, for example, since torture undermines the visibility of state-citizen relations, one cannot take (among other things) the juridical and penal practices of that state at their word, and it is therefore impossible to know what that state might be capable of doing.

In this case, judgments regarding international human rights (those pertaining to the legitimacy of given concentrated [state and/or corporate] practices before the world) make a demand of those implicated in the necessity of those judgments (meaning those who communicate effectively and whose communications—as "citizens"—are given, in principle, an a priori legitimacy). Such judgments demand that the "speaker" recover and clarify the terms and conditions within the political forms enabling such communications that make pacts, alliances, covenants, and other modes of cooperation (in the name of peace and justice) necessary and possible. What, in other words, already places any speaker in a position of international judgment?

Political actions aimed at international human rights must make yet another move, constituting the outside itself as a space where the contrast between principles and practices brought to light by human rights organizations are given the form of political judgment. The autonomy of states (or, for that matter, "medicine") has its legitimacy in human rights law, as does the inviolability of rights—but only when that legitimacy is constituted by a making visible of the necessity of that autonomy in relation to the heteronomy constitutive of its grounding in other autonomies. The outside is constituted when the functionality of an individual's position (one is compelled to speak about x as a citizen, as a doctor . . . , as one seeking pacts, alliances, and covenants in the name of peace and justice) requires that he or she step beyond that functionality in order to make visible what has been occluded by the concentration of political-economic and ideological violence (the organization through mutual protection of autonomous states, property owners, institutions, etc.). In this case, in the name of the radical alterity of what has been violently rendered invisible and silent, one calls for the judgment of others as well as opening a political space for those lacking a priori legitimacy. More important, one also works to institute the co-constitution via the reciprocal polemic of actor and judge in world politics.

I will briefly address one recent and prominent instance of international human rights law and politics—the charges brought against and the detention of Augusto Pinochet. This example is productive to the extent that it splits Chileans into adherents of state sovereignty and those seeking international judgment, and it brings the scene of international judgment inside; it posits the citizens of the United States (in particular) as bystanders, who have taken responsibility for neither action nor judgment. And this was only possible insofar as the Spanish court relied very closely upon the letter of the law pertaining to its own rights of judgment (its right to pursue crimes committed against Spanish citizens, its extradition treaty with Great Britain, etc.). The unwillingness to step beyond this functionality, though, also accounts for the limitations of the actions against Pinochet: Liberal democracy as the rule of law is the implicit telos of human rights law and activism when there is no space for judging the judges. Here, I don't just mean corresponding actions against the criminals of Francisco Franco's regime, those in the British and U.S. administrations complicit in Pinochet's crimes, or public support for "taking the next step," i.e., extending the "same" juridical logic: A political response to the Pinochet case would make visible the political-economic and "Constitutional" limits to instituting the actor/judge split in, say, American politics in relation to its outside.

Returning to Cheah, I would point out that his understanding of radical alterity is, in fact, ontological rather than historical. As he states, the "foreclosure of the fact that it is in finitude that human beings qua finite corporal creatures are given life informs the culturalism and economism of old cosmopolitanisms and their new hybrid successors in postcolonial cultural studies" (1998, 323). Cheah, then, does not privilege the nation-state merely for what might appear to be a historically contingent reason: It is presently the only political agent with the capacity to offer at least some resistance to global capitalism. For him, the nation-state is a privileged site of responsibility within the cosmopolitical force field, a "responsibility to given culture [which] is (a)prior(i) to all forms of cultural agency that are based on the axiom of humanity's freedom from the given" (322). The nation-state is defended because of its privileged relation to culture, understood as a "sheaf [that] can denote a cluster of disparate strands as well as the process of gathering" (323). Culture, in other words, is the site of interwoven and incommensurable forces, and transcendence of the given is strictly banned: The global sheaf is not "the global capitalist system as a factual totality awaiting to be sublated into a global proletarian consciousness. . . . It is a non-transcendable moving ground extending across the globe in which political, cultural and economic forces are brought into relation" (324).

This further means that the postcolonial nation-state is not in any way in opposition to global capitalism: "The processes of globalization are not antipathetic to the postcolonial nation-state even though they threaten to recompradorize it" (Cheah 1998, 323). The postcolonial nation-state is a permanently vacillating one, "persistently modulating from being an agent for resisting international capital to being a collaborator of global economic restructuring" (324). The cosmopolitanism Cheah rejects as a founding principle can then return, sheaflike, as an uneasy support for the nation-state in the form of Third World feminists, who, although grounded in national culture, "remake the state in the image of a popular-feminist counter-nationalism only by linking up with a larger global network, all the while remaining aware that these persistently shifting global alignments can also undermine the postcolonial state that they are trying to save from neo-colonialism" (320–321). The postcolonial nationalism Cheah proposes can hence be seen to be working according to a series of negations: The nation-state negates global capitalism; the nation negates its naturally posited link to the state so as to challenge its always imminent if not actual subordination to global capitalism; cosmopolitan principles (e.g., feminism) negate the potentially fundamentalist and authoritarian tendency of the state (especially, although Cheah doesn't mention this, insofar as it actually tries to resist capitalism within the nation-state form); a specifically national feminism negates the cosmopolitan politics (the NGOs) tied to the metropole and capital; and, finally, the national feminist negates any attempt to complete or unify the nation, constantly struggling to maintain the readiness of the nation to challenge regressive, recompradorized state manifestations. The Third World feminist is therefore not relevant so much for the pertinence of the knowledge she provides or her ability to organize effectively revolutionary struggles but as a kind of "degree zero" of undecidability: The Third World feminist resists the closure of all the circulating sociopolitical categories and thus prevents the heterogeneous cultural forces from ever taking on a determinate form.

In this way, Cheah's work very effectively ties together the discourses on international civil society/public sphere and those of the alternatives of local culture by redescribing the nation-state as a site of undecidability and resistance to closure. Cheah's dependence upon Derrida's recent political thinking (in particular his "The Force of Law: The 'Mystical Foundations of Authority'") is implicit here, but it is more explicit in an earlier essay, "Violent Light: The Idea of Publicness in Modern Philosophy and in Global Neocolonialism." In that piece, Cheah articulates the relation between transcendence and immanence through Derridean undecidability and incalculability: "The necessity of the ethical would first and foremost be an openness or vulnerability to the constitutive possibility of newness to which reason then responds by articulating norms and ideals. The norms and ideals of reason are thus always marked by and undergo the test of an ineradicable because constitutive undecidability" (1995, 182). He also describes the Third World feminist as the site of "interminable renegotiation with the double-bind of her given culture" (182). Before concluding my discussion of Cheah, therefore, I will address Derrida's text.

Change, Derrida announces early on, is effected not "in the rather naïve sense of a calculated, deliberate and strategically controlled intervention, but in the sense of a maximum intensification of a transformation in progress" (1992, 9). As in all postmodern thought, the assumption behind Derrida's thinking is that since "the origin of authority, the foundation or ground, the position of the law can't by definition rest on anything but themselves, they are themselves a violence without ground" (14). Thus, because any founding is based on violence and "mystical foundations," one must not posit a will or purpose behind it; it is a fiction located beyond the question of legitimacy or illegitimacy. Justice, then, is deconstruction insofar as deconstruction resists the ultimate injustice of connecting doer with deed, of explicitly founding or deepening an earlier founding of a space of power and accountability. Instead, Derrida sets in place an "infinite" responsibility, which "exceeds calculations, rules, programs, anticipations and so forth" (27).

In opposition to Derridean "singularity," I would argue for political-economic universality. To make the contrast clear, I will examine Derrida's essay a bit more carefully. There, he argues that "not only *must* we calculate . . . but we *must* take it as far as possible, beyond the place we find ourselves and beyond the already identifiable zones of morality or politics or law, beyond the distinction between national and international, public and private, and so on" (1992, 28). So, the "decision to calculate is not of the order of the calculable, and must not be" (24); in other words, the decision to calculate (to follow rules, norms, knowledge, etc.) comes from the incalculable, and calculation itself, through a "maximum intensification," takes one back out to the incalculable. But the outside of calculation is its conditions of possibility, which are secured in advance of any decision to calculate. These conditions of possibility are, first, that rules and norms undergird political accountability rather than suppressing it: In other words, rules and norms are to open sites of judgment by setting boundaries around a space where questions can be focused and not by answering questions. So, calculation in the sense of applying and extending rules and norms doesn't lead to any "beyond"—it leads to the establishment of the historically pertinent question in its publicness. Second, knowledge, which does seek to answer questions, does so in order to present new, historically relevant questions: Arriving at the limits of knowledge also leads to no beyond but to qualified, eliminated, or strengthened courses of action, on one side, and to a renewed inquiry into theoretical presuppositions, on the other.

For Derrida, going beyond is not totally unregulated: Interminable but not total politicization requires that "each advance in politicization obliges one to reconsider, and so to reinterpret the very foundations of law such as they had previously been calculated or delimited" (1992, 28). Politicization is thus, at the same time, a return to, recovery of, and resituating of foundational categories. This all takes place on new historical terrain, and here is where Derrida takes the opportunity to say—against depoliticizing versions of deconstruction—that "nothing seems to me less outdated than the classical emancipatory ideal" (28). He also takes the opportunity to describe this new historical terrain, first of all stating that "beyond these identified territories of juridico-politicization on the grand scale, beyond all self-serving interpretations, beyond all determined and particular reappropriations of international law, other areas must constantly open up that at first can seem like secondary or marginal areas" (28).

What is *this* beyond? The classical emancipatory ideal is identified with those "identified territories" ("the Declaration of the Rights of Man . . . the abolition of slavery," etc.), so is opening a beyond of those territories a critique of politicizations that remain there? This tension, then, becomes an apparent conflict or contradiction between the grand scale and the seemingly secondary or marginal areas. Does one need to take sides here? First of all, let's look at these areas:

> laws on the teaching and practice of languages, the legitimization of canons, the military use of scientific research, abortion, euthanasia, problems of organ transplant, extra-uterine conception, bioengineering, medical experimentation, the social treatment of AIDs, the macro- or micro-politics of drugs, the homeless, and so on, without forgetting, of course, the treatment of what we call animal life, animality (Derrida 1992, 29).

What unites these areas aside from their seeming marginality, and how are they contrasted to the identified territories? And, again, are these areas beyond the classical emancipatory ideal (which would then be not outdated but strictly limited in its projections), or do they simply require more far-reaching reinterpretations? Should these marginal areas move to the center—or do they signify the absence of any center?

The main difference between the identified territories and the marginal areas is that in the former (the line leading from the Declaration of the Rights of Man to contemporary human rights documents), the law and politics are extended into areas that had previously been neutralized as constitutive of the domain of law and politics, such as the limits of state sovereignty. Thus, human rights can be formulated as the necessary condition for political freedom and international peace, which can, in turn, justify expanded human rights in the name of a more stable and viable mode of sovereignty. The marginal areas, meanwhile, involve the extension of law and politics into domains that had previously been regulated administratively, medically, and scientifically; that is, they involve "border disputes" between law, politics, knowledge, bureaucracy, and so forth.

Therein lies their undecidability: Scientific research is always already militarized; the military is always already "scientificized"; and if law and politics are to intervene in these negotiations, they must already be scientificized and militarized (and the other domains juridicalized and politicized) as well. But as soon as we formulate the distinction in this way (between territories already covered juridically/politically and areas with undecidable borders), we must immediately deconstruct it, as if the very crimes against humanity that led to the first major expansions of international law were not thoroughly implicated administratively, scientifically, medically, etc. So we are now faced with a single, postmodern problem— the marginal has moved to the center, meaning there is no center. We are left with this question: What happens when the various faculties, disciplines, boundaries, etc., can neither be thought outside of each other nor integrated and totalized in a new hierarchy and constitution of boundaries?

So, the identified territories lose their definition, and the classical emancipatory ideal is without any discernible location. This is confirmed by Derrida's dismissive reference to the "self-serving interpretations" located in the identified territories and even more so by the strikingly different form of politicization proposed for the marginal areas: "This marginality also signifies that a violence, indeed a terrorism and other forms of hostage taking are at work" (1992, 28). Is this, now, to be taken as a mode of reinterpreting the very foundations of law? It can only be the performative reenactment of the impossibility of any founding, since any founding "always maintains within itself some irruptive violence, it no longer responds to the demands of theoretical rationality" (27). The classical emancipatory ideal cannot be anything more than the effect, the retroactive positing established by this "irruptive violence."

Derrida is right, of course, to say that "justice . . . doesn't wait," in the sense that a "just decision"

> cannot furnish itself with infinite information and the unlimited knowledge of conditions, rules or hypothetical imperatives that could justify it. And even if it did have all that at its disposal, even if it did give itself the time, all the time and the necessary facts about the matter, the moment of *decision, as such*, always remains a finite moment of urgency and precipitation, since it must not be the consequence or the effect of this theoretical or historical knowledge, of this reflection or this deliberation, since it always marks the interruption of the juridico- or ethico- or politico-cognitive deliberation that precedes it, that *must* precede it (1992, 26).

But the decision interrupts a preceding deliberation by taking sides within that space of deliberation in the name of maintaining, protecting, and actualizing not an a priori incalculability but the conditions of possibility of knowledge, theory, and principled action structuring that space. That taking of sides renders the decision (along with knowledge, action, theory, etc.) finite and places it before an outside, which will, in turn, be interested in situating that space in relation to a different set of coordinates, cut short or enabled by that decision.

This set of relations (between knowledge, action, and theory) is refounded with every politicization, whereas Derrida's conception of politicization serves to further hybridize these boundaries. In this, of course, he is at one with powerful tendencies, which are also implicated in the marginal areas he cites. The purpose of focusing on the marginal areas, of bringing them to the center, and of using the principles of the center (the classical emancipatory ideal) to introduce the marginal areas as an irremediable decentering is precisely to singularize, pluralize, and exceptionalize that ideal and thereby reduce it to a representational mechanism within information flows, where the question suddenly becomes: Are you for maximum intensification or a conservative in favor of fixed boundaries? Maximum intensification is very attractive, and it allows for all kinds of esoteric mysteries and intimacies to coincide with managerial control and petit bourgeois privileges,[5] but its purpose is to undermine the classical emancipatory ideal. And it does so precisely by presenting the "New Times" in their overwhelming facticity: How, for instance, can the complications of the political, juridical, administrative, medical, and scientific in, say, reproductive technologies and practices be addressed otherwise than via a singular ungrounded act of judgment?

Assuming that one is not primarily interested in regulatory and managerial details (which have indeed been reduced to case-by-case methods), one has to ask how antipolitical violence—economic exploitation in its concentrated political form, aimed precisely at the conditions of political decidability (the historical and polemical articulation of theory, action, and knowledge)—appears on the same surface as the classical emancipatory ideal, both implicating and technologizing that ideal and suppressing its articulation on the new historical terrain. It is not impossible, for example, to explain how international conflicts over patents on pharmaceutical products articulate certain historical concepts of productivity, property, legality, science, bureaucracy, sovereignty, subjectivity, and so on so as to further alienate social capacities from needs. It is more difficult but still not impossible to theorize the co-constitution of those categories so that their relations are reconstituted in terms not of border crossing or hybridity but of the space of science *as* accountable to emerging contradictions in sovereignty and the space of legality *as* accountable to emerging antinomies in privatized science, etc., and, moreover, to do so in a way that defends the fundamental space of politics and theory (which makes reconstitution possible in the first place) against new concentrations of antipolitical violence. In other words, antipolitical violence tries to exclude and destroy not singularity but the conditions of power, accountability, and theory coming together. So, where Derrida places undecidability, there is pedagogical accountability.

To return to Cheah once more, I would argue that his refusal to reconsider the question of transcendence, as the theorization of the conditions of action as a prerequisite to legitimate action, leaves him with a completely formal description of the place of the nation-state. So, he cannot ask, for example, what kind of Third World feminism might take its implication in national culture and incompatibility with the consolidation of state power as an enabling (i.e., pedagogical) site. If this is something other than a site of undecidability, it is a site of class struggle, where, ultimately, one set of rules, norms, and knowledges contests another. Thus, positing sovereignty as a site of an undecidable double bind undermines the possibility of theorizing sovereignty as a site where internationally determined, class-articulated, and opposing agendas contend. This consideration might have brought Cheah closer to a theorization of the central contradiction of global capitalism: the surfacing of the categories of political-economic universality so that their recovery, seizure, and implication in their theoretical conditions is a precondition of action, versus their privatization and subordination to capitalist economic, political, and economic priorities. This is the form, I am contending, in which the contradiction between the forces and relations of productions appears today, and it is hence determinative of future forms of class struggle within, over, and against globalization.

Universality: Singular or Political Economic?

I will conclude by discussing Slavoj Zizek's most recent book, *The Ticklish Subject: The Absent Centre of Political Ontology,* and his challenge to oppose "universality" to "globalization." In this work, Zizek makes by far his most sustained political statement to date, developing the implications of the Lacanian-Marxist synthesis he has been defending for years across a very wide range of contemporary discourses and issues. He is most interested in what he asserts is an unfashionable defense of universality and the "Cartesian subject," and I will focus on these issues in my critique of Zizek as well. In dealing with his complex position, I will work through the various levels of his argument, in order to clarify exactly what he is defending and why. I will approach this as follows. First, I will address what we could call Zizek's general political horizon, as presented in his book: his explicit defense of Marxism's basic critique of capitalism and of socialist political aims. Second, I will consider what I would call his general political ethics; here, I will discuss Zizek's understanding of political space and the political act. Third, I will address his more conjunctural political positions, such as his article on the Kosovo conflict and a brief but symptomatic mention of sexual harassment. Fourth, I will discuss his defense of a Lacanian conception of subjectivity as part of his larger defense of the Cartesian-Kantian-Hegelian abstract subject. Fifth, I will consider his use of Lacanian mapping to sort out a variety of possible attitudes and responses to contemporary capitalism and the breakdown of "Oedipalization"—for example, his tracing of the ethical and political logics of desire versus drive. Sixth and last, I will discuss the specifically Lacanian ethics of "passion" that Zizek proposes. This final point is perhaps the key to grasping the viability and implications of Zizek's synthesis. My purpose in concluding here is to take Zizek up on his insistence that we place issues of global capitalism, universality, Marxism, and revolutionary politics squarely on the contemporary theoretical agenda. I also want, through a critique of his understanding of these issues, to propose a different way of doing so than Zizek would allow.

In *The Ticklish Subject*, Zizek defends some central Marxist theses far more forcefully than he has done elsewhere. Although he has always brought the logic of capital into his analyses, linking it to central tendencies within postmodern culture, to my knowledge this is the first explicit endorsement of the necessity of socialist transformation that Zizek has issued. In his critique, late in the book, of the ideologists of the "new risk society" for ignoring capitalism as the seemingly "natural" frame within which "risks" are taken, Zizek goes on to ask (rhetorically, of course),

> Is not the conclusion to be drawn that in the present global situation, in which private corporations outside public political control are making decisions which can affect us all, even up to our chances for survival, the only solution lies in a kind of direct socialization of the productive process—in moving toward a society in which global decisions about the fundamental orientation of how to develop and use productive capacities at the disposal of society would somehow be made by the entire collective of people affected by such decisions? (1999a, 350–351).

He further contends that "because *the depoliticized economy is the disavowed 'fundamental fantasy' of postmodern politics*—a properly political *act* would necessarily entail the repoliticization of the economy: within a given situation, a gesture counts as an *act* only insofar as it disturbs ("traverses") its fundamental fantasy" (Zizek 1999a, 355). Here, we can see the way in which he is uniting Marxian and Lacanian concepts, implicitly asserting their essential compatibility. At the same time, he makes it clear that "I am not preaching a simple return to the old notion of class struggle and socialist revolution," and he accepts "the breakdown of the Marxist notion that capitalism itself generates the force that will destroy it in the guise of the proletariat" (352). In fact, his call for "the subordination of the process of production to social control—the radical *repoliticization of the economy*" (353) is Zizek's preliminary answer to "the question of how it is really possible to undermine the global capitalist system"; this question, at any rate, "is not a rhetorical one—maybe it is not really possible, at least *not* in the foreseeable future" (352).

At this point, I simply want to raise a couple of questions. First, should we take Zizek's desire for a radical repoliticization of the economy as a disavowed one—that is, is the desire presented as a veil for the real desire, which is to declare it impossible? This matter should be considered because the relation between old notions and new conditions is a little uneven here: For example, Zizek urges us to "reassert the old Marxist critique of 'reification': today, emphasizing the depoliticized 'objective' economic logic against allegedly 'outdated' forms of ideological passions is *the* predominant ideological form, since ideology is always self-referential, that is, it always defers itself through a distance toward an Other dismissed and denounced as 'ideological'" (1999a, 355). Therefore, the old critique of reification is good, and so are ideological passions. Furthermore, "instead of celebrating the new freedoms and responsibilities brought about by the 'second modernity' it is much more crucial to focus on what *remains the same* . . . the inexorable logic of Capital" (354). Thus, many old things are equally relevant and valid today. Why, then, is class struggle and socialist revolution a genuinely dated concept against which Zizek's discourse defers itself? A second and related question involves the status of knowledge in the radical repoliticization Zizek supports—that is, is knowledge connected in any way to political struggle? I ask this question both as a way of beginning to address the rather spectatorial and ironic tone of Zizek's discussion and also as a way of considering the consequence of his argument that the "symbolic big Other" supportive of modern subjectivity is disintegrating (354). This exposes the central contradiction of Zizek's Marx-Lacan synthesis: his assumption that it is precisely the disintegrating subject that is the truth of modern subjectivity and hence the source of progressive possibilities.

The question of the old but relevant (the recovery or retrieval of fundamental possibilities or events) is central to Zizek's theorization of the conditions and specificity of politics. In his argument for a "progressive Eurocentrism" and a "leftist appropriation of the European political tradition" (1999a, 207), he argues that we can "identify as the core of this tradition the unique gesture of democratic political subjectivization" (207). In this, Zizek is drawing on Jacques Ranciere's understanding of the political as the act in which those "who have no part," (i.e., the dispossessed upon whose invisibility the political—for Ranciere, the "police"—order is founded) stage their exclusion and present it as the "whole." However, Zizek could just as easily have made this point by reference to the other thinkers he uses in his discussion of political subjectivization: Etienne Balibar and his notion of "equaliberty" as the founding moment of the political, Alain Badiou and his understanding of the "Truth-Event" as the emergence of the political founding act beyond the objectively given whole, or Ernesto Laclau's "hegemony." All of these thinkers provide some version of the singular universality that Zizek places at the center of the political. Rather than adhering to universal ideals and principles, the assertion of singular universality involves splitting the universal into its two sides: the abstract, objectivist, ultimately antipolitical side that supports the status quo and the assertion of the excluded part whose self-assertion falsifies the prevailing universal while representing its hidden truth and real basis.

Zizek's relation to these theorists of political subjectivization is complex. He supports their general project of theorizing the political in such a way so as not to reduce it to some prepolitical principle (of morality, ethnicity, community, distribution, etc.); he is also very sympathetic to the notion of the singular universal they all develop in different ways; and even more, he appropriates their problematics and vocabulary into his own discourse in a very systematic way throughout the book. At the same time, despite his own argument for a recovery of the political "as such," he points to what he sees as a contradiction in these theorists "between proposing a neutral formal frame that describes the working of the political field, without implying any specific *pris de parti*, and the prevalence given to a particular leftist political practice" (1999a, 174). Zizek's point is that the contrast between a properly political and political practices that are inauthentic in various ways is ultimately a kind of Kantianism that evades the issue of the contamination of the "purely" political with the possibility and actuality of the exercise of power and responsibility:

> "Justice," the rectification of the fundamental and constitutive ontological injustice of the universe, is presented as an unconditional impossible demand, possible only against the background of its own impossibility: the moment a political movement pretends to fully realize Justice, to translate it into an actual state of things, to pass from the spectral *dèmocratie á venir* to "actual democracy," we are in totalitarian catastrophe (233).

Thus, such a politics ultimately reinforces the place of the Master, the addressee of the impossible "demand."

Against this, Zizek argues that we must recognize that the antipolitical order of being is itself politically constituted. Put differently, what the "police" and the "Master" are doing is itself politics—a politics based on the disavowal of "the invisible support of its own public police apparatus" (1999a, 234) but a politics nevertheless. More generally, he contends, what the "proto-Kantians" miss "is the 'excess' of the founding gesture of the Master without which the positive order of the *service des biens* cannot maintain itself. What we are aiming at here is the 'non-economical' excess of the Master over the smooth functioning of the positive police order of being" (236). This Master "is ultimately an imposter," but nevertheless, the "heroism of the authentic Master consists precisely in his willingness to assume this impossible position of ultimate responsibility, and to take upon himself the implementation of unpopular measures which prevent the system from disintegrating" (237). Zizek invokes Lenin here, whose "greatness" lay in the way that, in contrast to hysterical revolutionary fervour caught in the vicious cycle, the fervour of those who prefer to stay in opposition and prefer (publicly or secretly) to avoid the burden of taking over, of accomplishing the shift from subversive activity to responsibility for the smooth running of the social edifice, he heroically embraced the onerous task of actually *running the state*— of making all the necessary compromises, but also taking the necessary harsh measures, to assure that the Bolshevik power would not collapse (237).

Was Lenin an imposter, albeit a necessary one, and was his mastery an illusion? This would seem to be the inescapable conclusion, insofar as Zizek, while referring to the authentic Master, doesn't offer any way of distinguishing him from the inauthentic one. Is Lenin's power constituted by "its own disavowed obscene supplement" (1999a, 235)? Zizek is making a necessary argument for political authority and responsibility against the "proto-Kantians," but, at this point, they seem to be functioning as his own disavowed supplement—they are the hysterics against which Lenin's mastery is deployed, even though they are the source of all of Zizek's political thinking in this book. Furthermore, Zizek seems to be falling into the trap he warned against in his critique of the proto-Kantians of positing some neutral field of mastery before any taking of positions. More specifically, his position here looks a great deal like Max Weber's "ethics of responsibility," as opposed to an "ethics of ultimate ends."[6] The ambivalence of the singular universal (hysterical or revolutionary?) corresponds to the ambivalence of the Master (authentic responsibility or fraud?).

Starting from these contradictions and looking forward to the next stage of the discussion, I will raise the following questions. First, what are the "ultimate responsibilities" that a rejuvenated Left will have to take upon itself? Second, which singular universals will contribute to the repoliticization of the economy and yet not simply impose empty demands upon the Master?

A preliminary response to these objections and answers to these questions would seem to be found in Zizek's claim that "*there is no Order of Being as a positive ontologically consistent whole*, the false semblance of such an Order relies on the self-obliteration of the Act. In other words, the gap of the Act is not introduced into the order of Being afterwards: it is there all the time as the condition that actually *sustains* every Order of Being" (1999a, 238). That is, the subjectivization of the universal does not come in opposition to some positive order of being, an impersonal, merely "technological" or bureaucratic structure; it is already constitutive of, even if suppressed within, that order. The split within and constitutive of the subject is the split constitutive of reality itself. The difference between progressive and reactionary politics would then, presumably, be that the latter hides behind the semblance of an ontologically consistent whole whereas the former openly recognizes the constitutive split—a position that, politically at least, would bring Zizek very close to Laclau and Butler. In that case, what precisely is the task of progressive politics? Should the Master be forced out into the open? And if so, why—to effect a genuine struggle between old and new Masters or to demonstrate the Master's fraudulence? To put it another way, is the assertion of the singular universal the initial move in the struggle against a real master? (In which case, what are the second, third, etc., moves? And will the assertion of one singular universal after another somehow lead to the heart of power?) Or is it a gesture indicating the fictionality of power and mastery or of sovereignty to remind ourselves of Butler's argument, with which Zizek is in great sympathy?

In the first case (i.e., the struggle against the Master is real), we would need a detour through theory and knowledge—which singular universal, why, and as part of what broader project? In the latter case, the struggle for power becomes both utterly naked and completely formal, a sheer "ethics of responsibility" at best, a simulacral struggle at worst. To put this yet another way: If the problem with the proto-Kantians is "the reduction of the subject to the process of *subjectivization*" (Zizek 1999a, 232), the difficulty for Zizek is determining whether the subject is a prepolitical force that reduces politics to a mere semblance of subjectivity or whether the subject is always already political, in which case wherein lies the specifically political logic in its striving toward "authentic Mastery"?

A good way to bring some of Zizek's more conjunctural analyses and polemics into the discussion at this point is through an examination of a brief reference he makes to sexual harassment. Zizek is discussing Lacan's claim that "there is no sexual relationship" (1999a, 285):

> The point of the scene of primordial seduction is not that adults accidentally infringe upon the child, disturbing his fragile balance with a display of their *jouissance*—the point, rather, is that the child's gaze is included, comprehended, from the very beginning in the situation of adult parental sexuality. . . . The parental sexual display, far from unintentionally disturbing the child's equilibrium, is in a way "there only for the child's gaze" (285).

The point of the larger discussion of which this comment is a part is to supplement Butler's account of subjectivity as equivalent to subjection. For Zizek, the gap or "fundamental fantasy, in which the subject is formed through the desire of the Other, precedes and anchors subjectivity" (1999a, 289). I will address the implications of this thesis in a moment. First, I will continue with the passage I began quoting:

We are dealing with the structure of a temporal loop: there is sexuality not only because of a gap between adult sexuality and the child's unprepared gaze traumatized by its display, but because this child's perplexity continues to sustain adult sexual activity itself. This paradox also explains the blind spot of the topic of sexual harassment: *there is no sex without an element of "harassment"* (of the perplexed gaze violently shocked, traumatized, by the uncanny character of what is going on). The protest against sexual harassment, against violently imposed sex, is thus ultimately *the protest against sex as such*: if one subtracts from the sexual interplay its painfully traumatic character, the remainder is simply no longer sexual. "Mature" sex between the proverbially consenting adults, deprived of the traumatic element of shocking imposition, is by definition *desexualized*, turned into mechanic coupling (286).

The topic of sexual harassment has a blind spot. First of all, then, the topic becomes subject—strangely, in the singularly universal claim of bringing private desire into the domain of law and politics, this act disappears into a reified topic, to be further reified as a blind topic/subject. Furthermore, this blind spot is one that presumably should not exist, for it calls into question the legitimacy of the subject, rather than being a productive site for democratic identifications. This is evident in the assumption that *sexual harassment* is not only a contradiction in terms (and it might also be observed that the same happens to rape if we read the passage carefully) but also a contradiction that must destroy its own conditions of possibility: If the topic has its way, there will be no sex at all to complain about, just mechanical coupling (a "positive order of being"?). Of course, a certain kind of feminist critique (like that of Catharine MacKinnon) could agree with Zizek's claim that the "topic" of sexual harassment is a protest against sex "as such" but only if we add to that sex as (presently) constituted as the eroticization of inequality and domination. This is the point for Zizek: Sexuality has to be constitutive; it can't be constituted. Even more important, it is precisely sex as a violent, irreducible remainder that is constitutive, and we need to trace the consequences of this position in Zizek's discourse.

If we continue the analysis of sexual harassment, we can make the case that this harassment corresponds to a central tendency in late capitalism—the transformation of private, presumably constitutive modes of violence into public questions. This tendency is parallel but, I will stress, not identical to the one that Zizek, early in his book, cites approvingly, albeit in a somewhat less celebratory manner than the advocates of "radical democracy" (first of all Laclau and Mouffe); i.e., it is the expansion of the universal through the infusion of an ever widening content. This is also a crucial conceptual hinge in the move from Marxism to post-Marxism, from the Marxist "symptomal reading" regarding the bourgeois content of human rights, a "quick dismissal of the universal for itself as ideological," to Laclau, who "insists upon the gap between the empty universality and its determinate content. . . . What about the human rights of women, children, members of non-white races, criminals, madmen? Each of these supplementary gestures does not simply *apply* the notion of human rights to ever new domains . . . but retroactively *redefines the very notion of human rights*" (Zizek 1999a, 180). For Laclau, this is the (radical) democratizing process intrinsic to modernity, producing more and more subjects in the struggle for hegemony; Zizek supports it because it renders visible the constitutive gap of subjectivity.

As I just suggested, though, making seemingly constitutive modes of (private) violence visible and public (slavery, the exploitation at the site of production, or in the case of sexual harassment, the maintenance of sexual difference as a means of enhancing and concealing inequality in the workplace) is parallel but not identical to the expansion of universal subjectivity. Its main effect is not to produce new subjectivities, whether free or split. To defend this point, I will focus on the broader notion of sexual harassment, that of the hostile environment, a concept that is obviously open to interpretation in any instance. What, exactly, is "hostile"? For whom? And what makes it systematic? Here, I will offer a couple of simple points. First, the more politicized a workplace is in feminist terms, the broader the applicability of the concept of hostility will be. Actions and words that might otherwise go unnoticed or be read in moral or psychological terms will instead be seen to be structuring the entire environment in ways supportive of inequality. In fact, there will be a presumption in favor of finding inequality, since one wouldn't be a feminist without this assumption.

This is what produces the guilty until proven innocent presumption that critics of political correctness focus upon so insistently. If we remain within the framework of subjectivity here, this condition can only be viewed hostilely, as is the case with Zizek: A coercive juridicalization produces a kind of bad faith, with potential victims and perpetrators alike (i.e., everyone) demanding ever more precise and detailed regulations and rules to enable the construction of a coherent representation before some possible tribunal. In other words, this intense formalization of formerly "spontaneous" relations only leads to the logic of deterrence if it remains within a juridical framework, a framework, furthermore, in which politics is both constitutive and disavowed. The only way to bring the politics back into sexual harassment is if accountability, as a political category, comes before subjectivity. Thus, any action (such as the private one of engaging in a sexual relationship with a coworker) is immediately a taking of a position on what counts as sexual harassment and, beyond that, on the constitutive questions founding sexual harassment itself: What are the relations between inequality, norms, and knowledge? In other words, one is always already in a polemical situation, where one is compelled, as a condition of speaking or acting, to theorize the political conditions of speaking or acting. Of course, one can foreclose this a priori, and it is precisely this violence that is constitutive of subjectivity today. And sexual harassment (along with the other categories of human rights) is productive precisely insofar as it forces these questions to the surface.

I will conclude my discussion of this point by briefly contrasting Zizek's remarks on sexual harassment with his embrace (right at the end of the book) of Mary Kay Letourneau, the teacher who, in a well-publicized case, was jailed for an ongoing sexual relationship with a fourteen-year-old student. For Zizek, Letourneau's is a "unique, passionate love affair," characterized by "ethical dignity" (1999a, 385); hers was, above all an "authentic *act*" (386). My aim is not to contest Zizek's critique of the public handling of this case as an instance of the use of a violent "medicalization" of Letourneau, on the one hand (in the constant claims that her actions were a result of mental illness, to be addressed with treatment), and "moralization," on the other hand—not only to denounce and condemn her but to obliterate her agency in the act. My point—and I will return to this in more detail in my discussion of Zizek's understanding of the act— is that, for Zizek, Letourneau is an authentic subject because and on the condition that she does not enter the terrain of knowledge, critiquing both medicalizing and moralizing discourses. At most, she can defend the authenticity of her emotions against these assaults. The point, then, is not primarily Zizek's sexism but that of which sexism is nearly always a sign—the need to hold on to some originary, prepolitical, and ultimately violent moment of undecidability.

Thus, there is something in Zizek's theoretical politics that locates the authentic act in a local, ultimately nostalgic manner. This comes out in many of the specific examples he uses: His call for a "leftist suspension of the law" is illustrated by the situation of an American journalist who decides to violate professional ethics by faking a photograph for the Sandinistas and by the German antifascist family who must commit a murder in moving from "empty moralizing" to "taking sides," "dirtying their hands" (1999a, 223), etc. Zizek is arguing that the "precise way the dimension of the universal is opposed to globalism" is that "the universal dimension shines through the symptomatic displaced element which belongs to the whole without being properly its part. For this reason, criticism of the possible ideological functioning of the notion of hybridity should in no way advocate the return to substantial identities—the point is precisely to assert the *hybridity as the site of the universal*" (225). Hybridity, in this case, is precisely when the subject is split, as in the aforementioned examples, between opposing conceptions of duty or political commitments and existing habits, comforts, and so forth: It always comes down to some existential choice. The difficulty for Zizek is in applying this principle in any other than either the hysterical way he critiques (raising the necessarily impossible demand reinforces the position of the Master as the one who must ultimately take care of the unpleasant details) or in the rather stereotyped and melodramatic examples he constantly falls back upon in his analysis.

This problem is evident in his essay on the Kosovo war ("Against the Double Blackmail"), published in both *New Left Review* (*NLR*)and *The Nation* (I will refer to the *NLR* version). Despite Zizek's unconditional claim, central to singular universality, that for the Left, "there is no . . . neutrality" (1999b, 223), it's hard to read his essay as anything but a plea for the neutrality of the Left in the conflict between NATO and Serbia. He calls for rejecting both sides on the ground that the two sides are really one, arguing that "phenomena like the Milosevic regime are not the opposite to the New World Order, but rather its *symptom*, the place at which the hidden *truth* of the New World Order emerges" (79). Perhaps this is so, but the whole point of singular universality is that one can only contest the whole by implicating its symptoms in its hidden truth, and rejecting the "double blackmail" doesn't explain how to do it. All Zizek has to propose is a rather vague question: "how to build transnational political movements and institutions strong enough to constrain seriously the unlimited rule of Capital, and to render visible and politically relevant the fact that the local fundamentalist resistances against the New World Order, from Milosevic to Le Pen and the extreme right in Europe, are part of it" (82). But the whole point of political theory, especially for Zizek, must be to understand which stances now are necessary for that building. He can't believe that we build now and take a stand later. In other words, what is the singular universal to be grasped now and articulated into a moment of responsibility, where the Left might act with real power?

At the same time, Zizek's neutrality in this essay is questionable. A careful reader will have good grounds for suspecting that his essay is really a disguised support for NATO intervention; if anything, Zizek, at one point, seems most concerned that the West has been too slow to act: "Why then," he asks, "the interminable procrastination of the Western powers, playing for years into Milosevic's hands, acknowledging him as a key factor of stability in the region, misreading clear cases of Serb aggression [etc.]?" (79). Even more important, he does, in fact, identify a singular universal that would define a genuine Serbian Left: "In today's Serbia, the absolute *sine qua non* of an authentic political act would thus be to reject unconditionally the ideological topos of the 'Albanian threat to Serbia'" (81). There is no similar sine qua non for American, British, French, and German (or, for that matter, Kosovar) leftists. Still, I would defend Zizek against charges of being pro-NATO because I think the problem runs deeper: What, exactly, would be the singular universal for the citizens of the NATO countries? The Serbian case provides him with a familiar narrative pattern, like the Nazis or a good noir film: The choice immediately presents itself. That will only work with the fundamentalist side of the New World Order; accounting for resistance within the Order itself can't easily be done in these terms. Even less will it be possible to account for the singular universals that will repoliticize the economy.

At this point, we need to examine Zizek's understanding of the act, which will also clarify his insistence on the necessity of Lacan for progressive theory and politics. We have already seen how Zizek connects the act with a suspension of morality, ethics, and law, which means taking direct responsibility for the act (one can't say "I was just following the rules") and its consequences, including the unwanted and unanticipated ones. He develops this point very forcefully near the end of his book, arguing that any genuine act involves a fundamental paradox that "lies in the fact that it is not 'intentional' in the usual sense of the term of consciously willing it, it is nevertheless accepted as something for which its agent is fully responsible—'I cannot do otherwise, yet I am none the less fully free in doing it'" (1999a, 376). Zizek pursues this much further, defining the act as both "miraculous" and "by definition catastrophic," meaning that there is "something inherently 'terroristic' in every authentic act, in its gesture of thoroughly redefining the 'rules of the game,' inclusive of the very self-identity of its perpetrator" (377). It follows from this that the worst kind of bad faith for revolutionaries interested in the "political act *par excellence*" (377) is to separate the "good," "ideal," and "innocent" revolutionary moment from its "abominable consequences" or "betrayal": "One should insist on the unconditional need to endorse the act fully in all its consequences" (377). Zizek is quite willing to follow this to its logical conclusion:

> A revolution is achieved (*not* betrayed) when it "eats its own children," the excess that was necessary to set it in motion. In other words, the ultimate revolutionary ethical stance is not that of simple devotion and fidelity to the Revolution but, rather, that of willingly accepting the role of "vanishing mediator," of the excessive executioner to be executed (as the "traitor") so that the revolution can achieve its ultimate goal (379).

Now, it would be very easy to raise a series of questions about what appears to be a kind of romantic nostalgia for Stalinism. Why isn't embracing the consequences of the act continuing to struggle for the realization of all its implications (e.g., proletarian democracy) against the attempt to choose some consequences (e.g., power in the hands of the party, state control over the means of production) over others, in particular its most universal ones (such as the internationalism abandoned by Stalinism)? Is Stalin more authentic *because* he "ate" Trotsky, whereas Trotsky would be the authentic one if the reverse were the case? These objections are valid, but, ultimately, they miss the point. In the description of the "Wo Es War" (Where It Was) series being edited by Zizek, in which *The Ticklish Subject* is one of the entries, we see the following: "The premise of the series is that the explosive combination of Lacanian psychoanalysis and Marxist tradition detonates a dynamic freedom that enables us to question the very presuppositions of the circuit of Capital."

Why does he mention Lacanian *psychoanalysis* (i.e., a theory) and Marxist *tradition*? The relation between Marxism and psychoanalysis posited here seems very similar to the relation between national and ethnic "traditions" (folklore, myths, sacred places, and the like) and nationalism—the latter "invents" the former by incorporating it within a modern state, educational, media, etc. system, as a functional means of reproducing an essentially modern social formation predicated upon the global preeminence of the capitalist mode of production. And the reasoning behind doing so is that such an irrationalist remainder is needed to provide the state with the indispensable element of will—people will be ready to sacrifice themselves for the "land where our fathers died," for this city or that shrine or event; who will do so to maintain a more or less efficiently functioning bureaucracy? To get at this another way, there seems, in Zizek's account, to be no singular universal within and constitutive of Marxism—no determination, in a given historical situation, that to defend *this thesis* is to defend Marxism *as such*; in Zizek's terms, this is essentially to remove Marxism from the sphere of the universal. Marxism, in other words, functions in Zizek's text as the "primordial 'passionate attachment' on which the very consistency of the subject's being hinges," or the "fundamental fantasy": "The 'attachment to subjectivization' constitutive of the subject is thus none other than the primordial 'masochistic' scene in which the subject 'makes/sees himself suffering,' that is, assumes *la douleur d'exister*, and thus provides the minimum of support to his being" (1999a, 265).

The repression of this scene is the primary repression or foreclosure upon which the secondary repressions rest. A crucial hinge of Zizek's project—the basis on which he supports a (reinterpreted) modern subjectivity against postmodern subjectivities—is that there are two ways of taking this fundamental fantasy on board. One is through "perversion," where one simply seeks to undo the repression and realize the repressed desire and thereby to deny repression as a totalitarian fiction interfering with the freedom of (refashioning) the self (Zizek aligns Deleuze, Foucault, and—with important qualifications—Butler with this project[7]). The other is "the open assuming/staging of the phantasmic scene" (1999a, 265), i.e., objectifying it and recognizing one's subjectivity within its constraints.

This distinction is crucial because, for Zizek, it marks the difference between reform and revolution. Perversion is ultimately reformist, and hence, it merely reconstitutes the power of the fundamental fantasy, the Master against whom one engages in simulated rebellions. The authentic act, though, traverses the fundamental fantasy. According to Zizek, Lacan recognizes, in a way that poststructuralist "anarchists" such as Butler don't, that

> radical rearticulation of the predominant symbolic order is altogether possible—this is what his notion of *point de capiton* (the "quilting point" or the Master-Signifier) is about: when a new *point de capiton* emerges, the socio-symbolic field is not only displaced, its very structuring principle changes. . . . Lacan leaves open the possibility of a radical recapitulation of the entire symbolic field by means of an *act* proper (1999a, 262).

This tells us more about the authentic act. It involves a transgression of the symbolic order, and in this sense, it posits an outside to it: The subject must "pay the price of psychotic exclusion, a passage through 'symbolic death'" (262).

The need to traverse the fundamental fantasy is Zizek's reason, as we have seen, for granting primacy to the repoliticization of the economic—that is, the depoliticization of the economic is, today, the fundamental fantasy of neoliberalism and multiculturalism alike. At the same time, to return to Zizek's discussion of Mary Kay Letourneau, we have "the sad reality of our late capitalist tolerant liberal society: the very capacity to *act* is brutally medicalized" (1999a, 387) and, as well, "juridicalized." The two are ultimately the same: The juridical form, applied to more and more behavior, must assume a bad intent; the medical disciplines diagnose the intent (a juridical reification) and reform it. Recovering the capacity to act, then, involves owning one's basic, compulsive, passionate attachment to *this* arbitrary thing, whatever it may be, which stands in for the whole. Somehow, for authentic political action, this passionate attachment must be for the singular universal (here and now, against the myth of the "Albanian threat") *and* for the repoliticization of the economy.

Zizek's book, as an act, is an attempt to traverse the fundamental fantasy common to neoliberalism/multiculturalism/New Ageism/postmodernism by reinstating Marxism as the fundamental fantasy of a renewed Left, positing "Capital itself as the Real of our age" (1999a, 276). All of Zizek's theses, including his most provocative ones, should be read as attempts to wrench the Left away from its implication in the depoliticized conditions of global capitalism. But we still have a contradiction between the singular universality of the passionate act and the repoliticization of the economy, which is constitutionally immune to passions and singularity except as marketing devices. This is the contradiction that Marxism as fundamental fantasy, aligned with Lacanian theory, is meant to resolve.

To consider how it might do so, let's return to the question of drive versus desire. Zizek, on one level, privileges desire over drive—for example, hysteria (which endlessly defers satisfaction and finds satisfaction in this endless deferral) over perversion (which tries to bypass repression and satisfy desire immediately). This is a distinction between progressive and reactionary stances or between a position that acknowledges the existence of necessity and systematicity and a libertarian individualism. But he also privileges the more revolutionary "death drive" over the ultimately reformist desire. Desire ultimately accepts the system, the Master, but drive takes upon itself the impossibility of desire and hence attains some distance from the Master-signifier. As Zizek puts it:

> While the subject of desire is grounded in constitutive *lack* (it ex-ists insofar as it is in search of the missing object-cause), the subject of drive is grounded in a constitutive *surplus*—that is to say, in the excessive presence of some thing that is inherently "impossible" and should not be here, in our present reality— the Thing which, of course, is ultimately *the subject itself* (1999a, 304).

And he exemplifies the "reversal of desire into drive" (298) with the "'making oneself chosen,' as in predestination" (299). This surplus transforms the subject itself into the object of its own striving to possess the whole. The cost of this, again, is a completely self-enclosed, inarticulate subject who must be Master (authentic or fraudulent) or nothing.

It is necessary to raise the following question at this point: How can we make sense of what is, on Zizek's part, essentially a defense of a leftist fanaticism with his consistently and certainly deliberately ironic or even ultraironic mode of writing? No one reading Zizek's urbane, witty, self-reflexive prose would ever mistake him for the "subject of drive"—he is clearly the "subject of desire," endlessly deferring definitive conclusions and cathecting the means of deferral themselves. This issue is connected to another: Where is transference in Zizek's psychoanalytic system? Transference is not only central to the arrival of the truth in the psychoanalytic situation, it is also one of the more useful concepts in terms of politicizing psychoanalysis and addressing issues of pedagogy, the intellectual, political leadership, and so on. Yet Zizek almost never discusses the topic and is, in fact, distinctly uncomfortable with it.

He informs us that "Lacan speaks of the 'desire of the analyst,' never of the 'drive of the analyst': in so far as the analyst is defined by a certain subjective attitude—that of 'subjective destitution'—the specificity of his position can be determined only on the level of desire" (Zizek 1999a, 297). To translate this along the lines I have proposed, the analyst is reformist but can enable the analysand to carry out the revolutionary act. If the revolutionary subject of drive is not to "abandon himself to the self-enclosed circuit of drive," there must be a

> desire that remains even after we have traversed our fundamental fantasy, a desire not sustained by a fantasy, and this desire, of course, is the desire of the analyst—not the desire to become an analyst, but the desire which fits the subjective position of the analyst. . . . The desire of the analyst is thus supposed to sustain the analytic community in the absence of any phantasmic support; it is supposed to make possible a communal "big Other" that avoids the transferential effect of the subject supposed to [know, believe, enjoy]. In other words, the desire of the analyst is Lacan's tentative answer to the question: after we have traversed the fantasy, and accepted the "nonexistence of the big Other," how do we none the less return to some (new) form of the big Other that again makes collective existence possible? (296).

This is essentially a Lacanian theory of revolutionary organization and postrevolutionary society. And in Zizek's discourse, it also accounts for the relation between Lacan and Marx and Zizek and his Left reader. The subject of drive is the motor of transformation; the subject of desire (of the analyst) moderates, channels, and makes drive "realistic." Zizek/Lacan shifts the Left reader to Marxism as drive, while maintaining an ironic distance. This relation is to be internalized within the Left: a series of passionate singular universalities held together by the desire of the analyst each embodies for the other. The theory, then, cannot be revolutionary, for revolutionary transformation is ultimately instinctual and atheoretical. In this case, Zizek is essentially deploying a Lacanized Marxism in order to ground more firmly the politics he shares with Butler and Laclau (the "exception to the series" [174] of contemporary post-Althusserian political theorists)—a politics based on "passionate attachments," jouissance, and desire; with the help of Lacan, Marx is cathected and made available to the postmodern Left.

This politics is based on a pre-, even antipolitical violent desire. Rather than a theoretical outside that places political action before the other, it is the "scopic drive"—the fundamentally masochistic "'middle way,' the attitude of 'making-oneself-seen,' of deriving libidinal satisfaction from actively sustaining the scene of one's own passive submission" (Zizek 1999a, 284)—that grounds "imagination" and therefore politics. Here, the polemic between Marx and Lacan could not be clearer: For Marx, it is the articulation of labor, politics, and theory, activities that relate one to the world in a transformative manner, that first of all make action and change possible. Thus, revolutionary action can be understood as action whose fundamental characteristic is enabling others to act, securing the conditions under which a more universal space of action—where doer and deed are commensurable in view of theory and its polemical field—is established.

One seemingly minor point that may clarify the issue is that the Marxist critique of "classic onto-theology . . . focused on the triad of the True, the Beautiful and the Good" is diametrically opposed to that of Zizek's Lacan: "What Lacan does is push these notions to their limits, demonstrating that the Good is the mask of 'diabolical' Evil, that the Beautiful is the mask of the Ugly, of the disgusting horror of the Real, and that the True is the mask of the central void around which every edifice is woven" (1999a, 161). For Marxism, society can be founded in a fundamentally just way, not merely in a way that self-reflexively neutralizes evil and manages the "Void." Thus, Zizek's claim that *there is no Power without violence* (191) is an unfounded dogma: The "obscene stain of violence" is not *constitutive* of power (in fact, Zizek equivocates on this claim, which would ultimately sink politics into pure drive). In this sense, there is a certain naïveté to political action, a literalness that nevertheless opens itself to critique precisely by setting in motion a polemic that awakens opposing ones.

Zizek's fundamentally nostalgic and experientially based politics can be seen in his explanation of postmodernism in terms of the decline of Oedipus:

> What occurs in today's much decried "decline of Oedipus" (decline of paternal symbolic authority) is precisely the return of figures which function according to the logic of the "primordial father," from "totalitarian" political leaders to the paternal sexual harasser—why? When the "pacifying" symbolic authority is suspended, the only way to avoid the debilitating deadlock of desire, its inherent impossibility, is to locate the cause in its inaccessibility in a despotic figure which stands in for the primordial *jousseur*: we cannot enjoy because he appropriates all enjoyment (1999a, 351).

As the link between the totalitarian leader and the paternal sexual harasser suggests, Zizek intends to cover a lot of ground here: In particular, the same historical shift accounts for the abandonment of politics (action, solidarity, judgment) *and* the politicization of new spheres of life, the engagement of previous neutrals as opponents. And, of course, it must—but without thereby making these phenomena politically equivalent, which is the consequence if the subject of the act is ultimately an inarticulate, pretheoretical one.

The decline of Oedipus leads to the "antinomy of postmodern individuality" (Zizek 1999a, 373): The more one is liberated from symbolic authority, the more one seeks, reflexively, to find new modes of authority. For example, as soon as one sets out to discover one's true self, one immediately submits to some expert in subjectivization. Along with this, one finds the externalization of feelings, the reign of simulacra, and other much noted postmodern phenomena. Postmodern theories of liberation, of course, view this as an opportunity for endless self-fictionalizations, free from normativity and grand narratives. Zizek resists this, affirming that *"there are acts . . .* they *do occur"* (375), that is, the "unity of the noumenal and the phenomenal" in which the subject *"posits himself as his own cause"* (375). However, he can only conceive of the act as evading the field of knowledge: The ironic subject of desire (of the analyst) and the existential subject of drive are maintained in an experiential, communal space, free from the polemical foundations of accountability. The ironic failure of polemic is why Zizek never actually gets anywhere near the "repoliticization of the economy." Not a single example, not a single analysis or conceptual articulation throughout the book even touches on the issue, and the contemporary phenomena he is most hostile to are precisely those (such as sexual harassment) that ground supposedly cultural issues and natural desire in political-economic relationships.

Although positing the repoliticization of the economy is necessary for traversing one fundamental fantasy and installing another, some notion of objectivity external to the subject is necessary to actually theorize it. The logic of Zizek's argument is that it is precisely the disintegrating late-modern subject who is most detached from foundations and hence especially singularly universal, able to reconnect with passionate attachments and the fundamental fantasy. What he therefore can't see is that the externalization of the subject, the formalization of lifeworlds, and the quasi juridification of natural relationships are all necessary products of the contradiction between the forces and relations of production. What is reactionary here is the shift in managerial power from bureaucratic experts to entrepreneurial postexperts; what is progressive is that a precondition of speaking or acting is assuming accountability to the pedagogical labor of clearing a political space where intentions, acts and consequences, and needs and capacities can be commensurated.

Zizek argues that

> from a truly radical Marxist perspective, although there is a link between "working class" as a social group and "proletariat" as the position of the militant fighting for universal truth, this link is not a causal connection. . . . To be a "proletarian" involves a certain *subjective stance* (of class struggle destined to achieve the Redemption through Revolution). . . . The line that separates the two opposing sides in the class struggle is therefore not "objective," it is not the line separating two positive social groups, but ultimately *radically subjective* (1999a, 227).

But in making this argument, he elides the fact that this radically subjective stance is a position on the boundary of theoretical polemics that, in turn, presuppose the specifically political appearance of the proletariat (what Trotsky called the "elements of proletarian democracy within bourgeois society" [1971, 367]). The difference between the working class (the constitutive capitalist drive toward dispossession and expropriation as precondition of exploitation) and the proletariat (the establishment of organizational and theoretical categories marking the boundary between capitalism and communism) is the objective space of knowledge, pedagogy, and organization as the site of collective critique, i.e., where causal relations are united with accountability. Revolutionary politics, in its universality, is precisely this articulation of political action actualizing the elements of proletarian power and/in the view of theory. Universality is not in the experiential singularity of the subject. Rather, universality is only in the ongoing struggle against the articulation of ideological and political-economic violence; the clarification of modes and boundaries of accountability; and, of course, experimental and hypothetical actions that crystallize and only thereby exceed thought by posing new questions.

Notes

1. In his *In Defense of Marxism*, Trotsky, explicating Lenin, puts it this way: "When economic processes, tasks and interests acquire a conscious and generalized ('concentrated') character, they enter the sphere of politics by virtue of this very fact, and constitute the essence of politics. In this sense, politics as concentrated economics rises above the day-to-day atomized, unconscious and ungeneralized economic activity" (1973, 123).

2. See Gills, Rocamora, and Wilson 1993.

3. See, in particular, his much debated "The Postcolonial Aura: Third World Criticism in the Age of Global Capitalism" (Dirlik 1997).

4. Here, I don't mean to minimize the Communist contribution to the defeat of Nazism, just to underscore who the ultimate beneficiary was.

5. An example of this is Spivak's claim that "from the infinite care and passion of learning we have bypassed knowledge (which is obsolete now) into the telematic postmodern terrain of information command" (1998, 343).

6. See Weber 1946.

7. Zizek's "critical remarks on Butler are based on a full endorsement of her basic insight into the profound link between—even the ultimate identity of—the two aspects or modes of reflexivity: reflexivity in the strict philosophical sense of negative self-relating, which is constitutive of subjectivity . . . and reflexivity in the psychoanalytic sense of the reflexive turn that defines the gesture of 'primordial repression' (the reversal of the regulation of desire into the desire for regulation, etc.)" (1999a, 290). Interestingly, the fundamental agreement between Butler and Zizek is on the impossibility of the regulation of desire: Any attempt to do so will simply transform the site of regulation into a site of desire and hence the basic

stake of subjectivity. The implication of this, to bring my critique of Butler in Chapter 2 to bear here, is that setting explicit limits on violent speech (more generally, on ideology) simply produces more such speech, in various implicit and explicit forms. What neither Zizek nor Butler consider is the possibility of making the causes of violence institutionally visible within a political frame openly built into (or deployed as a critique of) the institutional situation. The individual who begins a statement with "I know this isn't politically correct, but" is taking a political position in relation to knowledge and institutions, law and politics, and this position can be made explicit or "literalized" in a way that not only doesn't silence that individual but might free whatever he or she has to say from the infantilism of "anti-PC" rebellion.

WORKS CITED

Ahmed, Aijaz. 1992. *In Theory: Classes, Nations, Literatures*. London and New York: Verso.

Ahmed, Sara. 1998. *Differences That Matter: Feminist Theory and Postmodernism*. Cambridge: Cambridge University Press.

Althusser, Louis. 1990. *Philosophy and the Spontaneous Philosophy of the Scientists and Other Essays*. Trans. Ben Brewster et al. New York and London: Verso.

_____. 1971. *Lenin and Philosophy*. New York: Monthly Review Press.

Appadurai, Arjun. 1996. *Modernity at Large: Cultural Dimensions of Globalization*. Minneapolis and London: University of Minnesota Press.

Balibar, Etienne, and Immanuel Wallerstein. 1991. *Race, Nation and Class: Ambiguous Identities*. New York: Verso.

Baudrillard, Jean. 1993. "Toward a Principle of Evil." In *Postmodernism: A Reader*, ed. Thomas Docherty. New York: Columbia University Press, 355–361.

_____. 1985. "The Ecstasy of Communication." In *The Anti-Aesthetic: Essays on Postmodern Culture*, ed. Hal Foster. Port Townsend, Wash.: Bay Press, 126–134.

_____. 1983. *Simulations*. Trans. Paul Foss et al. New York: Columbia University Press.

Bauman, Zygmunt. 1998. *Globalization: The Human Consequences*. New York: Columbia University Press.

Beasley Murray, Jon. 1998. "Peronism and the Secret History of Cultural Studies: Populism and the Substitution of Culture for State." *Cultural Critique* 39 (Spring): 189–217.

Bhatt, Chetan. 1999. "Ethnic Absolutism and the Authoritarian Spirit." *Theory Culture & Society* 16, no. 2 (April): 65–85.

_____. 1997. *Liberation and Purity: Race, New Religious Movements and the Ethics of Postmodernity*. London and Bristol: UCL Press.

Brantlinger, Patrick. 1990. *Crusoe's Footprints: Cultural Studies in Britain and America*. New York: Routledge.

Brin, David. 1998. *The Transparent Society: Will Technology Force Us to Choose Between Privacy and Freedom?* Reading, Mass.: Addison-Wesley.

Buell, Frederick. 1994. *National Culture and the New Global System*. Baltimore: Johns Hopkins University Press.

Butler, Judith. 1997. *Excitable Speech: A Politics of the Performative*. New York and London: Routledge.

_____. 1990. *Gender Trouble: Feminism and the Subversion of Identity*. New York: Routledge.

Caughie, Pamela. 1997. "Let It Pass: Changing the Subject, Once Again." *PMLA* 112, no. 1 (January): 26–39.

Cheah, Pheng. 1998. "Given Culture: Rethinking Cosmopolitical Freedom in Transnationalism." In *Cosmopolitics: Thinking and Feeling Beyond the Nation*, ed. Pheng Cheah and Bruce Robbins. Minneapolis and London: University of Minnesota Press, 290–328.

———. 1995. "Violent Light: The Idea of Publicness in Modern Philosophy and in Global Neocolonialism." *Social Text* 43 (Fall): 163–190.

Cheah, Pheng, and Bruce Robbins, eds. 1998. *Cosmopolitics: Thinking and Feeling Beyond the Nation*. Minneapolis and London: University of Minnesota Press.

Chen, Kuan-Hsing. 1998. "Introduction: The Decolonization Question." In *Trajectories: Inter-Asia Cultural Studies*, ed. Kuan-Hsing Chen. London and New York: Routledge, 1–53.

Chen, Kuan-Hsing, ed. 1998. *Trajectories: Inter-Asia Cultural Studies*. London and New York: Routledge.

Chen, Kuan-Hsing, and David Morley, eds. 1996. *Stuart Hall: Critical Dialogues in Cultural Studies*. New York and London: Routledge.

Cohen, Tom. 1998. *Ideology and Inscription: "Cultural Studies" After Benjamin, De Man and Bakhtin*. Cambridge: Cambridge University Press.

Conner, Steven. 1989. *Postmodernist Culture: An Introduction to Theories of the Contemporary*. Cambridge: Basil Blackwell.

Cultural Studies. 1998. "Special Issue: The Institutionalization of Cultural Studies," ed. Ted Striphas, 12, no. 4 (October).

De Lauretis, Teresa. 1990. "Eccentric Subjects: Feminist Theory and Historical Consciousness." *Feminist Studies* 16, no. 1 (Spring): 115–150.

Derrida, Jacques. 1992. "The Force of Law: The 'Mystical Foundations of Authority.'" In *Deconstruction and the Possibility of Justice*, ed. Drucilla Cornell, Michel Rosenfeld, and David Gray Carlson. New York and London: Routledge, 3–67.

———. 1978. "Structure, Sign and Play in the Discourse of the Human Sciences." In *Writing and Difference*. Trans. Alan Bass. London and Henley: Routledge and Kegan Paul, 278–293.

Di Leo, Jeffrey R., and Christian Moraru. 1997. "Posttheory, Cultural Studies and the Classroom: Fragments of a New Pedagogical Discourse." In *Class Issues: Pedagogy, Cultural Studies and the Public Sphere*, ed. Amitava Kumar. New York and London: New York University Press, 237–244.

Dirlik, Arif. 1997. "The Postcolonial Aura: Third World Criticism in the Age of Global Capitalism." In *Dangerous Liaisons: Gender, Nation & Postcolonial Perspectives*, ed. Anne McClintock, Aamir Mufti, and Ella Shohat. Minneapolis and London: University of Minnesota Press, 501–528.

———. 1996. "The Global in the Local." In *Global/Local: Cultural Production and the Transnational Imaginary*, ed. Rob Wilson and Wimal Dissanayake. Durham, N.C., and London: Duke University Press, 21–45.

Dixon, Marlene. 1983. *The Future of Women*. San Francisco: Synthesis Publications.

Eagleton, Terry. 1996. *The Illusions of Postmodernism*. Oxford and Cambridge: Blackwell.

Ebert, Teresa. 1996. *Ludic Feminism and After: Postmodernism, Desire and Labor in Late Capitalism*. Ann Arbor: University of Michigan Press.

Featherstone, Mike. 1995. *Undoing Culture: Globalization, Postmodernism and Identity*. London: Sage Publications.

Fiske, John. 1992. "Cultural Studies and the Culture of Everyday Life." In *Cultural Studies*, ed. Lawrence Grossberg, Cary Nelson, and Paula Treichler. New York: Routledge, 154–173.

_____. 1989. *Understanding Popular Culture*. Boston: Unwin Hyman.

Foucault, Michel. 1990. "Governmentality." In *The Foucault Effect: Studies in Governmentality*, ed. Graham Burchell, Colin Gordon, and Peter Miller. Chicago: University of Chicago Press, 87–104.

_____. 1980. *Power/Knowledge: Selected Interviews and Other Writings—1972–1977*. Ed. C. Gordon, trans. C. Gordon et al. New York: Pantheon.

Fox, Bonnie, ed. 1980. *Hidden in the Household: Women's Domestic Labour Under Capitalism*. Toronto: The Women's Press.

Fraser, Nancy. 1990. "Rethinking the Public Sphere: A Contribution to the Critique of Actually Existing Democracy." *Social Text*, no. 25–26: 56–80.

_____. 1989. *Unruly Practices: Power, Discourse and Gender in Contemporary Social Theory*. Minneapolis: University of Minnesota Press.

Fraser, Nancy, and Linda Nicholson. 1992. "Social Criticism Without Philosophy: An Encounter Between Feminism and Postmodernism." In *Feminism/Postmodernism*, ed. Linda Nicholson. New York and London: Routledge, 19–38.

Friedman, Thomas L. 1999. *The Lexus and the Olive Tree*. New York: Farrar Strauss Giroux.

Frow, John. 1995. *Cultural Studies and Cultural Value*. Oxford: Clarendon Press.

Gills, Barry, Joel Rocamora, and Richard Wilson, eds. 1993. *Low Intensity Democracy: Political Power in the New World Order*. London and Boulder: Pluto Press.

Giroux, Henry. 1992. "Resisting Difference: Cultural Studies and the Discourse of Critical Pedagogy." In *Cultural Studies*, ed. Lawrence Grossberg, Cary Nelson, and Paula Treichler. New York: Routledge, 199–212.

Gray, John. 1998. *False Dawn: The Delusions of Global Capitalism*. New York: The New Press.

Grossberg, Lawrence. 1998. "The Cultural Studies' Crossroads Blues." *European Journal of Cultural Studies* 1, no. 1 (January): 65–82.

_____. 1997a. *Bringing It All Back Home: Essays on Cultural Studies*. Durham, N.C., and London: Duke University Press.

_____. 1997b. "Cultural Studies, Modern Logics and Theories of Globalisation." In *Back to Reality? Social Experience and Cultural Studies*, ed. Angela McRobbie. Manchester, England, and New York: Manchester University Press, 7–35.

Grossberg, Lawrence, Cary Nelson, and Paula Treichler. 1992. "Introduction." In *Cultural Studies*, ed. Lawrence Grossberg, Cary Nelson, and Paula Treichler. New York: Routledge, 1–22.

Grossberg, Lawrence, Cary Nelson, and Paula Treichler, eds. 1992. *Cultural Studies*. New York: Routledge.

Habermas, Jurgen. 1987a. *The Philosophical Discourse of Modernity*. Trans. Frederick Lawrence. Boston: MIT Press.

_____. 1987b. *The Theory of Communicative Action*, vol. 2: *Lifeworld and System: A Critique of Functionalist Reason*. Trans. Thomas McCarthy. Boston: Beacon Press.

Hall, Stuart. 1992. "Cultural Studies and Its Theoretical Legacies." In *Cultural Studies,* ed. Lawrence Grossberg, Cary Nelson, and Paula Treichler. New York: Routledge, 277–294.

———. 1988. *The Hard Road to Renewal.* London: Verso.

———. 1980. "Cultural Studies: Two Paradigms." *Media, Culture, Society,* no. 2: 57–72.

Haraway, Donna. 1992. "A Manifesto for Cyborgs: Science, Technology and Socialist Feminism for the 1980s." In *Feminism/Postmodernism,* ed. Linda Nicholson. New York and London: Routledge, 190–233.

Hardt, Michael. 1996. "Introduction: Laboratory Italy." In *Radical Thought in Italy: A Potential Politics,* ed. Paolo Virno and Michael Hardt. Minneapolis and London: University of Minnesota Press, 1–10.

———. 1995. "The Withering of Civil Society" *Social Text* 45: 27–44.

Hartsock, Nancy. 1992. "Foucault on Power: A Theory for Women?" In *Feminism/Postmodernism,* ed. Linda Nicholson. New York and London: Routledge, 157–171.

———. 1983. *Money, Sex and Power: Toward a Feminist Historical Materialism.* Boston: Northeastern University Press.

Harvey, David. 1996. *Justice, Nature and the Geography of Difference.* Cambridge and London: Blackwell.

Hill, Mike. 1997. "Cultural Studies by Default: A History of the Present." In *Class Issues: Pedagogy, Cultural Studies and the Public Sphere,* ed. Amitava Kumar. New York and London: New York University Press, 148–162.

Hoggart, Richard. 1992. *The Uses of Literacy.* New Brunswick, N.J.: Transaction.

———. 1970. *Speaking to Each Other.* New York: Oxford University Press.

Jameson, Fredric. 1991. *Postmodernism, or the Cultural Logic of Late Capitalism.* Durham, N.C.: Duke University Press.

Jenness, Linda. 1972. *Feminism and Socialism.* New York: Pathfinder Press.

Kellner, Douglas. 1989. *Jean Baudrillard: From Marxism to Postmodernism and Beyond.* Stanford: Stanford University Press.

Kipnis, Laura. 1996. *Bound and Gagged: Pornography and the Politics of Fantasy in America.* New York: Grove Press.

Kumar, Amitava. 1997. "Introduction." In *Class Issues: Pedagogy, Cultural Studies and the Public Sphere,* ed. Amitava Kumar. New York and London: New York University Press, 1–6.

Kumar, Amitava, ed. 1997. *Class Issues: Pedagogy, Cultural Studies and the Public Sphere.* New York and London: New York University Press.

Laclau, Ernesto. 1990. *New Reflections on the Revolution of Our Time.* London and New York: Verso.

Laclau, Ernesto, and Chantal Mouffe. 1985. *Hegemony and Socialist Strategy: Towards a Radical Democratic Politics.* New York: Verso.

Larrain, Jorge. 1996. "Stuart Hall and the Marxist Concept of Ideology." In *Stuart Hall: Critical Dialogues in Cultural Studies,* ed. Kuan-Hsing Chen and David Morley. New York and London: Routledge, 47–70.

Larsen, Neil. 1997. "Theory at the Vanishing Point: Notes on a Pedagogical Quandary." In *Class Issues: Pedagogy, Cultural Studies and the Public Sphere,* ed. Amitava Kumar. New York and London: New York University Press, 77–86.

Lenin, V. I. 1940. *"Left Wing" Communism, an Infantile Disorder: A Popular Essay in Marxist Strategy and Tactics*. New York: International Publishers.

_____. 1939. *Imperialism: The Highest Stage of Capitalism*. New York: International Publishers.

Lowe, Lisa, and David Lloyd. 1997. "Introduction." In *The Politics of Culture in the Shadow of Capital*, ed. Lisa Lowe and David Lloyd. Durham, N.C., and London: Duke University Press, 1–32.

Lowe, Lisa, and David Lloyd, eds. *1997. The Politics of Culture in the Shadow of Capital*. Durham, N.C., and London: Duke University Press.

Lyotard, Jean-Francois. 1997. *Postmodern Fables*. Trans. George van Den Abbeele. Minneapolis and London: University of Minnesota Press.

_____. 1988. *The Differend: Phrases in Dispute*. Trans Georges Van Den Abbeele. Minneapolis: University of Minnesota Press.

_____. 1984. *The Postmodern Condition: A Report on Knowledge*. Trans. Geoff Bennington and Brian Massumi. Minneapolis: University of Minnesota Press.

MacKinnon, Catharine. 1989. *Toward a Feminist Theory of the State*. Cambridge, Mass., and London: Harvard University Press.

Marchak, M. Patricia. 1991. *The Integrated Circus: The New Right and the Restructuring of Global Markets*. Montreal and Kingston, Canada: McGill-Queens University Press.

Marx, Karl. 1973. *Grundrisse: Foundations of the Critique of Political Economy*. Trans. Martin Nicolaus. New York: Vintage Books.

_____. 1970. *A Contribution to the Critique of Political Economy*. New York: International Publishers.

_____. 1906. *Capital: A Critique of Political Economy*. Charles Kerr.

Marx, Karl, and Frederick Engels. 1942. *Selected Correspondence: 1846–1895*. New York: International Publishers.

Massumi, Brian. 1998. "Requiem for Our Prospective Dead (Toward a Participatory Critique of Capitalist Power)." In *Deleuze and Guatarri: New Mappings in Politics, Philosophy and Culture*, ed. Eleanor Kauffman and Kevin Jon Heller. Minneapolis: University of Minnesota Press, 40–64.

McGuigan, Jim. 1992. *Cultural Populism*. New York and London: Routledge.

McRobbie, Angela. 1992. "Post-Marxism and Cultural Studies: A Postscript." In *Cultural Studies*, ed. Lawrence Grossberg, Cary Nelson, and Paula Treichler. New York: Routledge, 719–730.

McRobbie, Angela, ed. 1997. *Back to Reality? Social Experience and Cultural Studies*. Manchester, England, and New York: Manchester University Press.

Mercer, Kobena. 1992. "'1968': Periodizing Postmodern Politics and Identity." In *Cultural Studies*, ed. Lawrence Grossberg, Cary Nelson, and Paula Treichler. New York: Routledge, 424–449.

Minnesota Review. 1998. Ns. 48–49, December.

Montag, Warren, and Ted Stolze, eds. 1997. *The New Spinoza*. Minneapolis: University of Minnesota Press.

Morley, David. 1998. "So-Called Cultural Studies: Dead Ends and Reinvented Wheels." *Cultural Studies* 12, no. 4 (October): 476–497.

Nelson, Cary. 1997. *Manifesto of a Tenured Radical*. New York: New York University Press.

Nelson, Cary, ed. 1997. *Will Teach for Food: Academic Labor in Crisis*. Minneapolis and London: University of Minnesota Press.

Nicholson, Linda, ed. 1992. *Feminism/Postmodernism*. New York and London: Routledge.

Ong, Aihwa. 1999. *Flexible Citizenship: The Cultural Logics of Transnationality*. Durham, N.C., and London: Duke University Press.

Parry, Benita. 1994. "Resisting Theory/Theorizing Resistance, or Two Cheers for Nativism." In *Colonial Discourse/Postcolonial Theory*, ed. Francis Barker, Peter Hulme, and Margaret Iverson. Manchester, England: Manchester University Press, 172–196.

Philipson, Ilene J., and Karen V. Hansen. 1990. "Women, Class and the Feminist Imagination: An Introduction." In *Women, Class, and the Feminist Imagination: A Socialist Feminist Reader*, ed. Ilene J. Philipson and Karen V. Hansen. Philadelphia: Temple University Press, 3–40.

Robertson, Roland. 1992. *Globalization: Social Theory and Global Culture*. London: Sage.

Robinson, William. 1996. *Promoting Polyarchy: Globalization, US Intervention, and Hegemony*. Cambridge and New York: Cambridge University Press.

Rorty, Richard. 1991. *Objectivity, Relativism, and Truth*. Cambridge: Cambridge University Press.

Ross, Andrew. 1992. "New Age Technoculture." In *Cultural Studies*, ed. Lawrence Grossberg, Cary Nelson, and Paula Treichler. New York: Routledge, 531–555.

Ross, Robert J.S., and Kent C. Trachte. 1990. *Global Capitalism: The New Leviathan*. Albany: State University of New York Press.

Ryan, Michael. 1989. *Politics and Culture*. Baltimore: Johns Hopkins University Press.

Sargent, Lydia. 1981. *Women and Revolution: A Discussion of the Unhappy Marriage of Marxism and Feminism*. Boston: South End Press.

Sassen, Saskia. 1996. *Losing Control? Sovereignty in an Age of Globalization*. New York: Columbia University Press.

Scott, Alan. 1997. "Introduction—Globalization: Social Process or Political Rhetoric?" In *The Limits of Globalization: Cases and Arguments*, ed. Alan Scott. London and New York: Routledge, 1–22.

Slack, Jennifer Daryl. 1996. "The Theory and Method of Articulation in Cultural Studies." In *Stuart Hall: Critical Dialogues in Cultural Studies*, ed. Kuan-Hsing Chen and David Morley. New York and London: Routledge, 112–127.

Sloterdijk, Peter. 1987. *Critique of Cynical Reason*. Minneapolis: University of Minnesota Press.

Social Text. 1997. Vol. 51 (Summer).

Spivak, Gayatri Chakravorty. 1998. "Cultural Talks in the Hot Peace: Resisting the 'Global Village.'" In *Cosmopolitics: Thinking and Feeling Beyond the Nation*, ed. Pheng Cheah and Bruce Robbins. Minneapolis and London: University of Minnesota Press, 329–348.

_____. 1993. *Outside in the Teaching Machine*. New York and London: Routledge.

Stabile, Carol. 1997. "Pedagogues, Pedagogy and Political Struggle." In *Class Issues: Pedagogy, Cultural Studies and the Public Sphere*, ed. Amitava Kumar. New York and London: New York University Press, 208–220.

Strauss, Leo. 1958. *Thoughts on Machiavelli*. Glencoe, Ill.: The Free Press.

Strickland, Ronald. 1997. "Pedagogy and Public Accountability." In *Class Issues: Pedagogy, Cultural Studies and the Public Sphere*, ed. Amitava Kumar. New York and London: New York University Press, 163–176.

Trotsky, Leon. 1973. *In Defense of Marxism*. New York: Pathfinder Press.

_____. 1971. *The Struggle Against Fascism in Germany*. New York: Pathfinder Press.

Turner, Graeme. 1990. *British Cultural Studies: An Introduction*. Boston: Unwin Hyman.

Virno, Paolo. 1996. "Virtuosity and Revolution: The Political Theory of Exodus." In *Radical Thought in Italy: A Potential Politics*, ed. Paolo Virno and Michael Hardt. Minneapolis and London: University of Minnesota Press, 189–210.

Virno, Paolo, and Michael Hardt, eds. 1996. *Radical Thought in Italy: A Potential Politics*. Minneapolis and London: University of Minnesota Press.

Visker, Rudi. 1995. *Michel Foucault: Genealogy as Critique*. Trans. Chris Turner. New York: Verso.

Waite, Geoff. 1996. *Nietzsche's Corps/e: Aesthetics, Politics, Prophecy, or, the Spectacular Technoculture of Everyday Life*. Durham, N.C., and London: Duke University Press.

Wald, Alan. 1997. "A Pedagogy of Unlearning: Teaching the Specificity of U.S. Marxism." In *Class Issues: Pedagogy, Cultural Studies and the Public Sphere*, ed. Amitava Kumar. New York and London: New York University Press, 125–147.

Waters, Malcolm. 1995. *Globalization*. London and New York: Routledge.

Weber, Max. 1946. "Politics as Vocation." In *Max Weber: Essays in Sociology*, ed. H. H. Gerth and C. Wright Mills. New York: Oxford University Press, 77–128.

Williams, Jeffrey. 1997. "Renegotiating the Pedagogical Contract." In *Class Issues: Pedagogy, Cultural Studies and the Public Sphere*, ed. Amitava Kumar. New York and London: New York University Press, 298–312.

Wilson, Rob, and Wimal Dissanayake. 1996. "Introduction: Tracking the Global/Local." In *Global/Local: Cultural Production and the Transnational Imaginary*, ed. Rob Wilson and Wimal Dissanayake. Durham, N.C., and London: Duke University Press, 1–18.

Wilson, Rob, and Wimal Dissanayake, eds. 1996. *Global/Local: Cultural Production and the Transnational Imaginary*. Durham, N.C., and London: Duke University Press.

Wolfe, Cary. 1998. *Critical Environments: Postmodern Theory and the Pragmatics of the "Outside."* Minneapolis: University of Minnesota Press.

_____. "Getting the Dirt on the Public Intellectual: A Response to Michael Berube." *Public Intellectuals and the Future of Graduate Education*. Available: http://humanities.uchicago.edu/humanities/maphchj/symposium.html.

Zizek, Slavoj. 1999a. *The Ticklish Subject: The Absent Centre of Political Ontology*. London: Verso.

_____. 1999b. "Against the Double Blackmail." *New Left Review* 234 (March–April): 76–82.

_____. 1989. *The Sublime Object of Ideology*. New York: Verso.

INDEX

Printed in the United States
by Baker & Taylor Publisher Services